Tell This in My Memory

STORIES OF ENSLAVEMENT
FROM EGYPT, SUDAN,
AND THE OTTOMAN EMPIRE

Eve M. Troutt Powell

STANFORD UNIVERSITY PRESS
STANFORD, CALIFORNIA

Stanford University Press
Stanford, California

Library of Congress Cataloging-in-Publication Data

Powell, Eve Troutt, author.
  Tell this in my memory : stories of enslavement from Egypt, Sudan, and the Ottoman Empire / Eve M. Troutt Powell.
      pages cm
  Includes bibliographical references and index.
  ISBN 978-0-8047-8233-3 (cloth : alk. paper)
  ISBN 978-0-8047-8864-9 (pbk. : alk. paper)
  1. Slavery—Egypt—History—19th century. 2. Slaves—Egypt—History—19th century. 3. Slavery—Sudan—History—19th century. 4. Slaves—Sudan—History—19th century. 5. Slavery—Turkey—History—19th century. 6. Slaves—Turkey—History—19th century. I. Title.
  HT1371.P69 2012
  306.3′620962—dc23

                        2012019391

Typeset at Stanford University Press in 9.5/15 Palatino

*This book is meant to dignify the history
of those who find themselves refugees.*

Contents

Illustrations

Maps

Figures

Acknowledgments

If it takes a village to raise a child, the number of people who helped me research, write, and finish this book would fill an entire city; these words cannot encompass my deep gratitude to everyone who assisted me. I was fortunate to receive significant institutional funding and support from the John D. and Catherine T. MacArthur Fellowship Foundation, the Center for Arabic Studies Abroad, the Radcliffe Institute for Advanced Study, and the University of Pennsylvania. I have been equally fortunate with the opportunity to work with Kate Wahl, the executive editor of Stanford University Press, who somehow manages to make comments and suggestions that are inspirational while being helpful. Joa Suorez and Clementine Gannett Breslin put up with the hysteria of pre-production, and I am also deeply grateful to Carolyn Brown and Cynthia Lindlof for the final editing process. I also must thank the anonymous readers, who treated this book with mercy.

My beautiful friend Yar Deng led me years ago to a celebration of Joseph Bakhita's life. The paths of the former slaves in this book led me to the help of Abuna Ibrahim Riyadi, of the Church of the Sacred Virgin in Cairo, Egypt, and also to the resources of Ashraf Miladi, an Egyptian immigration lawyer with many insights about the situation of Cairo's Sudanese refugees. Father Celestin of Saint Joseph's Church in Zamalek (Cairo) warmly opened the doors of the library to me. The clergy of Sacred Heart Cathedral in Abbasiya (Cairo) welcomed me into the Josephine Bakhita Center, where Abuna Ibrahim and I were able to interview a group of women, all Sudanese refugees, all generous in sharing their experiences and time with me. But I could not have found Abuna Ibrahim without the institutional support of the Center for Arabic Studies Abroad and the guidance of its directors at the time, Mahmoud al-Batl in the United States and Zeinab Taha in Cairo.

In Rome, the gracious sisters at the headquarters of the Canossian Daughters of Charity did their utmost to share as many documents about Saint Josephine Bakhita as I could carry. I must thank in particular Mother Erika and Mother Velia for their tremendous efforts to share Saint Bakhita's intellectual life with me, as well for putting me in touch with Jeffrey Tiner, an inmate in Oregon who has become, after years of prayer and study, a true scholar of Saint Bakhita. The welcoming brothers of the Comboni Archive in Rome, notably Father Joaquim, also helped me find material on Father Daniel Sorur Pharim Deng and helped me understand the intellectual depth of this priest's spirituality.

In the Sudan Archive at the University of Durham in the UK, Jane Hodgson worked tirelessly to help me find photographs of Sudanese slaves and to find as much material as possible on Salim C. Wilson. This is my second book project that I could not have completed without Jane's kindness and support.

This project began as an idea at the University of Georgia in 2003. John Morrow, David Schoenbrun, Miranda Pollard, and John Inscoe were kind enough to listen, and Diane Batts Morrow was particularly generous with her ideas about the role of black women in the Catholic Church. Many of my earlier ideas about the book—that it would revolve only around Saint Josephine Bakhita—were completely transformed by my fellow members at the Radcliffe Institute. I learned so much from Vince Brown, Salem Makuria, Tera Hunter, Susan Terrio, and Betty Shamieh that my project grew to incorporate the narratives of other former slaves and other former slave owners. Two sisters from Radcliffe, Kathy Peiss and Barbara Savage, have become my sisters in the History Department of Penn as well. Kathy listened carefully as the research changed, and Barbara read and reshaped my pages. I know that this book is so much better than it would have been without their care. Penn has been a wonderful place in which to grow a book, where I have been able to absorb the comments of colleagues who study different parts of the world, like Cheikh Babou, Peter Holquist, Firoozeh Kashani-Sabet, Steve Feiermann, Lynn Hollen Lees, Bruce Kuklick, Tukufu Zuberi, Ali Ali-Dinar, and Anne Norton. And without the administrative help of Deborah Broadnax, Joan Plonski, and Joslin Ham in the History Department, and Camille Charles, Carol Davis, and Gale Garrison in the Center for Africana Studies, I would simply have collapsed.

I can say with confidence that much of the research that went into this book could not have been finished without a stellar group of research assistants, both undergraduate and graduate students. Nicole Carter was of tremendous help while I was beginning the research at Radcliffe. Ori Pleban was a tireless assistant at Penn. Without Daniel Lammendola's translation of the Italian documents, I could never have unearthed so much about Saint Bakhita or her role in Italian society (or understood the recent movie about Bakhita without Daniel's simultaneous translation; the film made us both cry). Manal Taha's research and comments have added depth and great help with Arabic translations as well. Ashley Freeman and Pasha Gol have also been monumental and instrumental in their research help in the last stages of the book.

I have learned so much from my graduate students and their fearless comments about slavery studies and Sudanese, Egyptian, and Ottoman history, and I can only hope that my help with the work of Marie Brown, Ceyda Karamursel, Katie Hickerson, Elizabeth Dyer, and Jeremy Dell is equal to their help with mine. I also deeply appreciate Shehab Ismail's help and attentiveness to all questions about 'Ali Mubarak Pasha.

I have tried to track my acknowledgments through the cities and institutions where these dear colleagues and friends work, but I have to differently acknowledge those who are always there, no matter where I am or they are. Leslie Peirce, Michael A. Gomez, and Ehud Toledano shared so much wisdom. There is no archive where information about slaves in the Middle East is stored that Terry Walz has not discovered, and he always shares whatever he has. Herman Bennett and Jennifer Morgan literally helped me reorient myself. Beth Baron has been a guide all along the way. Israel Gershoni carefully, critically, and dependably read chapters sent in haste and anxiety. Roger Owen was there for almost every talk I gave. Sahar Bazzaz and Bill Granara have been friends like the best inns—each always finds room for me.

It has meant a great deal to me to see my in-laws, David and Lucia Powell, smiling at me from audiences with the kind of warmth and pride I have missed since my mother's death. Living closer now to my sister,

Margot Troutt Keys, and my brother, David Troutt, has better helped me translate the power of love and kinship that many of the former slaves in this book searched for. My sons, Jibreel and Gideon, have watched this book grow as I have watched them grow. They are the ones who have trained me to be truly productive, have forgiven me for research trips (unless they could come along), and have been the reason to keep on pushing.

And finally, I must thank my husband, Timothy Powell, for absolutely everything. Never have there been stronger hands to hold, throughout this entire process, Timmy, than yours.

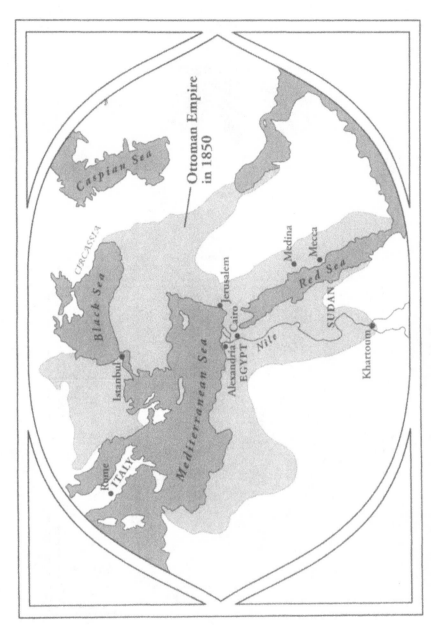

The Ottoman Empire in 1850. Map by David E. Chandler.

Egypt and the Sudan. Map by David E. Chandler.

The Caucasus. Map by David E. Chandler.

Prologue

In the fall of 2005, a group of Sudanese refugees erected a makeshift camp on the grass of Mustafa Mahmud Square in the middle-class Cairo neighborhood of Muhandiseen. They had chosen this site for its proximity to the offices of the United Nations High Commission for Refugees (UNHCR), and their camp was set up in protest against the legal limbo in which they found themselves and for which they held the UNHCR responsible. Most of them, having fled the long civil war in the south of Sudan or the newer war in Darfur, had lived in Cairo for months or even years without being legally recognized as refugees. This status kept them from being able to find jobs or to gain access to education for their children. They lived in poverty along Cairo's margins.[1]

But Mustafa Mahmud Square is not a marginal urban site: it is a bustling hub in the middle of the city. Across from the refugees' shantytown, on the other side, stands the grand Mustafa Mahmud Mosque. For months, the refugees relied on the charity of the mosque, which offered food and showers. Many in the neighborhood supported the refugees' attempt to make their voices heard, but patience wore out after three months and three thousand refugees had spread across the square. The UNHCR offered the refugees better apartments and reviews of their status, but the refugees insisted they be granted the means, and documentation, to leave Egypt. In answer to the impatience of Muhandiseen's residents and the employees of the UNHCR, police ended the stalemate and charged the camp early in the morning of December 29. They hosed the refugees with water cannons and dragged others away to buses. The *New York Times* reported the next day that twenty-three refugees were killed, several of them children.[2]

In the messy diplomatic aftermath, officials from the UNHCR and the Egyptian government wrestled with questions about the refugees. The government's spokesman, Magdy Rady, offered this apology: "We are sorry. What happened is unfortunate, it is sad, but it was not the intention of the police. The Sudanese pushed us to do this. They do not want to settle in Egypt. They want to move to another country. We did not know what else to do. It was a very difficult situation." Mr. Rady admitted to being mystified by the intransigence of the Sudanese. "I do not understand. What were they fighting for?"[3]

Later investigations explained with more clarity why the Sudanese wanted so badly to leave Egypt. Not only had their legal limbo made economic mobility all but impossible; these southern or Darfuri Sudanese daily faced discrimination. Gamal Nkrumah described their situation a few weeks later:

> Questions are now being raised about how Egypt has failed Sudanese asylum-seekers. And it is not only the authorities who are implicated, but the public as well. Sudanese people, particularly southerners, face daily harassment in the streets of Cairo. They are subjected to racist taunts, and insults hurled from the unemployed. Egyptians are understandably angry at the deplorable conditions they face, including joblessness and disenfranchisement, and it appears they have been unable to resist the temptation of scape-goating the estimated five million Sudanese residing in the country.[4]

An Egyptian columnist for *Al-Masry al-youm* echoed the indignation of Gamal Nkrumah in an opinion piece published several years later, in which she described watching a young Egyptian woman harass a southern Sudanese woman while riding on the Cairo Metro. The reporter, Mona Eltahawy, intervened only to have the Egyptian girl and her mother berate her and tell her it was none of her business. The young Sudanese woman thanked her. Eltahawy responded in her article: "I could only imagine other times she'd been abused publicly. We are a racist people in Egypt and we are in deep denial about it." Looking back over recent history, she continued, "What else but racism on Dec. 30, 2005, allowed hundreds of riot policemen to storm through a makeshift camp in central Cairo to clear it of 2,500 Sudanese refugees, trampling or beating to death 28 people, among them women and children?"[5]

Many Sudanese refugees would welcome the sensitivity of Nkrumah and Eltahawy but may have wondered, as I did reading these accounts, why none of these reporters repeated the exact insults hurled at refugees on Cairo's streets. As I learned from interviews with Sudanese refugees even before the Muhandiseen incident, the most painful epithet was *'abid*, the Arabic word for "slave," a word intended for darker-skinned people of African descent. I think the silence around this word, even between the most caring of observers, reflects a larger silence about the legacy of slavery that connects Egyptian history to Sudanese history. When the Egyptian government's spokesman, Mr. Rady, expressed his bafflement about what the Sudanese refugees were fighting for, he also disclosed a lack of awareness about how the southern Sudanese are connected, painfully, to Egyptian society.

The refugees also expressed their determination to leave Egypt and their exhaustion at carrying a history on their backs about which they, too, had little understanding. Their large and loud presence in Muhandiseen dredged up clumsily articulated historical memories of earlier generations of Sudanese forcibly migrated to Egypt and other parts of the Ottoman Empire. The refugees have followed, unfortunately, in the footsteps of thousands of slaves who crossed the same paths hundreds of years before. They are caught in the grips of a historical geography. When they arrive in Cairo, they look like the people who once labored as slaves, in the eyes of a population that attributes a particular kind of social and cultural darkness to the south of Sudan or Darfur. This imagined map has distorted and perverted "their understanding of the world."[6]

The following chapters will attempt to fill in these gaps in historical geography by exploring the maps made by slaves caught in the slave trade, from the south of Sudan, to Egypt, to Ottoman cities in Anatolia, and to Europe. By looking at the narratives of a group of people who were born within a decade of each other in the late nineteenth century and died by the 1960s, I hope to show how slaves and the experience of slavery affected each one and how they told their stories to very different audiences. Each of the former slaves discussed in the book traveled thousands of miles, to different cities and homes, learning different religions and languages that helped them integrate socially as best they could. Each of the former slave owners narrated how slavery was an experience of childhood; what was more challenging, as their writings show, was how to make the transition into a different, "modern," and postcolonial political environment in which, to use Frederick Douglass's phrase, "the old things of slavery" had no place.[7]

Chapter 1 focuses on the topographical textual map of Cairo that 'Ali Mubarak wrote between the years 1886 and 1889 while he was minister of public works and commissioned to tear down and rebuild the parts of Cairo deemed too old and unsustainable. Through the pages of his famous *Al-Khitat al-tawfiqiya al-jadidah*, 'Ali Mubarak explored the impact slaves had on Cairene, Egyptian, and his own personal history. From 'Ali Mubarak we learn how some Egyptians divided slaves racially and ethnically, often in oversimplified ways. But never is their participation in history ignored.

I move from Egypt to Sudan in Chapter 2, which analyzes the narrative of Babikr Bedri, a one-time fighter in the Mahdi's army, a trader in Sudan, a well-known educator who founded a school for girls in the north of the country, and a longtime slave owner. Babikr Bedri's lively memoirs tell another side of the history of slavery in Sudan. They also reveal how contentious the issue of slavery became as the British grew more involved in the administration of the country, particularly after 1925. A slave-owning nationalist like Babikr had to confront British contempt for his leadership (even from officials who liked him) because of the structure of his household.

Chapter 3 examines the memoirs of Salim C. Wilson, a Dinka man enslaved in the south of Sudan, who confronted the religious rebellion of the Mahdi personally and who left Sudan for England under the sponsorship of British Protestant missionaries. Salim was a contemporary of Babikr Bedri and would have recognized many of the historical experiences narrated by Babikr, but from a deeply different perspective. And unlike Babikr, Salim's own name, like that of many Sudanese slaves, mapped stages of his journey out of his homeland—Salim was the name his first owner gave him, and Charles Wilson was the name of the missionary who gave him his first home in England. He learned Arabic as a slave and English as a free man and worked as a lecturer in England, telling the story of his enslavement. He published his narrative in several editions, each time working to prove how Christianity had civilized him. But Salim also remembered his life before slavery and worked equally as hard to prove himself an authority on the anthropology of his own people.

Chapter 4 explores the intimate connections between family life and enslavement that are also made clear in the memoirs of Huda Sha'rawi and Halide Edib Adivar, national leaders who, like Babikr Bedri, grew up in households where slaves helped raise them. Huda was one of the founders of the Egyptian women's movement, and her Ottoman contemporary, Halide, was a leading voice among Turkish women. Both were nationalist pioneers who grew disappointed with their male colleagues' lack of commitment to issues and laws concerning the rights of women. Both also grew up in households in which there were Sudanese, Ethiopian, and Circassian slaves, reflecting the larger network of the slave trade found in Cairo and in Istanbul. To different degrees in their memoirs, both Halide and Huda confronted how slavery reflected on their own maturity, personally and politically, as they grew into outspoken national figures.

Chapter 5 studies the lives of a group of Sudanese former slaves who were freed by Italian Catholic missionaries in Khartoum and trained, linguistically and theologically, to become missionaries themselves. All of them became nuns or priests and moved from Sudan to Egypt, sometimes to Jerusalem, then to Italy for their training. Only a few of them returned to Sudan, but when they did, they were figures who commanded respect. One of them, Father Daniel Sorur Pharim Deng, wrote articles that explored the philosophy of slavery and the meaning of abolition. Father Daniel also wrote and lectured about what enslavement had done to his Dinka family and the damage caused particularly between him and his mother. Father Daniel and the other black sisters discussed in this chapter wrestled with racist European attitudes, much as Salim C. Wilson did in England, but most were able to make their homes there.

The final chapter outlines the symbolic power of one of the world's most famous former slaves, Saint Josephine Bakhita. Many of the refugees from the southern Sudan who fought the police in Muhandiseen sought refuge afterward in Saint Bakhita Centers throughout Catholic and Protestant churches in Cairo. Her life has been emblematic for Sudanese refugees for decades, never more so than when Pope John Paul II canonized her in 2000.

Like the former slaves who preceded her, as discussed in Chapter 5, Bakhita became a Catholic in Italy. But she was sold to an Italian consul in Sudan and went to Italy with him to escape the Mahdi's armies. Barely educated and never fluent in Italian, Bakhita fought to become a nun, and her case became a cause célèbre in late nineteenth-century Italian society. Once free and a woman religious, Bakhita, too, toured the country, showing her scars and sharing her experiences. She dictated these to another sister, and her translated memories have been reprinted at least ten times, in numerous languages. Although she may have been the least articulate of the former slaves in this study, spiritually she was by far the most eloquent. Even though they all traveled just as far, it is Bakhita's history that has been retold the most times to refugees who see in her life and the work she was forced to do a model for their own circumstances. To some scholars, she has redefined the very historiography of slavery. With her smiling image found on many church doors in Cairo, perhaps she adds to the history that 'Ali Mubarak first began writing down.

Public Workers, Private Properties

SLAVES IN 'ALI MUBARAK'S HISTORICAL RECORDS

The yellowed pages of the first editions of *Al-Khitat al-jadidah al-tawfiqiyah li misr al-qahirah* resemble woven tapestries, with regular patterns of sentences printed in very small font that form a block of text that continues for pages and pages, seldom relenting into separated paragraphs. These twenty volumes were first published in Cairo between 1886 and 1889; following their lines requires patience on the part of the twenty-first-century reader. There are few of the modern printer's merciful rest stops (paragraphs, illustrations, double-spacing, or frequent punctuation). The reader must learn, page by page, to trust her guide, 'Ali Mubarak, to lead her eyes into the streets of Cairo and the villages of Egypt, through some of the most vivid descriptions of different eras of life in the country. But eventually, through the tightly ruled print, emerge images of temples, mosques, canals, castles, and the people who walked through them or worked in them over hundreds of years of history.

Many of these people, as 'Ali Mubarak unfailingly observed, were slaves. Some of those found in these pages were elite, military slaves who helped establish, build, and shape the city of Cairo under the Fatimid Empire in 969. Others contributed to battles that raged across the city, before the end of the Fatimids in 1171. Some of the slaves built armies, palaces, and infrastructure for the Mamluk Empire that ruled Egypt until the Ottomans conquered it in 1517. And while 'Ali Mubarak covered their centuries-old legacy over Cairo's palaces and streets, he also offered his readers details about the circumstances of slaves that his contemporaries owned, slaves that he himself owned, and the lives of notable ex-slaves who found new ladders to prominence in his lifetime.

Because there are no pictures in *Al-Khitat*, 'Ali Mubarak counted on a cultural connection he could share with his readers, one in which author

and audience shared a profound sense of place. It is my sense that the historical and contemporary presence of slaves in *Al-Khitat* strongly exem-
plifies this bond with readers in his lifetime and leaves readers of later
generations (and perhaps from other cultures) struggling to understand
the racial and ethnic diversity of the enslaved in Egypt. In this chapter, I
explore 'Ali Mubarak's understanding of slavery in Egypt. The ways in
which he identified slaves—as *'abid* or *mamluk*, black or white—reflected
the social, legal, and cultural understandings of slaves' identities then current among him and his readers (many of whom also owned slaves). Contemporary historians of Egypt and of slavery have depended on him for
so long, I believe, that as outsiders to the historical moments that so en-
gulfed him, we have sometimes failed to see just how intimately connected
to slavery our longtime guide was and how that connection influenced his
vocabulary about slaves. Extricating the details of particular slaves' lives
from the tight lines of *al-Khitat* requires a complicated close reading.

Reading 'Ali Mubarak

Other readers have noted the visual challenge presented by 'Ali Mubarak's
Khitat.[1] There are no maps or illustrations in these volumes, which were
printed at least seventy years after the publication of the brilliantly illustrated *Description de l'Égypte*, the French-commissioned topographical
study of Egypt published in Paris in 1809, after the failed French invasion
of Egypt. Instead, as Nezar AlSayyad has noted, 'Ali Mubarak

> starts the section on Cairo by slowly building through his narrative a full map
> of the city. He first introduces the concept of sea level, and invokes the differ-
> ent flood levels that the city had experienced in recent history. Having estab-
> lished this horizontal plane, he then outlines the main streets of the city and
> the structures that they lie on. It is a method that allows the reader to mentally
> construct the topography of the city in relationship to specified coordinates—
> akin to building a three-dimensional physical model with only the important
> landmarks.[2]

The reader's mental construction of Cairo's topography is work that,
AlSayyad remarks, proceeds unaided by "a single illustration or diagram,"
even though 'Ali Mubarak "was a skilled draftsman who drew and used

maps." Perhaps, AlSayyad speculates, "Mubarak felt that his audience did not need, or would not have understood, such a medium."[3] Perhaps he also intuited that his readers understood the theory and practice of writing a *khitat*. Literally, this word can be translated as "a plan," "a survey," or "topography." Literarily a *khitat* represented a historiographical genre established centuries earlier throughout the medieval Arabic-speaking world, a tradition especially well practiced by Egyptian historians.[4] This genre originated as a survey, assigned by authorities to document the resources of a particular area. Samia Mehrez has analyzed this genre as one particularly sensitive to "a patron whose interests it served and represented."[5] This is clear even in the title of 'Ali Mubarak's topography—*Al-Khitat al-jadidah al-tawfiqiyah li misr al-qahirah*, which means "the new plans of [Khedive] Tawfiq for Cairo Egypt"—referring to the ruler of Egypt, Tawfiq, at the time of Mubarak's writing. And his learned readers would have recognized the literary tradition to which 'Ali Mubarak's twenty volumes referred; his work was built on the fourteenth-century *khitat* written by al-Maqrizi, particularly because

> according to him, the Cairo described by al-Maqrizi was hardly recognizable any more. The city had expanded, its topography, geography and demography had changed and new structures had been erected, all of which needed to be recorded. In addition, there seems to be another equally valid reason for undertaking the project of re-writing, namely, the change of authority in the city, and the need to represent that new authority.[6]

'Ali Mubarak's audience of contemporaries would have read *Al-Khitat* at a time of great cultural and political change in Egypt, much of it engineered by the author himself. 'Ali Mubarak's own life mirrored the decades of dramatic change experienced by Egyptians in the middle to late nineteenth century. Born in 1823, he was the proud product of a secular educational system introduced to the country by the Ottoman governor (*wali*) Muhammad (Mehmet) 'Ali Pasha in the 1820s and 1830s. Although born in the Egyptian Delta to a family of religious teachers (*shaykhs*), 'Ali Mubarak flourished when he began a secular curriculum and excelled as a student in Muhammad 'Ali's School of Engineering (the Muhandiskhanah). His talents earned him a place in one of the educational missions that Muhammad 'Ali sent regularly to France. After

Muhammad 'Ali's death in 1848, 'Ali Mubarak held different positions in education and in the military, valued for his engineering expertise but vulnerable to the changing politics of Muhammad 'Ali's successors.[7] It was only after Muhammad 'Ali's grandson, Khedive Isma'il, took over the throne that 'Ali Mubarak's role in influencing the physical infrastructure of Cairo soared. In 1868, Isma'il appointed him minister (*nazir*) of both public works and education. It was a position with onerous duties; Khedive Isma'il had assigned to him the following gargantuan tasks: "(1) supervising the execution of plans for the quarter of Isma'iliyah; (2) redeveloping the older and vacant lands peripheral to Azbakiyah; and (3) drawing up a master plan for the entire city in accordance with the style of Paris."[8] This meant, as Nezar AlSayyad has noted, that "he was no doubt the chief planner and architect of Cairo during its transformation before the twentieth century."[9]

This also means that those readers who had the opportunity to read *Al-Khitat* when it was first published could have walked the streets 'Ali Mubarak described and would have recognized the corners of streets, perhaps at the tip of Shari'a 'Abdin, as indicated by the author's careful directions, where a palace used to be, yet "now it is destroyed and there is not a trace of it that informs of the history of its foundation."[10] If these readers were adults of a certain age, they may have remembered small alleys in old neighborhoods of Cairo that had, at the time of their reading, been removed upon order of the author. Although the author relied on his fellow Egyptians' familiarity with the topography of their country, he put little trust in their historical education or their memory of the past. He did not believe that his contemporaries, Cairenes in particular, knew the facts of their history. He wrote, in the beginning of *Al-Khitat*, of Cairo:

> We have found no one among the sons of Egypt who can interpret for us these changes or instruct us in the causes thereof, or guide us aright in understanding the country's notable monuments. We look upon these works but do not know who made them . . . how many the mounds that were once towering buildings, the ravines that were once splendid gardens, the tombs that lie hidden along the narrow lanes and the shrines scattered in the open country, which the common people are wont to misidentify. . . . How many the mosques that are ascribed to

men who did not build them, and temples to persons who had not even seen
them. . . . But it is our duty to know these things, for it is not fitting for us to remain in ignorance of our country or to neglect the monuments of our ancestors.
They are a moral lesson to the reflective mind, a memorial to the thoughtful soul.
. . . For what our ancestors have left behind stirs in us the desire to follow in their
footsteps, and to produce for our times what they produced for theirs; to strive
to be useful even as they strove.[11]

In *Al-Khitat*, his great duty is pronounced clearly: bringing this history to
his fellow Egyptians. As we read through this history, it is interesting to ob-
serve where he maintains silence and where he includes anecdotes of his
personal experience. 'Ali Mubarak admits very little about his own vast administrative power in these volumes but spends pages on the details of the
ruin of his disastrous second marriage. He places his own life story firmly
in the middle of the story of his natal village, Birinbal (where he retired and
where he wrote *Al-Khitat*), but says nothing about the political upheaval
that had disrupted his patron's authority—the early nationalist movement
of Colonel Ahmad 'Urabi Pasha in 1881, a powerful political drive that protested the glass ceilings imposed by the khedive and his highest officials on
indigenous Egyptians and called for Egypt for the Egyptians. There is no
mention that the British occupied the country in the fall of 1882, in response
to the 'Urabi rebellion; this may well be due to his significant role negotiating between the khedive's officials, 'Urabi's followers, and British agents;
the sensitivity that the rebellion elicited (he began publishing *Al-Khitat* only
a year after the British occupation); and the fact that 'Ali Mubarak spent
years in debate with European officials about the preservation of medieval
architecture in the neighborhoods of Cairo.[12]

Because 'Ali Mubarak's *Khitat* has served as a seminal text for more than
a century, and because, I believe, historians of Egypt have trusted him as a
unique and deeply insightful guide, this absence of social commentary has
left careful readers wanting much more. Nezar AlSayyad sees the problem
as one brought by the genre: "His earlier *khitat* reflects the imaginary of
Egypt and Cairo's built legacy through the lens of a planner. Though it does
document Cairo's architectural heritage with great faithfulness, however,
his *khitat* does not pay adequate attention to social reality, presenting its

built fabric as a closed chapter of the city's history."[13] Samia Mehrez also faults the genre of *khitat* writing for its inherent and repeated use of the passive voice—"it is said that" (*yuqalu inna*):

> The interesting aspect of the passive voice and reported speech is that both stylistic devices introduce a kind of polyphony in the text. Statements of "fact" are relegated to voices other than that of the author; as much as they appear to be objective statements, they do not allow for *one* reliable source of information. On a different level, the direct asides to the reader serve to reinforce the dialogic aspect of the text, where author and reader engage in a kind of direct exchange.[14]

This is true, which makes it even more significant that 'Ali Mubarak did pay close attention to particular groups of people whose lives in Cairo most dramatically reflected social realities—slaves. In these pages, in this narration of a capital city whose streets and buildings reverberated between what was old, beautiful, and worthy of preserving and what was old, decrepit, and necessarily destroyed, live the slaves. They are among the ancestors who, as mentioned earlier, built the monuments and the mosques. Their presence also populates the project between antiquity and modernity that 'Ali Mubarak and Khedive Isma'il tried so hard to build. Their presence is often felt in those particular neighborhoods that have been commissioned for dismantling or in the houses of notables on the rise in Muhammad 'Ali's, or Isma'il's, Egypt. Slaves figure prominently in 'Ali Mubarak's topographical description of Cairo and Egypt—the markets where they were sold, the buildings that they erected, the armies in which they fought, the country over which they ruled for centuries. Although their presence is felt very strongly in Mubarak's discussion of contemporary times—he himself owned slaves—it is my impression that slaves in *Al-Khitat* represent an institution that Mubarak knows will be dismantled, although he had nothing to do with that razing. For as his contemporary readers knew, by the time of *Al-Khitat*'s publication, Khedive Isma'il's projects had plunged the treasury into bankruptcy; his successor, Tawfiq, had only barely overcome a nationalist rebellion; and the British government, with a keen eye toward abolition, had invaded and occupied Egypt. 'Ali Mubarak's readers would not have been surprised by the presence of slaves, in either the distant past or in representations of Egypt's present, or in their own homes. One wonders, though, when reading these volumes so filled with sensitivity to the timing of urban decay and renewal, what 'Ali Mubarak considered to be the legacy of slavery and of the slaves. With many of them having built the monuments and great edifices of Egypt, could they be claimed as ancestors? As movers and shakers in Egypt's past? Could they be included as participants in Egypt's future?

The Many Topographies of Slavery

'Ali Mubarak's openness about slaves and slavery serves as an important guide to how slavery was remembered in the Egyptian society of 1889, and would be remembered by later generations of Egyptians. Written after the completion of his commissioned projects of municipal destruction and rebuilding, 'Ali Mubarak's *Khitat* describes, it can be argued, textual sites of memory. Although not nearly as mournful of the past as al-Maqrizi was when writing his own *Khitat*, 'Ali Mubarak makes his pages realms of memory (*lieux de mémoire*) by reconstructing Egypt's historical past in as physically vivid terms as possible to ensure that Egyptians will understand the significance of their environment's past.[15] His volumes offer us a glimpse into a unique moment in Egyptian history, when different traditions of slavery had not been eliminated but were losing their relevance. The perceived wisdom about slaves that 'Ali Mubarak offers from within the changing traditions of his society permit us, I believe, a rare look at an institution in the process of being remembered before it is erased or before it is monumentalized as "history." As Pierre Nora wrote,

> Memory and history, far from being synonymous, appear now to be in fundamental opposition. Memory is life, borne by living societies founded in its name. It remains in permanent evolution, open to the dialectics of remembering and forgetting, unconscious of its successive deformations, vulnerable to manipulation and appropriation, susceptible to being long dormant and periodically revived. History, on the other hand, is the reconstruction, always problematic and incomplete, of what is no longer. Memory is a perpetually actual phenomenon, a bond tying us to the eternal present; history is a representation of the past.[16]

I think 'Ali Mubarak catches just this moment, between history and memory, in regard to the slaves he describes and the effects of their actions, or even their presence in particular positions in society. Here are slaves, like 'Anbar Effendi, whose voice the reader can almost hear, as remembered by 'Ali Mubarak. Yet there are slaves, like the black Fatimid slave soldiers, fully rendered as historical markers of an important and changing Cairo neighborhood.

Almost all studies of the phenomenon and experience of slavery in the late nineteenth century draw on *Al-Khitat* for insights into the roles that slaves played in Egypt.[17] We know from 'Ali Mubarak that slavery had existed in Egypt for many centuries, that the Fatimids employed slave soldiers of different ethnicities, and that the Mamluks who built much of Cairo in the fourteenth and fifteenth centuries were themselves slave soldiers.[18] Volume 1 of *Al-Khitat* traces the roles of slaves in state building through the Ottoman conquest of Egypt and the conquests and reforms of Muhammad 'Ali to the end of the 1880s. Throughout these centuries, being a slave did not exclude one from either power or, as 'Ali Mubarak presents the circumstances of his own century, knowledge. In *Al-Khitat*, 'Ali Mubarak presents knowledgeable slaves who know where they come from, such as the *mamluk* slave woman resisting her Coptic master, and 'Anbar Effendi, a confident and powerful administrator whose education is the envy of people who otherwise would not have considered him a peer. So, in continued reflection of Pierre Nora's statement about the place between memory and history, it is clear that contemporary historians of slavery in the Middle East must rely on 'Ali Mubarak's own sense of the historical role of slaves, as well as on his vivid and powerful memories of slaves he knew.

'Ali Mubarak's texts remain monumental sources about the complicated positions and interactions of slaves in Egyptian society, but his terminology for the different kinds of slaves to be found is almost Manichean in its simplicity: black slave (*'abid*) and white slave (*mamluk*).[19] I chose to begin this study of slavery's remembrance and legacy with Egypt because so many different slave routes ended there and thousands of slaves who originated in different cultures eventually made their homes there. Once settled, all that diversity is erased in *Al-Khitat*: 'Ali Mubarak describes them as "white" (*mamluk*), or "black" (*'abid*); this elides who they were and where they came from. It is also somewhat surprising to me, because 'Ali Mubarak wrote *Al-Khitat* at a time when slavery was under much discussion in Egyptian society, and Egyptians found the structure of their society and their homes under both the uncomfortable scrutiny of the British administration that had occupied the country in 1882 and the glare of politically powerful abolitionist societies in London.[20] I will return to how he navigated his memories between the tumultuous politics of the last decade of his life at the end of this chapter, but let us first break down what and who it meant to be a black slave or a *mamluk,* in Egypt in the late nineteenth century.

Slaves and Destruction in Medieval Cairo

As we explore 'Ali Mubarak's investigation into the past, it is important to bear in mind that he followed in the literal footsteps of the medieval Egyptian historian al-Maqrizi, who spent the years between 1417 and 1440 writing his own *khitat* (known in Arabic as *Kitab al-mawa'iz wa-l-I'tibar bi-dhikr al-khitat wa-l-athar*). 'Ali Mubarak relied heavily on al-Maqrizi, particularly for information about Cairo during the Fatimid and Mamluk Empires. Taqi al-Din al-Maqrizi was a scholar, teacher, and historian. Unlike 'Ali Mubarak, he did not bear the great administrative authority over the city about which he wrote, serving more as a witness to its changes.[21] Moreover, al-Maqrizi brought a sense of dread to his text concerning what he feared would be the imminent destruction of his beloved city due to neglectful rulers and incompetent administrators. As Nasser Rabbat writes, "A heightened sense of loss imbues him with an urgent desire to capture cherished memories—both his own and those of the denizens of Cairo—before they slip away with the disappearance of the places and buildings to which they are attached."[22] One historical event, long past even by al-Maqrizi's time, served as an apocryphal warning if a ruler's care in governance faltered. This was the civil war between black slave troops and Turkish-speaking soldiers that ravaged Cairo in 1062 during the reign of the Fatimid caliph al-Mustansir.[23] Al-Maqrizi called this years-long armed struggle "days of calamity and death" (*ayam al-shidda wal-ghala'*).[24] As presented by Mubarak, however, a malaise and disorder infected the city before the days of calamity had begun. Al-Mustansir's predecessor had lost his senses, and there was an increased widespread fear "of the immorality that had raided the neighborhoods and plundered the countryside, and the greed of the slaves ['*abid*] had increased and overtaken them."[25]

This disruption of order led to what 'Ali Mubarak calls "the great struggle in the era of al-Mustansir" (*al-fitnah al-'adhimah fi 'ahd al-Mustansir*). Tensions between the black slaves of the government (*'abid al-dawlah*) and Turkish-speaking soldiers (*'asakir al-turk*) worsened into a state of violence during which ministries were burned, markets destroyed, and disease spread. In fact, as 'Ali Mubarak states, all of the chaos and violence would ultimately lead to the end of the Fatimid Empire and Europeans would seize control of Egypt.[26]

What caused the internal war between black slave soldiers and Turkish soldiers? Part of the blame lay in al-Mustansir's neglect of his own retinue. Part lay in an incident in which a drunken Turkish soldier, armed with a knife, stabbed a recently purchased black slave. The slaves quickly assembled and killed the Turkish soldier. The slaves also gathered to ask al-Mustansir whether he had ordered the killing, but he denied the accusation. Then the Turks arose to attack the black slaves, massacring many of them. And here, Mubarak places much of the responsibility for the disruptive ambition or greed (*tami'a*) of the slaves on the caliph's mother, Sayyida Rasad, herself "a black slave girl."[27] Sayyida Rasad was deeply affected when the slaves were killed because, 'Ali Mubarak writes, of their shared ethnicity (*li kawnha min jinsihim*):

> It was she who was the reason for their great numbers in Egypt. It was she who, out of her ample love for them, bought them from every possible place, until it was said that their numbers exceeded 50,000 slaves. After that battle, she secretly supported them with money and with weapons. She had ruled in the country, and her word was enforced. She goaded the slaves into killing the Turks, and the strife began again, and the violence lasted until the year 459 [1067].[28]

This is a fascinating passage for what it says about ethnicity, slavery, and authority. Sayyida Rasad clearly commanded extraordinary powers, having served as regent when al-Mustansir was too young to rule. In his historical survey of this period, Yaacov Lev writes that a previous Fatimid caliph, al-Zahir, had bought her and that she had her former master, a Jew, appointed minister years later. In this passage, not only does she use her money and authority to create a force loyal to her but she does so out of ethnic affiliation.

Such an expression of ethnic belonging raises important questions about Fatimid society and the political roles played by slave elites. It is well known that slaves of all races could attain high office in the Fatimid Empire, as in other Islamic empires in the premodern world of the Middle East. Al-Mustansir's mother was able to take what seems to have been extraordinary advantage of her position and "worked with slave dealers to build an even larger military force" of African slaves who served as cavalry. But this appears to have provoked unusually hostile racial relations: "The appearance of African cavalry created a major racial and political conflict with the light-skinned Central Asian Turkish-speaking *mamluk*s who saw the African cavalry as a direct threat to their role as the leading military contingent in the army of Egypt."[29] Was it the promotion to cavalry, and not only their increase in numbers, that threatened the white soldiers (often slaves themselves)?

'Ali Mubarak does not specifically cite the promotion to cavalry as part of the growing problem between the Turkish-speaking soldiers and the black slaves, but it is clear from his text that a crucial part of the order of the social fabric had been shattered and could not be righted until the Turks finally defeated the *'abid*. What interests me is how 'Ali Mubarak defines these expressions and terminologies and how his usage and understandings of these terms reflect his nineteenth-century sense of ethnic and racial belonging. The very term *'abid*, used so often by 'Ali Mubarak, has historically in Egypt been used to define black African slaves. When Sayyida Rasad makes sure to have a lot of black slaves around—people, it is implied, like her—does she do so because of a racial consciousness already pronounced in the late eleventh century? Or does it reflect 'Ali Mubarak's own sense of racial or ethnic hierarchies in the society of his day? 'Ali Mubarak describes her protectiveness as her great love for them, because she was one of them, but who are they? He points out that she bought them from every possible place, but where did they come from? What languages did they speak? Is it possible that her "love for them" came from a tribal affiliation, even if they came from so many different places? And did the Turkish soldiers share a similar esprit de corps? Their fight for social standing and political survival seems less surprising, in *Al-Khitat*, than that of their black enemies.

The struggle between these armies raged for seven years. Many of the black slaves were pushed out of Cairo. As 'Ali Mubarak puts it, the country-side of the Delta and parts of upper Egypt fell into the hands of the slaves (*wa saar al-ṣa'id bayn aydi al-'abid*). In *Al-Khitat*, those areas of Egypt under black slaves' control lost their beauty and their property value. Cairo itself was divided and destroyed by the fighting, and those remaining black slave soldiers were forcibly moved out of the center of the city into an area Mubarak describes as bereft of real buildings or settled development (*khali'an min al-bina' al-bitah*). Half of this area, Birkat al-'Azbakiyah, consisted of gardens, and the other half, "substantial lakes" and "numerous smaller ponds"; those buildings that had been standing had been obliterated by the civil strife between slave armies.[30] The defeated black slaves built up a section there, first known as the neighborhood of the black slaves (*haarat al-'abid*) and later known as the neighborhood of the thieves (*haarat al-lusus*).[31]

Over time, Birkat al-'Azbakiyah was reintegrated into Cairo as an elite neighborhood. 'Ali Mubarak mentions that one of Salah al-Din al-Ayyubi's first investments in the architectural and developmental growth of Cairo was the demolition of *haarat al-'abid* and the planting of gardens there.[32] The banks of the ponds were filled with silt deposits from the Nile's annual flooding over the centuries, until they were completely dried out by the middle of the fifteenth century. In 1470, a Mamluk prince, Azbak, built a palace there and reflooded the pond, as did later princes and merchants who moved there. The area became one of the most fashionable districts of Cairo, populated now by Mamluk princes, the most elite slave soldiers of Egypt.[33] When Napoleon Bonaparte invaded Egypt in 1798 and seized homes and buildings from the ruling Mamluks, it was in Birkat al-'Azbakiyah that the French general and his top aides situated their headquarters. By this time, the shores of Birkat al-'Azbakiyah were "surrounded by magnificent gardens [built] during the 16th and 17th centuries for the pleasure and the comfort of the rich and the famous."[34]

One of the greatest heroes of reform in 'Ali Mubarak's *Khitat*, Muhammad 'Ali, turned his eyes on Birkat al-'Azbakiyah in the 1830s and had the area drained while diverting canals away from it and planting more gardens there.[35] Decades later, even though all the ponds were by then long gone, Khedive Isma'il, Muhammad 'Ali's grandson, saw in Birkat al-'Azbakiyah a site "ripe for the development that was soon to take place."[36] He dreamed of creating in the old Birkat al-'Azbakiyah a formal garden, modeled perhaps on the Bois de Boulogne and the Champ de Mars in Paris.[37]

Birkat al-'Azbakiyah was thus an area once made notorious by black slaves who, in 'Ali Mubarak's view, practically turned it into a slum; then it was gentrified by the elite and royal slaves of the Mamluk Empire and finally redesigned to fit the architectural expectations of a European-minded khedive in 'Ali Mubarak's own lifetime. As his *Khitat* makes clear, 'Ali Mubarak considered the eleventh-century battle between the slaves and the Turkish soldiers so important an event in the city's history that it introduces Mubarak's readers to a neighborhood with which they must have been quite familiar by the 1880s, even had they not known of its historical antecedents. What irony may he have hinted at by teaching his readers that this chic, once-again beautiful neighborhood, made ready to meet foreign visitors' needs when the Suez Canal opened in 1869, had once been a ghetto of rebellious black slave soldiers? What would this mean for his representation of later, more contemporary slavery?

Mamluks

> Most wealthy, urban and urbane Ottomans encountered slaves in their own houses and in those of their friends and relatives. They could pretend that this was where a slave's story actually began and make believe that whatever had happened to that slave before belonged to another world—one that was uncivilized, unruly and beyond their control.
>
> Ehud Toledano

'Ali Mubarak identified himself strongly as an Egyptian, but the society in which he lived was intimately connected to the Ottoman Empire, as were most of the slaves about whom he wrote. Like the "urbane Ottomans" that Ehud Toledano describes,[38] 'Ali Mubarak lets his readers know about how different slaves were purchased (as in the description of Sayyida Rasad's buying black soldiers from all parts of Africa), but his *'abid/mamluk* binary also erases their pre-enslavement past. Although it is a stock phrase now in historical descriptions of Islamic slave systems to say that this was a multiracial and multiethnic trade, very different from the Atlantic slave trade or the institution of slavery in the United States or the Caribbean, using *mamluk* as a phrase to characterize white slaves tells us as little of the many places from which these slaves came as *'abid* does for slaves coming from vastly different parts of Africa. Slaves were more than just memory bearers for late nineteenth-century Egyptian or Ottoman society; they also carried within them the history and memories of other places that, if possible, should no longer be ignored.

Ottoman and Egyptian traditions of slavery intertwined, particularly after the Ottoman conquest of Egypt in 1517, when two kinds of slavery actually collided. Until that point, Egypt had been governed by dynasties of Mamluks (the word itself means "owned" in Arabic), and refers to an institution in which young Christian boys were captured by Muslim military rulers, converted to Islam, and received the finest military training. When they finished their training, they were usually manumitted and organized in different households (*bayts*), who competed for political control of Egypt and dominated the country from 1250 to 1517.[39] "The Mamluks can be classified as slaves who became masters and belonged to the uppermost layer of Muslim military society," as David Ayalon has stated. "Their overwhelming majority was brought over to the Muslim world from countries situated beyond its borders, which means they were born infidels." For quite some time, these territories meant Central Asia and its environs.[40] And there were, throughout the Islamic world, other empires that employed military slaves: for example, the Fatimids, as we have seen; the Ayyubids; and the Seljukids. When the Ottoman Empire began to regularize its armies in the fifteenth century, it also employed a system of military enslavement called the *devshirme*, in which young boys from the Balkans, and later from regions of the Caucasus and Georgia, were appropriated, trained in Turkish (as were the Mamluks), and also given the best training the military had to offer. As Stanford Shaw describes, "Most Christian subjects outside Istanbul were liable to the levy, with agents going periodically through the provinces, conscripting the brightest subject youths for service to the sultan. Each group of recruited children was turned over to a *surucu* ('driver'), who brought them to Istanbul or Bursa."[41] The most gifted were given specialized training that prepared them to "enter particular branches of the Ruling Class." Although their service originated in enslavement, they were groomed to rise to the top of Ottoman society, "subjected to strict discipline, isolated from the outside world as well as their families, and cut off from women under the guard of the white palace eunuchs." When they completed their training, they were freed, "for entry as full members of the Ruling Class or as subjects." Significantly, no matter how far up the Ottoman hierarchy these former slaves climbed, they "always considered themselves bound to their old masters, acting for mutual advantage whenever it was possible for them to do so."[42]

Before the Ottomans conquered Mamluk Egypt, the rigid separation between Mamluks and the people they ruled made "it easy to tell Mamluks from non-Mamluks." This ruling class was exclusively Turkish speaking; as Michael Winter has written, "Turkishness was their distinguishing mark: they alone in Egypt . . . had Turkish names and they spoke Turkish."[43] The hierarchy was rigidly maintained; the children of Mamluks could not themselves become Mamluks and were always given Arabic Muslim names, not the Turkish ones of their fathers.[44] Those Mamluks who were actually Circassian and spoke their own language were educated in Turkish and considered to be Turks by the indigenous, Arabic-speaking population over whom they ruled. Turkish was thus "the language of the ruling caste." This rigid hierarchy grew complicated, however, when the Ottoman armies invaded Egypt. This army was filled and run by former children of the *devshirme,* also raised in a Turkish-speaking environment and also members of a proud and powerful ruling elite. The Ottoman defeat of the Mamluks blurred the social and linguistic dividing lines so jealously guarded by the Mamluks.[45] Over the years, however, as the Ottomans governed in only the highest offices (such as governor), as the *devshirme* system fell apart, and as the Mamluk system continued, Mamluks continued to occupy important military and administrative positions in Egyptian society.[46]

Thus, for the rulers of premodern Egypt, ethnic and racial distinctions played a central role in the ordering of society. Stereotypes of different groups "were central to the social concepts of the people at that time." As Michael Winter sees it, "All sources, literary and official alike, emphasize the distinctions between Circassians and Turks, Arabs and Turks."[47] By the late eighteenth century, new groups entered the ruling classes of Egypt through slavery. These youths were not levied—the *devshirme* system had died out.

Instead, they had been kidnapped from villages in the Caucasus and from Georgia. Others were actually sold by feudal lords. And even if they had been kidnapped as teens and knew exactly where they came from, who their parents were, and what their previous social status had been, they still lived in Egypt as Mamluks.[48] This diversity did little to change their linguistic identity for those they ruled. These distinctions between the Turkish-speaking rulers and the Arabic-speaking subjects were still strong by the time Muhammad 'Ali became the Ottoman governor of Egypt in 1805; even after he wiped out the Mamluk forces in Cairo in 1811, *mamluk* as a word still signified a Turk or a Circassian (or a Georgian or a Greek).

What did it mean to be "Circassian"? The Turkish word *Çerkes* is an umbrella appellation that refers to the indigenous tribes and clans of the North Caucasus. They had their own dialects and lived in social structures that "varied from tribe to tribe." Generally, Circassian society "was composed of four classes: princes (*pshi*), nobles (*vork, ozden*), freemen (*tokav, tlfokotl*) and serfs (*pshitl*)." It was not a system with a centralized authority: Circassians lived in tribal confederations and resisted foreign domination.[49] In the 1850s, Russia attacked the eastern section of Circassia, in the Caucasus. After the attack, the Russians expelled "a very large free and slave population from the Caucasus," which had a "major impact on the Ottoman slave market."[50] This flooding of the market with Circassians reintroduced agricultural slavery and expanded the "traffic in young female slaves intended for elite harems." These girls were integrated into different roles depending on their "looks and talents and as circumstances (or luck) determined."[51] Some became concubines; others were married or were employed. As Ehud Toledano writes,

> After their settlement in the empire, Circassian parents continued to sell their daughters through slave dealers or, less frequently, directly to buyers. Although such dealings were largely conducted within the slave class—that is, slaveholders selling their slaves' children owing to the hardships and opportunities created by their forced dislocation—a growing number of freeborn children were also being traded and reduced to slavery.[52]

These were men and women who also belonged to 'Ali Mubarak's society, who were in some of the houses he visited as both owners and as slaves.

Although none of this history can be gleaned from his calling them *mamluk*s (rarely does he use the term *çerkesi* to describe them), he does render faithfully the unique ways in which this group integrated into Egyptian households. Calling these slaves "white," he mentions them as gifts exchanged as symbols of high esteem, as in the case discussed later of Dr. Nabrawi and the slave he received from the khedive's mother. 'Ali Mubarak, in fact, respects the strictly observed privacy of Muslim families while still explaining how generations of Circassian or Georgian slaves had been freed and married others like themselves, creating a family tree of enslavement and entitlement, an oxymoronic relationship to most Western observers that was one of the most common and strongest traditions linking these families.

Classic examples of this type of merging can be found in well-explored nineteenth-century court documents. In one example from 1851, Muhammad Quftan Pasha, a wealthy member of the Council of Egyptian Judicial Rulings, established a religious endowment (*waqf*). He and his wife had no children but owned several homes in the province of Beni Sueif and in Cairo. He himself had twenty freed slaves at the time of the *waqf*'s establishment: "eleven males (three Circassians, four Ethiopians, and four blacks) and nine females (five Circassians and four blacks). His wife had three freed female slaves, one Circassian and two blacks." It is important to highlight that both Muhammad Quftan Pasha and his wife (nameless in this historical account) had once been slaves themselves. He was "a freed slave of the former *wali* of Egypt, who was married to a freed slave-girl of his former master."[53] He was an elite slave, a member of the *kul* system, in which military slaves became part of the upper ranks of civil bureaucracy in both the Ottoman Empire and its vassal state Egypt. As Ron Shaham points out, *kul* slavery was seen by Ottoman society "as an *origin*, rather than a *status*, whereas domestic and agricultural slavery definitely constituted a *status*." This means that "Ottoman society treated *kul* slavery as one of the paths to patronage, like kinship, marriage, adoption, or suckling. Therefore, the dichotomy between patronage and slavery, one voluntary and the other not, was alien to Ottoman realities."[54]

This kind of ease between being owned and owning is one of the most striking things about Ottoman systems of slavery, certainly for the *kul*s (as they were known in Istanbul) and *mamluk*s or "Turks" (as they were often called in Egypt). 'Emad Hilal also describes this cyclical system in which many of the slave owners were notables with slave roots, and an owner of a slave had often been himself once a slave; he notes that this kind of circular chain of enslavement could continue for at least four or five generations.[55] Within this system, even the most elite masters often bore children with slave women, who were recognized as mothers and freed. The majority of Muhammad 'Ali's sons were born of slave mothers. The same held true in less elite households, and the mothers could be of any race or ethnicity, although the further down in the economy one passed, the greater the likelihood that the slave mother would be Ethiopian or "zanjia" (black or "negro").[56] In complex and intimate ways, then, elite slaves shared the world of their masters. Through bearing and caring for children, their own (fathered by their masters) or their masters', born to other mothers, they became officially recognized members of the household. There was little if any secrecy about their origins as slaves, and these roots became part of families' legacies. Going further than the conventional wisdom that slaves were more like family in Egypt than slaves, repeated in a European guidebook about Egypt in 1885, I suggest that those slaves who were "treated more like members of the family than like servants" were intrinsically part of the family and had many opportunities to remind their "families" who they were.[57] By 'Ali Mubarak's time, as we will explore in more depth later, Circassians came as slaves or concubines to Egypt without the protection of these institutions—the distinctions between Turkish speakers and Arabic speakers could be blurred and was blurred if a native-born Egyptian was wealthy enough to buy or be given a Circassian concubine and have children with her, children who would be of Egyptian nationality.

Thus, for centuries white slaves came to Egypt through both the Mamluk and the Ottoman military systems. This had strongly deteriorated by the late nineteenth century, when generations of slaves and their masters, descended from Circassian or Georgian communities, shared a unifying experience, belonging (after manumission, after the birth of recognized children, after many such passages of life) to the same culture of Ottoman traditions. These generations of slaves and former slaves had outlived many aspects of the institutions that had maintained them as elites. Mamluk traditions of succession to power were eliminated once Muhammad

'Ali was able to bequeath the throne to his successors. One historian has gone so far as to say that "there was no trace of the Mamluk heritage, no sign of a behind-the-scene influence of the army."[58] But the parlance of Egypt's most influential historian and administrator, 'Ali Mubarak, undermines that statement. Even as they were transformed, the slave traditions that had long undergirded Ottoman society in general and Egyptian society in particular were cemented in the social divisions in which all elite slaves were "white" and called *mamluk*.

'Abid

Trade between Egypt and Sudan originated in antiquity, and the most famous route, traveled for centuries by the merchants and traders in huge caravans, was the ancient Forty Days Road (*darb al-'arba'in*). By the middle of the eighteenth century, caravans came to Egypt from two major trading centers, Darfur and Sennar.[59] As Terence Walz has listed, the staples of trade between Egypt and Sudan were "from the interior, slaves, camels, ivory, feathers, gold, vegetable and mineral raw goods and a few exotic luxuries such as animals and birds; from Egypt, textiles, metals, hardware, beads and semi-precious materials and, in the post-medieval period, firearms."[60] There were many other routes that took African slaves to Cairo and Istanbul. After Muhammad 'Ali's armies conquered Darfur, Sennar, and much of the rest of Sudan in 1820–21, thousands of slaves traveled the Forty Days Road. Thousands more enslaved Africans of many different tribes from Ethiopia, what is now Uganda and Tanzania, were forced to set sail from Red Sea coastal ports to the markets of Arabia, such as Jiddah and Mecca, or traveled farther east to be sold in the markets of Indian Ocean ports. By the middle of the nineteenth century, in 'Ali Mubarak's lifetime, the Egyptian trade in African slaves was far larger than the trade in Circassians, even when we account for the influx of forced migration after the Russian invasion of the Eastern Caucasus.[61]

An exploration of all of the routes, destinations, and experiences of African slaves coming from central and eastern parts of the continent to central cities in the Ottoman Empire and Egypt is a subject worthy of its own book. In this study, however, I focus attention mostly on the trade in and experience of slavery in Sudan, Egypt, and Ottoman Istanbul. I do this in part because the history of these particular routes and trade networks is well documented; there is much to be found on these subjects in the archives of Cairo, Khartoum, and Istanbul. More important, however, I choose to keep my attention on these routes because both slaves and slave owners who walked them, or traded in them, wrote about these experiences. In ways that differed from the trade in Circassian slaves but that were still as strong, the trade in Sudanese slaves united many elements in Egyptian and Ottoman households. Slaves who walked across routes that divided continents often lived together in elite households, as 'Ali Mubarak has shown us. I have not seen any historical record, however, that describes the arrival of new Mamluk or Circassian slaves with the same grandeur with which Egyptians in the eighteenth century met the slave-bearing caravans of Sudan:

> The arrival of the great Dar Fur caravan . . . was a momentous occasion. Upon entering the frontier of Egypt, it was greeted by a representative of the governor of Upper Egypt, usually a subaltern carrying the title *kashif*, who was entrusted with the responsibility of registering taxable goods. The encounter took place at Baris, the southern outpost of Kharga oasis, to the accompaniment of fireworks, and before the *kashif* and his clerks could scrutinize the merchandise, the *habir* and leading merchants of the caravan were given coffee and presented with a *binis*, a long ceremonial gown which was worn over the caftan. (This custom continued for many years and was enacted in the mid-nineteenth century in Asyut where merchants called upon the governor and were given caftans and pelisses.) The bestowal of ceremonial gowns, which has a long history in the East, may be considered an indication of respect for caravan officials and merchants following the *darb al-'arba'in*.[62]

After the wonderful greeting given to the merchants and caravan officials, the slaves were sent to markets in Daraw, Asyut, and Cairo.[63] Buyers purchased them for varying prices, depending on the slaves' age and gender and what was understood to be their ethnicity. Baer sums it up in the following way:

> Usually the price of black girls was a little higher than that of boys, although exceptions to this rule have been registered. The price of black adults was higher than that of boys by 50–100 percent. Eunuchs fetched double or three times the

price of black male adults. The price of Abyssinian boys was a little higher than that of Negro boys, and the difference grew with the age of the slave, reaching 100 percent. There were great variations in the difference between the price of Abyssinian girls and that of Negro girls, figures in our sources showing differences between 25 and 600 percent. The highest class was of course that of white females (Circassians), who were sometimes up to ten times as expensive as Abyssinian girls.[64]

Baer argues that the different values set for the price of different kinds of slaves fluctuated throughout the nineteenth century. He, too, diminishes the tribal distinctions of the slaves, dividing them into categories of "black," "Negro," and "Abyssinian," which his readers would presumably understand. But it is certainly true that in Darfur, the sultanate waged wars and raids against tribes it considered pagan—not Muslim and not monotheistic like other "people of the book." In Darfur these people were considered suitable for enslavement and often known as the "Fartit."[65] Over the decades of the nineteenth century, other non-Muslim groups were also forcibly absorbed into this category of "enslaveable"; people from the Nuba Mountains and from the many tribes of the Dinka, Azande, and Shilluk (to name only a few) from the southern Sudan were thrust into these labels, and into enslavement, by religiously based racial and ethnic assumptions that originated in Sudan itself.[66]

Muhammad 'Ali's invasion of Sudan in 1820–21 fueled the engine of slavery and its uses. Slaves were seized originally to form the backbone of the reformed army that the ruler of Egypt was trying to build. Although the original experiment in making slave soldiers out of Sudanese slaves did not fulfill Muhammad 'Ali's expectations, slave regiments known as the *jihadiya* remained an important part of the Egyptian and Sudanese military well into the twentieth century. Sudanese slave soldiers served long and dutifully; "they 'were recruited for life' as the official circumlocution put it."[67] Sudanese slaves were increasingly imported to Egypt to work in the agricultural fields of Muhammad 'Ali and his successors, and the trade flourished.[68] In the 1850s, a generation after the conquest of Sudan, an enterprising trader named al-Zubayr Rahman created his own slave-trading enterprise in the Bahr al-Ghazal region of Sudan, which sent slaves by the thousands directly to Egypt. He grew powerful enough to conquer Darfur in 1875, but this put him into direct confrontation with Khedive Isma'il, who defeated him and imprisoned him in Cairo (al-Zubayr was able to obtain the title of pasha for his suffering).[69] Ismai'il himself owned hundreds of slaves, who lived in his palaces and in the harems and who worked the vast agricultural lands he controlled. He and other large landowners (themselves former *mamluks*, as 'Ali Mubarak would describe them) put these slaves to work in fields given over to cotton, especially in the years of the American Civil War.[70] Another major use to which slaves were put, particularly slave women, was as domestic laborers in the households of Egyptian society. By the 1880s, being able to own a slave had become more possible and a more important step toward upward mobility for Egyptian notables—this privilege had been forbidden them under the Ottomans.[71] And what did this mean for Sudan, where slaves were so cheap that almost every household could own at least one? "It transformed the land of Sudan into one big raid: poaching, marketing and trading of slaves and slave caravans."[72]

Slaves Who Gentrify

Slaves who lived just before and during 'Ali Mubarak's lifetime can be found throughout the twenty volumes of *Al-Khitat*, in the many villages and towns in Upper and Lower Egypt that he described. Sometimes they serve in the background—exemplars of their masters' wealth; as anonymous Sudanese beings bought and sold in particular towns and villages; as Circassian slaves given as gifts or rewards to loyal subjects of the royal family. Sometimes, however, the slaves become the protagonists of 'Ali Mubarak's stories, literally transformed into the most visible faces and the most distinguishable voices in the villages where they lived. And in one notable case, they change 'Ali Mubarak's life completely.

In his entry for the village of Nabrah, 'Ali Mubarak focuses on the industrious life of Ibrahim Bey al-Nabrawi, a life that also bordered the transition Egypt made, in the middle of the nineteenth century, to secular-based education and professional training. During these decades of Muhammad 'Ali's rule (1805–48), new echelons of Egyptian society were encouraged to adapt to social reform, much of it inspired by Europe.[73] As a very young man, Ibrahim Bey al-Nabrawi began his education in the village Islamic primary school (*kuttab*) learning to write. After that accomplishment, his family sent him to Cairo, during the reign of Muhammad 'Ali, to sell watermelons. He failed to accumulate any profit (*ra's al-mal*, as Mubarak called it) and was too frightened of his family's reaction to return to Nabrah. He stayed in Cairo, where he studied medicine at the Islamic university Al-Azhar and was so successful that he accompanied a delegation of young men to France to learn more about science and law.[74] When Ibrahim Bey returned, Muhammad 'Ali appointed him teacher at the new medical school of Qasr al-'Aini. He was soon named chief physician (*hakimbasha*) and accompanied Muhammad 'Ali himself to Europe. Ibrahim Bey continued to advance through the patronage of Muhammad 'Ali and his successor, 'Abbas I, and even accompanied 'Abbas's mother when she performed the *hajj* (official pilgrimage to Mecca).[75]

The gift of a Circassian slave crowned his achievements. While in France, Ibrahim Bey had married a French woman who returned with him to Egypt. She bore him two children but died after his return from the *hajj*. In consolation, 'Abbas's mother sent him one of her finest slaves, with whom he shared a happy life until he died of asthma in 1879. 'Ali Mubarak describes the wealth of land that he left and how it was divided among the children of his different wives, including the daughter of his "white slave" (*al-jariyah al-bayda'*),[76] who received six hundred feddans in the district of Minya al-Farmawi. The sons of his other marriages supervised and administered this land.[77]

'Ali Mubarak sees this wealth and reward as fitting for a man who had pioneered medical practice like no other Egyptian before him. Other Egyptians, too, particularly under the aegis of Muhammad 'Ali, gained great wealth, as shown in their ownership of many slaves. Sayyid Ibn 'abd al-Rahman died in the village of Umm Duma in AH 1280 (1863–64 AD) after having reached the rank of *nazir* (overseer or director) of the district; he was a man with distinguished friends, one who possessed fine articles and many slaves. The sayyid owned so many slaves that it was said if he were riding, behind would also be riding thirty slaves or more, all dressed in cashmere shawls and robes of thick broadcloth with sleeves hemmed in silk. Only the sayyid's own dress was more impressive.[78]

Sayyid Ibn 'abd al-Rahman riding and parading his slaves becomes a landmark event in the description of Umm Duma. For the city of Asyut, it is eunuchs who distinguish the landscape or, as presented by 'Ali Mubarak, once did: "in older times (*al-zaman al-sabiq*) slaves were brought from Sudan to Asyut, to be prepared for service to the highest ladies."[79] Unlike any other presentation of enslavement in *Al-Khitat*, 'Ali Mubarak portrays this particular kind of slave etymologically, emphasizing the quaintness of the eunuch by tracing the history of the word for eunuch—*tawashi*— through Egyptian history. He lists whom al-Maqrizi meant by *tawashi*, whom the Mamluks meant by it, how many of them were owned by the Mamluk princes, what each one cost, and how the word is spelled in Turkish.[80] These very expensive slaves seem obsolete, relegated firmly to the past with their archaic name and no longer found in Asyut by 1886.

'Ali Mubarak did not employ the same past tense when mentioning where slaves were traded, as in the Siwa oasis or in the village of Kirdassa, not far from Giza.[81] And slaves figure, angrily and dramatically, in his description of the "events of Gaw," a small community near Asyut that is part of al-'Uqqal. These events escalated into a rebellion against the authorities of Khedive Isma'il, perhaps when 'Ali Mubarak was in office as minister of public works. Beginning his recitation of the events with a list of the vast properties left by the district head (*qa'imaqam*) who had eventually stopped the rebellion, Mubarak relates that a man from the upper Sa'id, claiming to be a holy man (*shaykh*), persuaded many of the villagers to follow him. Tensions were therefore already high between the villagers and the local authorities when a young Muslim slave woman (*mamluka*) complained to the self-proclaimed holy man that her master, a Coptic Christian (referred to in the text as *al-nasrani*), wanted to have sexual relations with her.[82] The Christian was brought in and told that he had the choice of either freeing her or selling her, but not the choice to be intimate with her—that was forbidden by Islamic law. The Coptic master insisted on his right to ownership. The *shaykh* (considered a somewhat dubious character by 'Ali Mubarak) would find no compromise and seized the woman from the Christian. The foreigner filed a formal complaint with the government, and the authorities asked the *shaykh* to surrender the woman. This he refused to do, and now agitation increased between the *shaykh*, the village, and the govern-

ment's agents. The *mudirs* (directors) of both Jirja and Asyut tried to intercede, troops were sent in (some of the soldiers were Sudanese *jihadiya*), and
fighting broke out. The *shaykh* was killed, along with many of his followers.
Others escaped into areas of the White Nile (Sudan). Many were pardoned
later by Khedive Isma'il, and the property seized from them was returned.[83]

"And thus we have related the talk about the village of Gaw," suc-
cinctly concluded 'Ali Mubarak.[84] Because of the complaint of a slave
woman, who refused to submit to her foreign master's sexual domination,
an entire town rose up against the government, and many were killed or
exiled. It is particularly interesting that the owner, a Christian, defended
what he considered his physical rights with his slave by appealing directly
to Egypt's government, who sent in troops to honor his claim to his slave.
These events also raise questions about the slave herself, identified as a
"white Muslim" (*muslima bayda mamluka*). The unnamed slave's objections
and seeming self-protection stand out on these pages where slaves rarely
are heard. From *Al-Khitat* and other accounts, it seems clear that she defied
her master's advances because of his religion. It must have been unusual
for an elite slave (as a white *mamluk* slave would have been) to be sold into
a situation such that a non-Muslim Egyptian could afford her.[85] Lucie Duff
Gordon mentions that the slave was known to have memorized the Qur'an;
clearly she used her knowledge of Islamic law to publicly protest her situation.[86] This slave's contemporaries seem to have recognized that her plight
was rare, but did they also see her outspokenness as unusual? What would
the situation have been like if she had not been an elite, white Muslim slave
but a dark-skinned Sudanese girl?

One can see in this account how the relationship between Egyptian
subjects, their ruler, and their government was changing during Isma'il's
rule (1863–79). When this village took on the mobilized armed forces of the
khedive, the heavy taxation of the farmers (*fallahin*) had become an onerous burden, whereas foreigners had the ability to take advantage of the
Mixed Courts to regularize their property and status in Egypt by appealing
to a government increasingly beholden to European banks for the intense
building and development Isma'il was introducing to the country.[87] After
decades of secular education, a new socioeconomic class of native-born
Egyptians was rising to the top of society. Egypt's elites looked increas-

ingly to Europe as a model for scientific, legal, and cultural progress, while also patterning their advancement along Ottoman cultural practices. And within this massively changing system, a Coptic Christian could appeal to the government to uphold his legal rights as a slave owner, and a slave could use popular opinion and the sanctuary of a self-elected holy man to uphold her inviolability as a Muslim woman. But solving the murky problem of who could legally be a slave, and of whom, sometimes was decided in different ways in the court of public opinion and in the official courts in the village of Gaw in 1865.

'Ali Mubarak situates himself firmly in the class of rising elites in the mid-nineteenth century and acknowledges with gratitude and a great deal of astonishment that a former slave opened the doorway to all of his education and accomplishments. When the topographic, biographic train of *Al-Khitat* reaches Birinbal, his native village, Mubarak takes several pages to describe his childhood, his education, and the man who really changed his life's course.[88] Writing that he will follow the pattern he has already created of listing the achievements and careers of the dignitaries of each of Egypt's cities and villages, 'Ali Mubarak identifies Birinbal as his home (phrased more quaintly as *masqat ra'si*, or "my native land") and says that he was born there in 1823 into a family of men who worked, traditionally, as imams, *qadi*s (judges), and religious speakers (*khutaba'*), with little connection to the local farmers or administrators (*wa lam yakun 'alayhim mima'ala al-fallahin wa la lahum 'ala'iq 'and hukam al-jihah*). This made them a rather weak family economically.[89] When 'Ali Mubarak was six years old and just learning how to read, political difficulties forced his family to leave their village. His father, a learned man, negotiated with the Arab tribe of al-Khaysh to become their *faqih* (in this case, teacher of the Qur'an). 'Ali Mubarak describes this as a social demotion for his father, who had to thus come down from the "august and the powerful" (*al-akram wal-ajlal*). His father's religious and moral sincerity endeared him to the Bedouin tribe, who built him a mosque and made him their imam, which enabled him to begin the education of his son.[90] So, early in the presentation of his life, 'Ali Mubarak illustrates his family's ability to be flexible when necessary, as well as their deep consciousness of social standing and hierarchies.

'Ali Mubarak's first teacher was a *shaykh* from a nearby village who hit him so often that Mubarak fled after two years of memorizing the Qur'an. Unfortunately, this set the pattern for the rest of his early religious and professional preparation. Some jobs were too debilitating: repeatedly, the teacher (*mu'allam*) or the scribe (*katib*) to whom he was apprenticed would cheat, verbally abuse, slap, or publicly humiliate the young 'Ali, to the point where he would either complain to his father or run away.[91] Other jobs taxed his maturity: he once worked as a junior scribe in a jail, writing letters for prisoners who took pity on him for his young age. But his father had heard that the military administrator of the district needed a qualified scribe. 'Ali had to send him an example of his handwriting, and when his application was accepted, he went to meet the administrator (*ma'mur*) himself. The appearance of this commander, 'Anbar Effendi, immediately challenged 'Ali's deepest social expectations:

> He was Ethiopian black [*aswad habashi*] as if he was a military slave ['abd mam-luk] yet he was generous, dignified, and venerated. I saw shaykhs and judges of the area standing respectfully before him [*waqifan bayn yadayhi*] while he issued orders and warnings to them. I hesitated before entering, then stood in front of him and kissed his hand. He addressed me in elegant, perfect Arabic [*bikalam raqiq 'arabi fasihi*] and said: "Do you wish to be my scribe and earn a salary of 75 *qurush* per week?" I answered him yes and then left his presence.
>
> I sat down outside with the servants. I knew that some of the shaykhs I had seen gathered before 'Anbar Effendi were some of the most eminent in the region, with great wealth and many servants, dependents, and slaves. Therefore, I was surprised by their worshipful behavior as they stood in his presence. I had never witnessed such a thing before. Maybe they were Turks for whom such a custom was not strange. I stayed there, shocked, wondering what forces could make these esteemed personages stand before a slave holding out their hands like that. I struggled mightily to figure this out [*harastu kull haras 'ala al-wuquf 'ala hatha-l-sabab*].[92]

The next day, 'Ali Mubarak's father was called to the *ma'mur*'s presence, where the arrangements for 'Ali's employment were finalized. When they returned home, 'Ali, still trying to grasp the incongruity of a dark-skinned man having so much power in Egyptian society, asked his father if 'Anbar

Effendi was a Turk. His father answered that maybe he was an emancipated slave. "But can a slave become a judge if even the grandees of the village cannot be?" When his father explained that perhaps 'Anbar Effendi's advancement was due to his decent morals and his broad knowledge, 'Ali remained unpersuaded. "Maybe he had been a slave at Al-Azhar?" his father ventured. "Would the education at Al-Azhar lead to this career as a *hakim* [doctor]?" Ultimately his father concluded, "My son, we are all slaves of God, and God raises up whom he wants."[93]

After he had been working for the *ma'mur* for a little while, he discovered the secret of 'Anbar Effendi's rise: When he was a child, he had been bought by one of the wealthiest, most prominent women of Egyptian society, who then enrolled him in the prestigious school Qasr al-'Aini in Cairo. This was the preparatory school where only young *mamluks* and Turks (as 'Ali Mubarak called them), children of elites who were close to Muhammad 'Ali, could attend (for years, no Egyptian student was enrolled).[94] 'Anbar Effendi gained from his state-of-the-art education at this secular preparatory school the skills for his impressive professional ascent: the handwriting necessary for a scribe but also useful skills such as Turkish and accounting. He proved his talents and advanced in ways that were unprecedented—even for a free farmer (*fallah*), even for an ambitious native-born literate young Egyptian like 'Ali. It was on the unusual but inspiring career of a slave that 'Ali Mubarak modeled his ideas for his own future. It was then that 'Ali Mubarak began to desire to attend the Qasr al-'Aini school.[95]

His path to enrollment was, perhaps, harder than 'Anbar Effendi's, but 'Ali Mubarak did go to Qasr al-'Aini, the flagship school of the educational institutions launched by Muhammad 'Ali. As F. Robert Hunter summarized about the life of this remarkable man: "Perhaps because he was the first native Egyptian to attain 'ministerial' rank in an administration dominated by Turks, Mubarak's career reveals an instability remarkable even for mid-nineteenth-century Egypt." Hunter asserts that unlike the other officials he explores in his study, "there were far more abrupt twists and turns in his official life." Yet, looking back over his whole life, "the aged Mubarak must have felt the quiet satisfaction of having surpassed the wildest expectations of his youth."[96] I agree with this and have also chosen to look at

'Ali Mubarak's representation of Egypt's past and of his own for the same reasons that Hunter did. But in his account of 'Ali Mubarak's insistence on enrolling in Qasr al-'Aini, Hunter attributes the desire to 'Ali's meeting current students from the preparatory school and admiring their clothes.[97] Nowhere in the pages of Hunter's insightful and interesting account of 'Ali Mubarak's education can the significant presence of 'Anbar Effendi be found. But as *Al-Khitat* shows, the ability of a former slave to transform himself from very low social expectations to a military commander of formidable power was just as profound as 'Ali Mubarak's ability to live up to his own huge ambitions. And significantly, when these ambitions were challenged, slaves were there to bear witness. For instance, 'Ali Mubarak's second marriage to a young, orphaned, Turkish-speaking woman became a nightmare, as her guardians used every legal challenge they could to keep her wealth from him (they suspected that the not very wealthy Mubarak was interested in her property). After years in court, 'Ali Mubarak walked away from the house he had built for his wife "without taking a thing with me, even leaving my slave girls who had long been in my possession— I cleansed myself from what linked me to these suspicions."[98] This proud man could still measure his success or failure, his prosperity or poverty, by the possession of slaves. It was on the life of a former slave that 'Ali Mubarak patterned his own trajectory, although he remembered this always with surprise.

·   ·   ·

The ownership of slaves had become an essential means of social, political, and economic promotion by the time 'Ali Mubarak finished *Al-Khitat*, creating households in which links of enslavement were also part of the family's bond. But 'Ali Mubarak's description of slaves as either *mamluk* or *'abid* glossed over more than the ethnic and cultural provenance of the enslaved—it hid the increasing complications of ethnic and political identity among their Egyptian owners as well. Let us return briefly to the Mamluks who had remained in Egypt; "culturally tied to the Ottoman Turks through their shared use of Turkish rather than Arabic, the Circassians formed part of a Turco-Circassian elite in Egypt that enjoyed a monopoly on force and the major state offices despite their small numbers." But over the decades of the nineteenth century, "the children of Turco-Circassians began to be raised as Arabic-speaking Egyptians."[99] And for those Arabic-speaking Egyptians whose grandparents and great-grandparents had also always spoken Arabic, but who were able to gain entry into the secular preparatory schools of Muhammad 'Ali and Khedive Isma'il, it was increasingly possible to achieve high rank in the civil administration of Egypt. 'Ali Mubarak's life serves here as a case in point. He had become part of a new, indigenous elite, formally recognized as such by Isma'il and his son Tawfiq through state grants of land and through significant administrative appointments.

> On the official level of interaction, this new elite was placed side by side with the older and transformed Turco-Circassian component of the elite. Not only did they work together with the latter in their official duties, but, due to their new vested interests in property, they found common cause with them in seeking to protect their gains. This intimacy *cum* economic interest led both components to forge bonds of alliance and identification that enabled them to combine efforts to protect and advance their economic goals. Intimacy and cooperative effort, however, would have easily foundered, had not the two groups also been united by a common language.[100]

Ibrahim Abu-Lughod saw this language as Arabic, whose official usage spread through more branches and offices of the Egyptian government in the decades of the 1860s and 1870s. Arabic became the language of instruction throughout the entire system of education, not only religious instruction: "Books translated from European languages and intended as teaching manuals, were, for the most part, rendered into Arabic."[101] Isma'il proclaimed Arabic to be the official language of Egypt in 1869. Only members of the high command of the army were permitted the exclusive use of Turkish for official communications.[102]

The army elites blockaded themselves as the last defenders of Turkish linguistic distinctiveness and, in so doing, helped provoke a profoundly influential political rebellion in Egypt. Although some Egyptians did move up to midlevel ranks, they hit a linguistic glass ceiling. As Andrew McGregor has written, "Long after the use of Arabic and French had become common in many ministries, the Egyptian Army retained Turkish as the language of command, allowing Turco-Circassians some leverage in keeping a lingering grip on their previous monopoly on force."[103] Arabic-speaking Egyptian officers protested this discrimination in 1879. By 1881, these protests had become a full-blown rebellion under the leadership of Colonel Ahmad 'Urabi Pasha. And the 'Urabi Rebellion began what would be a very complicated decade for 'Ali Mubarak. 'Urabi Pasha and his colleagues appealed to 'Ali Mubarak for support, and he did approach Khedive Tawfiq on their behalf. But their insistence on more indigenous Egyptian participation in government enraged the khedive and threatened other interests supporting Tawfiq as well. 'Ali Mubarak withdrew his support.[104] And those other interests behind the Egyptian throne, the governments of Great Britain and France, disliked 'Urabi's message of "Egypt for the Egyptians." They saw in this a threat to the ability of the Egyptian government to repay the staggering loans borrowed by Isma'il, on which Egypt had defaulted in 1876. They saw, too, a threat in the protest against their increased oversight of the Egyptian treasury.[105] And by 1881, European military, financial, and cultural advisers could be found everywhere in Egypt.

In an area closer to his heart than the ambitions and indignation of the 'Urabists, 'Ali Mubarak had to struggle with British and French advisers over restorations in Cairo, especially after the creation of the Comité de conservation des monuments de l'art arabe in 1881. This committee was set up to restore what its experts considered "medieval" Cairo. The Comité's participants were European, its business was conducted in French, and it worked to classify the mosques, fountains, and other older edifices of Cairo. Directed by Viollet-le-Duc, the Comité was commissioned to decide which parts of Cairo were "Tulunid, Fatimid, Mamluk—as comprising the period known as medieval, Arab, and Mohammadan."[106] It created museums out of mosques, established the first Egyptian museum of Arab art, and designed projects to delineate, for both transportation and tourism, the physical space between "old" and "modern" Cairo.[107] And, unlike 'Ali Mubarak, the Comité "left copious photographic documentation of its work."[108] In *Al-Khitat*, "no medieval or Islamic place existed separate from others." As Irene Bierman summarizes, the Cairo of 'Ali Mubarak "was filled with buildings and streets where social interaction took place, where collective memory was built, and in which the actions of peoples existed in words."[109]

Men and women making history always people the buildings in *Al-Khitat*; they do not sit as silently as the beautiful but muted monuments in the Comité's photographs. As we have seen, slaves fight, protest, conquer, or submit to domesticated lives in the ornate and complicated pages of *Al-Khitat*. Their own languages are lost, their identities oversimplified by Arabic terminology, but they are not silent—we just have to turn to sources other than 'Ali Mubarak to really hear them.

Babikr Bedri's
Long March with Authority

My grandfather used the edge of his gown to wipe away the tears that
had run down his face from laughing so much, and after giving me time
to settle myself into the gathering, said, "By God, that's some story of
yours, Wad Rayyes." This was a cue to Wad Rayyes to continue the story
my entrance had interrupted. "And afterwards, Hajj Ahmed, I put the
girl in front of me on the donkey, squirming and twisting, then I forcibly
stripped her of all her clothes till she was as naked as the day her mother
bore her. She was a young slave who'd just reached puberty—her breasts,
Hajj Ahmed, stuck out like pistols and your arms wouldn't meet round
her buttocks. She had been rubbed all over with oil so that her skin
glistened in the moonlight and her perfume turned one giddy."

Her weeping would be made the subject of one of Wad Rayyes' famous stories about his many women with which he regales the men of the
village. The rage in my breast grew more savage. Unable to remain, I left;
behind me I heard my grandfather calling but I did not turn around.

Tayib Salih, *Season of Migration to the North*

This chapter moves south from Cairo to the northern Sudanese society of
Babikr Bedri. Babikr Bedri was a young man at the time 'Ali Mubarak was
completing his *Khitat* and faced social transformations in Sudan that were
equal to, if not more dramatic than, the 'Urabi rebellion or the British occupation of Egypt. During those same years, a massive rebellion known as the
Mahdiyya had swept across northern Sudan, inspiring its followers with
religious revivalism and anti-Egyptian protests.[1] The Mahdiyya launched
Babikr into a public life that would last for many decades. And, like 'Ali
Mubarak, when he grew old, Babikr Bedri put his life down on paper. In

his memoirs, the cultural topography of Sudan in the late nineteenth century comes alive, with power and sensitivity akin to 'Ali Mubarak's great imagination.

The differences between the two men are multiple and dramatic, yet in each man's narration, similarities between them emerge. Like 'Ali Mubarak, Babikr Bedri came from a deeply religious family, and his early education took place in a *kuttab*. Profoundly faithful, Babikr also learned to respect and eventually promote secular education as a critical step for Sudan's development; this would become his great mission. Both authors directly addressed their readers, asking for judgment or sympathy; both hoped to demonstrate how they reached spiritual maturity. Each man imbued his memoir with a strong sense of connection to his own community: 'Ali Mubarak to Egypt, and Babikr to the newly independent nation of Sudan.

Other similarities between the two contemporaries are that both had to negotiate vastly different kinds of authority and belief systems as they became prominent professionals, and British authorities often stood in each of their ways as they tried to pursue their careers. Babikr had been a strong believer and soldier for the Mahdi, and after the British conquered Sudan in 1898, he had to struggle against British regulations and limitations in order first to work as a trader and then to become an educator. 'Ali Mubarak struggled with the threat to Khedive Tawfiq's authority once the British had occupied the country. Babikr wrestled with British authorities over the intellectual legacies of the Mahdiyya and over control of the secularization of the Sudanese educational system.

Whereas the arc of 'Ali Mubarak's younger life was sharply altered by the example and influence of a former slave, the path of Babikr Bedri's life was transformed by his increasing sympathy for women in Sudanese society. The many slaves in his life, however, marked him differently. Slaves passed in and out of every aspect of his life. This brought no shame to him in his lifetime or to his legacy. Babikr is remembered and highly respected in Sudan for being a pathbreaking educator. He founded the first secular schools for girls and the first college for women, Ahfad College. His memoirs contain an unparalleled look at the cultural and social life of Sudan through three of the country's most significant political eras—the Mahdiyya, the defeat of the Mahdiyya after eighteen years, and the institutionalization of the Anglo-Egyptian Condominium, when the British assumed control of the administration of Sudan. As we shall see, many scholars, myself included, have written about the political and social importance of Babikr Bedri's *Tarikh hayati* (The story of my life). But few have discussed the many experiences with slavery and slaves that Babikr included in *Tarikh hayati*. He did so as an insider, addressing, like 'Ali Mubarak, other insiders who would understand his relationships and his history; he wrote his memoirs in Arabic with a Sudanese Arabic-speaking readership in mind, and these achieved much acclaim. For this audience, no apologies were necessary about the presence or ownership of slaves. Slaves punctuated every phase of his life, and he included them fastidiously in the details of his experience. This chapter therefore takes a different approach to Babikr's account of his life, to examine how he wrote about the many slaves in his life and why.

The Master Narrative

Babikr Bedri began writing his memoirs in Arabic in 1944 and finished them nine years later, months before his death at age ninety-four.[2] By the time he died, his decades of work in education had made him a broadly respected figure in a country on the cusp of independence (Babikr died three years before Sudan achieved independence). As a young man in his late teens, he joined the religious movement of Muhammad Ahmad, the Mahdi, and participated in the siege of Khartoum in 1884–85. During the years between the fall of the Ottoman-Egyptian administration of Sudan and the British reconquest, Babikr became a merchant. Once the British took over governance of Sudan, he worked for many years as a daring and creative educator in Khartoum under the Anglo-Egyptian Condominium and pioneered education for northern Sudanese Muslim girls. The first volume of his memoirs describes his youth, most notably his years under the Mahdiyya, and Babikr makes the voices and faces of his early life quite vivid. Even in English, it is clear that Babikr could hear those conversations of many years past; in the Arabic version, the rhythms and vernacular of late nineteenth-century northern Sudanese culture vibrate through the text. As his son described, Babikr wrote his memoirs in a style quite unlike that of his professional writings: "The vocabulary and style also of the Arabic

which he uses in this first volume—very different from those of his educational writings or of his account of his later life—reflect the outlook of a
young man in an unsophisticated and bygone environment."[3]

This vibrancy and color affected almost all of the reviewers who en-
thusiastically noted the memoirs' historical significance. In a review article that explored the state of historiography on Sudan, G. N. Sanderson
wrote that the publication of the autobiography was "an event of great
importance for the historiography of education in the Sudan, and of social
history generally" (Sanderson actually wrote the historical introduction
for the second translated volume of *Tarikh hayati*).[4] Another commentator,
Nasr el Hag Ali, wrote in 1967: "There is no trait of Sudanese society and
no element that makes the life of the individual, spiritually or physically,
that cannot be traced to what the characters in Babikr Bedri's autobiography did, said, or experienced."[5] Elizabeth Hodgkin noted that the memoirs
were not written until well into the author's old age, yet they have "the
freshness of a totally unselfconscious recall, with the result that many of
the anecdotes throw a most illuminating light on the contemporary attitudes to women, parents, travel, food, marriage, tax evasion and death."
She reviewed the first volume in translation and noted how fresh the language was "in the way they keep a Sudanese 'feel' and yet are in a convinc-
ing English doggerel."[6] Talal Asad paid close attention to where Babikr fit
into Arabic historiographical and literary traditions, noting that "there is
nothing quite like these memoirs in the first-hand literature on the Sudanese Mahdiya." The other accounts Asad includes (such as that of Na'um
Shuqayr, a Syrian chronicler of the Mahdiyya) "lack the vivid detail of
everyday life and the sense of immediate involvement in the social up-
heavals."[7] Asad goes so far as to say that the moving way in which Babikr
described triumphs and misfortunes exudes "the zest and wit reminiscent
of some of the best stories of *A Thousand and One Nights*."[8]

Talal Asad's comments lead to the question of the literature that Babikr
read, and how he situated himself in traditions of writing about the self.
Throughout the first volume of his memoirs, he makes reference to classical
Arabic poetry, such as the poems of al-Mutanabbi, to emphasize his point
or his analysis of a particular situation.[9] In other examples, he read canoni-
cal Arabic works on history for pleasure. He regularly read the *Muqadimma*

of Ibn Khaldun aloud to an appreciative friend.[10] He composed love poetry to one of his wives along the model set by the medieval Arabic tale of
Majnun Layla.[11] Books mattered to Babikr. Whenever possible, he packed
them away. They provided refuge from stress and offered lessons for battles and struggles he was about to confront. Not long before the battle of
Omdurman, in which the Mahdist forces led by the khalifa would face a
much stronger British-led army, Babikr retreated into the world of the mind:

> I read the poems of Ibn al-Farid with the commentaries of al-Burini and
> al-Nabulusi, much of the Koran commentary *al-Kashshaf*, the first volume of
> al-Shihab's marginalia upon al-Baydawi's Koran commentary, al-Jamal's gloss
> on the *Hamziyya* and al-Bajuri's gloss on *al-Burda*. I also had al-Zawzani's com-
> mentary upon the *Mu'allaqat*; but I was not particularly attracted to it—not be-
> cause of any defects in it, but because it did not stir one's heart to religious fer-
> vour as did Ibn 'Abbad's book on *al-Hikam* of Ibn 'Ata'allah, which I continued
> to pore over until I had almost memorized all the sayings. For men were pre-
> paring their souls for death; and daily the news of terrifying happenings deaf-
> ened one's ears. You could not join any gathering where you were not asked for
> news, and even if you invented it people would believe it and spread it, though
> they had reason to suppose or even knew for certain that you had invented it.[12]

If Babikr could take advantage of his clearly substantive library to fortify
himself both spiritually and intellectually with classical Arabic books, there
is no reason not to consider that he took advantage of the same rich intellectual heritage when constructing his life in manuscript.

Nicole Grandin perceived in Babikr Bedri's autobiography a historic
and literary revolution, because stylistically it broke with what she saw as
a Muslim tradition "in which a biography can only be a hagiography" and
where the literary form of autobiography is "unknown in classical Arabic
literature." She asserts that Babikr Bedri "adopted a Western tradition" and
that he therefore positioned himself on the cusp of two different traditions
of self-narration.[13] His choice of autobiographical style came from his ethic
about cultural reality. The memoirs were written when the British were in
firm control of the Sudanese government and he himself was increasingly
in conflict with them; thus, Babikr had become "a Sudanese personality in
public view, for whom the work of modernization and the self-development

of education were at the same time a boon for his people and a weapon against the colonial power."[14] Grandin considers that by writing his life out in this way, Babikr gave his life a "militant coherence" that narrated the daily life of a Mahdist's jihad while also continuing to participate in a jihad. Grandin sees Babikr writing "under the 'I' native to the West, foreign to his own culture" as a kind of "ruse of war" in which the author legitimized those who fought against the British, in the literary framework, if not the exact language, of the British.[15]

The idea that Babikr would use a Western literary trope as a linguistic weapon against the British is both interesting and provocative, but I disagree that autobiographical writing has no antecedents in Arabic literary traditions; we have seen in Chapter 1 that 'Ali Mubarak Pasha, like his historical predecessors, inserted autobiography into his *Khitat*. I would go further to argue that the very nature of the struggle between Egyptian forces, the Mahdi, and the British inspired a small but politically powerful set of memoirs, written by the turn of the century, by important Egyptian, Sudanese, and European figures.[16] Although Nicole Grandin does not mention them in her article, other men were caught between these political forces in the late nineteenth century and had to negotiate with British culture over the terms in which they narrated their lives.

One of the most famous of these was the northern Sudanese trader al-Zubayr Rahman Pasha, who in 1874 seized control of Darfur and with great efficiency made it a center of the slave trade between Sudan and Egypt. The victims of this enhanced trade, those kidnapped in raids and sold from his compounds, were predominantly non-Muslim, non-Arabic-speaking members of some of the region's tribes. At that time, Egypt controlled most of Sudan, though its hold on Darfur was fragile. The Egyptian ruler, Khedive Isma'il, had recently enacted laws drawn up in negotiation with British politicians and the powerful lobby of the Anti-Slavery Society that prohibited the trade in slaves in both Egypt and Sudan. Al-Zubayr's success as a raider, trader, and government administrator embarrassed Egypt's monarch and increasingly complicated relations between Great Britain and Egypt. News of al-Zubayr's slave raids reached and provoked audiences in Great Britain concerned with slavery's abolition in the Nile Valley, and humanitarian activists in organizations like the British Anti-Slavery Society directly petitioned the Egyptian khedive to exert as much effort as possible to exterminate the trade and make Egypt and its territories a "free country."[17] Isma'il responded to these petitions and pressure by hiring General Charles Gordon to conquer Darfur, in the name of stamping out the slave trade, and, once subdued, the defeated Zubayr Pasha was committed to house arrest in Cairo.[18]

Western accounts of al-Zubayr's activities in Darfur described them as violent acts committed by Arabs against vulnerable and victimized black Africans, and this was worsened by the "toleration of Arab governors."[19] But even as the personification of the evils of slavery, al-Zubayr Pasha fascinated English audiences. He was both vilified by and perplexing to the English press. Gordon had chased him out of Darfur in 1876, much to the satisfaction of the Anti-Slavery Society in England. Gordon, in fact, wrote many entries in his diaries about al-Zubayr Pasha, and these diaries were almost immediately published after Gordon's death in Khartoum in 1885.[20] Contrary to the expectations of the Anti-Slavery Society, however, these entries were deeply respectful of al-Zubayr's leadership abilities; Gordon repeatedly and strongly recommended to the British government that al-Zubayr be appointed governor of Sudan, as the only possible counter to the forces of the Mahdi.[21] Here is one example (out of approximately nineteen in the first volume of his journals) of Gordon's estimation of al-Zubayr: "We choose to refuse his coming up because of his antecedents *in re* slave trade; granted that we had reason, yet as we take no precautions as to the future of these lands with respect to the slave trade, the above opposition seems absurd. I will not send up A. because he will do this, but I will leave the country to B. who will do exactly the same."[22]

After the British occupied Egypt in the fall of 1882, al-Zubayr was removed from house arrest and sent to Gibraltar. And there, in 1887, the young and soon-to-be famous female journalist Flora Shaw, who had begun her career writing about slavery and would end her professional life as the wife of Lord Lugard, colonial ruler of Nigeria, discovered the great slave trader in exile. They conducted many long interviews, meeting once a week for four months. Shaw described the scene in which they sat opposite each other at his house—al-Zubayr by the window, smoking, "dark, slight, tall, looking all the taller when he rose for the draperies of Eastern dress." She sat opposite him, where she "industriously scribbled."

And most vividly, she described the people moving in between: "Between us the interpreter, on whom the whole story depended, sat bending forward, equally attentive to one and the other; while round our chairs black servants, some of them natives of the countries of which we spoke, stood in attendance. When the narrative grew dramatic, they listened eagerly. Now and then, on a question from the Pasha, one or the other could offer some bit of information about his country or people."[23] Even though Shaw worried that the interpreter did not speak English very well—"I realize there must be many discrepancies between what was told and what was heard"—she presented the interviews as al-Zubayr finally telling, in his own words, his dramatic story.[24]

The life that emerges is one fully shaped by the slave trade. Shaw dismissed al-Zubayr's self-proclaimed origins as so much snobbery: "Amongst the Arabs it appears that a man is not held to be of noble birth unless he can count back his ancestry, as such, for ten generations."[25] She was much more interested in how he arrived at monopolizing such a large sector of the trade. Al-Zubayr Rahman Pasha may have committed crimes against slaves, but Shaw was not persuaded by the humanity of those caught up in the trade. She rationalized al-Zubayr's actions by placing him in an African context characterized by deep and far-ranging barbarity. "In order to understand his own view of the work he did," Shaw wrote, "it is necessary to understand the condition of the people over whom he ruled." Shaw described these people as almost "all blacks" and cannibals in a cultural situation in which slavery "was already flourishing, in the outlying provinces, and man-hunting was everywhere a common practice, whether for purposes of eating or selling." The only occupation these Africans had, she claimed, was fighting—"their ignorance was indescribable."[26]

In his answers to Shaw, al-Zubayr justified his conquest of Darfur with the explanation that he "had opened new channels for the commerce of the civilized world" and that by ordering the roads and allowing caravans to pass through, he had played a role in the suppression of "man-hunting."[27] She noted with irony that these same objectives were shared by General Charles Gordon and that "it was a curious experience to hear Zebehr Pasha speak of these same things as not only his ideal, but in some degree the accomplished work of his lifetime."[28] So successful was al-Zubayr, in fact, at creating better systems of trade and communications between the "chiefs and slave-hunters" of Darfur that everyone profited from his leadership, unfairly earning him his "wide reputation for slaving."[29] The Zubayr Pasha who emerges in these pages refused to connect himself directly with responsibility for the slave trade. Shaw presented herself as a polite but tough interlocutor, and al-Zubayr insisted on his own integrity:

> It was upon entering into these commercial questions that we first spoke freely about the slave trade. The Pasha absolutely denies that participation in it with which he is usually accredited. I spared him none of the reports generally spread about him on the subject. "I am not a baby, and I thank you for being honest with me," was his answer to an apology with which I prefaced the reading of the hard passages which refer to him in Gordon's early letters and diaries.[30]

Perhaps it was not clear between them what it meant to actually be involved in the raiding and trading of slaves. Perhaps al-Zubayr knew that by 1882, Gordon's opinion of him had changed to a position of great respect. And perhaps al-Zubayr felt he had already answered to British suspicions, with his son having been killed by Gordon's aides soon after his own arrest and by years of exile. But one looks up from these pages wondering exactly who was responsible for the enslavement of thousands in Sudan. Even Shaw, in a way, excused al-Zubayr's feints and dodges by likening him to British citizens of her grandfather's generation: "Zebehr's mind appeared to be in the attitude which was taken by the ordinary English mind in the second decade of this century, when we had carried through successful negotiations with Spain and Portugal for putting down the slave-trade, and still refused to contemplate the abolition of slavery in our colonies. He argued that no order is possible in a country where slave-hunting is permitted."[31]

But where had he been during the sales of slaves or during their being herded into the famous compounds of El-Fasher, his capital city? Al-Zubayr denied any connection to the trade, with all of the passion of antislavery orators: "I cannot explain to you how impossible it would have been to me to sell my people . . . unless you realize that a king is indeed father of his people." His sense of connection and belonging to the people of Darfur was even more vividly articulated when he explained, "I happen to be fond of children, and often when I have been in the villages I have carried the babies in my arms. If I had sold the young men and women I should have had the mothers hanging upon my shirts, and weeping, saying 'Give me back my son, give me back my daughter that you have sold.' My steps everywhere would have been accompanied by tears. Life would not have been endurable."[32] Here one wonders how the relationship between Flora Shaw, the interpreter, and al-Zubayr influenced these last published statements. What did it mean to each of them when the term "my people" arose? Al-Zubayr did not identify himself with those communities and villages considered eligible for slave raids, groups he (or Shaw) wrongly identified as "Nyam-Nyam," people whom al-Zubayr considered to have no God.[33] Shaw had already made clear her belief that the polytheistic tribes were peoples with no culture, beliefs, or trade. And it is interesting, too, that al-Zubayr paints a scene about which most former slaves could only dream: if the pasha had himself stolen children, how dogged he would be by the mothers of kidnapped children having the access to plead personally with the ruler of Darfur for their return. But the imagined plea comes from a mother who is one of "his people," over whom he was king. The resolution of some of al-Zubayr's distancing himself from the crimes of slavery may be found in the loopholes of antislavery laws in the Nile Valley at this time and the fact that it was illegal to kidnap and sell people, but it was not specifically illegal to buy them.[34] Men like al-Zubayr Pasha could interpret their purchase of slaves as a means of civilizing them; he certainly saw no shame in buying many. Immediately after claiming that his footsteps would have been dogged by tears everywhere had he sold slaves, he "stated without apology that he had bought upwards of 20,000 slaves while he was at Mandugba."[35] Not only did his purchase of slaves civilize them but it also contributed to the increasing cultural and economic sophistication of al-Zubayr himself:

> "In those countries," he said, "especially as you get farther from centers of civilization, the natives have not learned the use of steam or water, and everything is done by means of slaves. The only motive power is slave-power. If you cut off slave-power, the result would be the same as the cutting off of steam and water from England." . . . He could only say with regard to the present time, that when

the Mussulmans of Cairo or Constantinople spoke with Western statesmen of the entire abolition of slavery in these countries, they spoke of what they knew in their hearts to be impossible. They are well aware that the country is not yet prepared for it.[36]

Al-Zubayr could denounce the kidnapping of people for enslavement. Al-Zubayr strongly pronounced his intolerance for the part of the trade that brought attendants to the harems of Ottoman and Egyptian rulers. He could speak of this to a young British journalist in a language that, despite the obstacles presented by careless or uninformed translation, she and her audiences could understand if they looked at their own history of only a few previous generations. In this sense, he performed the linguistic sabotage of autobiographical expression that Nicole Grandin earlier ascribed to Babikr Bedri. Al-Zubayr was able, with the complicit help of Flora Shaw, to present contemporary conditions of Sudanese slavery in British historical terminology. And thanks to her interviews, the British government released al-Zubayr from his gilded exile in Gibraltar and returned him to Cairo, where he was able to provide patronage for Flora Shaw as she continued her reportage on the Middle East and East Africa.[37] Despite the difficulties with translation, it paid for al-Zubayr Pasha to narrate his life to an increasingly influential political journalist like Flora Shaw. He won greater political freedom and the protection of imperial officials, protection against the continuing suspicions of abolitionists. In 1899, after the British-led conquest of Sudan, he returned home and prospered as a wealthy landowner and "valuable counselor of the new government."[38]

Slaves and the Life of Babikr Bedri

Al-Zubayr Rahman Pasha's figure loomed large across Sudanese communities as well. During and especially after the Mahdiyya, many appealed to him for financial help and political support while he was in exile in Cairo, particularly those who had been captured by the Egyptian army and sent to Egypt as prisoners of war.[39] Babikr Bedri also came to know al-Zubayr relatively well; they were distant cousins, and al-Zubayr married a beloved but divorced former wife of Babikr's. When Babikr went to Cairo to try to reclaim this wife, he came face-to-face with al-Zubayr, who at that time was probably the wealthiest of all Sudanese. Babikr negotiated with al-Zubayr (who emerges in these pages as very powerful and haughty) but doubted that his wife would ever return to him after living "in the house of the Pasha, the greatest of all the Sudanese today" (she did not).[40] To his face, Babikr called al-Zubayr the greatest of Sudanese, but Babikr's narrative shows that men and women with different, more spiritual depths aroused his real appreciation and respect. This was a man whose family was relatively poor when he was a child, who loved his teachers at the *kuttab*, and who, accompanied by his mother, devoted himself early to the religious teachings and movement of Muhammad Ahmad, the Mahdi. Al-Zubayr's fame arose from his monopolization of an important part of the slave trade between Sudan and Egypt, but there is no discussion in his narrative about the spiritual journeys of his life. Slaves formed a part of every aspect of Babikr's life, from his childhood well into his maturity, but all along he threw himself into Qur'anic study and tried to live a life of devotion. His support for the Mahdiyya was religious as long as the Mahdi lived; it became political once the British took control of Sudan. And within this powerful and complicated belief system of Babikr Bedri lived his slaves. In *Tarikh hayati*, there are no justifications and no apologies for his role in the enslavement of others. Slaves were a part of the life of this faithful man, even, at times, a part of how he expressed his faith.

In the first volume, Babikr describes a bustling landscape and social life in northern Sudan, in which slaves are everywhere. Someone else's slaves are washing laundry in the river when the very young Babikr loses his robe (*tob*) while swimming, so he is able to steal another from them.[41] Slaves work on his family's farm, are frequently borrowed by other people, nurse Babikr back to health when he is very ill, and share the family's poverty when times get difficult.[42] Slaves are used as intimidators against enemies, and their lives are also symbols of debasement—to be called one is an insult.[43] Slaves are brought into Babikr's and others' households as children.[44] The purchase of young female slaves punctuates the most important events in Babikr's life; they are bought as gifts and wet nurses when his wives give birth.[45] Throughout his narrative, most slaves could be seen but not heard, served often in the background, and were living gifts marking life's passages. There were times, though, when Babikr and his family depended on brave and loyal slaves and considered a few as dear companions.

When Babikr and his mother first heard the call of the religious leader Muhammad Ahmad, they were deeply moved and joined his movement. As the rebellion grew more successful, Babikr and all of the men in his family adopted the *jibba* (the patched robes worn by the Mahdi and his followers) and joined the Mahdi's army in the siege of Khartoum. As Ahmad Sikainga has written, the majority of those who followed the Mahdi were "small traders, poor farmers and herders," people like Babikr Bedri, his parents, and his family. Sikainga discusses how British officials assumed that the antislavery laws pushed through in the late 1870s provoked such widespread support for the Mahdiyya, but the enthusiasm that Babikr and others shared for the Mahdi's message actually came more from disenchantment with the policies (usually economic) of the Turco-Egyptian administration. Interestingly, as Sikainga points out, many slaves also responded positively to the Mahdi, "who promised them freedom and salvation."[46] As we shall see in Babikr's account, this was often a source of conflict between slave owners and particular slaves they had possessed for years. Although the Mahdiyya cut Sudan off from most of the borders of its neighboring, slave-buying countries, and al-Zubayr Rahman Pasha had been removed as a major trader, the internal slave trade continued. Even as the movement weakened under the Mahdi's successor, Khalifa al-Ta'ishi, and was defeated, slaves accompanied Babikr and other supporters throughout.

Slaves in the Background

After British-led armies defeated the forces of the khalifa and as British officials formed the administration of the Sudanese government, British officials and soldiers paid close visual attention to Sudanese slaves. Individual officers explored Khartoum, Omdurman, and the rest of the country, taking pictures such as the one shown here of a slave woman washing clothes. Although the camera focuses not on her face but on her labor and the movement of her arms as she works, the woman is centered in the photograph—she is foregrounded and highlighted.

Babikr rarely saw his slaves in such a central light or narrated their presence so closely. But they formed the background of his narrative, and

few pages pass in the memoirs without some mention of slaves. He introduces slaves early in his narrative, after he has gone to hear the Mahdi for
the first time. His father had been summoned to help lay siege to Khartoum
and wanted Babikr to stay home to supervise work on the family farm.
Babikr remembered:

> But passion for Holy War had mastered my mind, and I embarked my mother
> and my wife and my father's second wife and all the sesame in a boat which I
> had hired, and sailed to Jirayf, leaving my brother Musa Bedri and the slaves
> that were with him to work the farm. At Jirayf I disembarked and went to the
> camp by myself, and when my father saw me he was astonished.
>
> "Why on earth have you come here?" he said. "In whose care did you leave
> the farm?"

Anonymous photograph of a slave woman washing, n.d. Sudan Archive, Durham,
SAD-1/116.

"In God's care," I replied. "The Holy War is more important than farming."

In response to Babikr's zeal, and his leaving the supervision of the farm to one brother and many slaves, his father shook his head, "whether in astonishment or admiration I do not know."[47]

The bodies of other slaves, probably former slave soldiers hired by Gordon to fight for the Egyptian government on the other side of the siege walls, warranted Babikr's closer attention when they were dead:

> While we were looking at the enemy dead, most of whom were blacks, someone noticed that some of the corpses were on fire, and called our attention to one of them. I saw that its wounds were very red, then it turned black, then a little foam came out of it, then smoke like the smoke of a cigarette, and finally it caught fire and became all charred.[48]

A few years later, after many difficult experiences under the khalifa's rule in Omdurman, Babikr went to his mother, then living with his half brother Sa'id under conditions that Babikr thought disrespectful to his mother. Babikr was unhappy with this:

> At sunset Sa'id invited me for the evening meal. He had in front of him some sweet millet-stalks, and I picked up some of them and said to his small slave girl, "Take these to my mother." I do not know whether such terrible extravagance angered him, or whether it was for some other reason, but after that he never invited me to eat with him again.[49]

Slaves also served in the background as Babikr begins to realize his talent for trade and as he wrestled with the complicated taxes of the khalifa's bureaucracy. His cleverness with math helped his uncle Malik prosper, and throughout their dealings, Malik's slave Ma'mun runs the errands, carries the inventory, and brings Babikr's much-loved mother closer to him, back from his half-brother Sa'id's home.[50] What do these quick glimpses—the agricultural workers, the small girl serving at the table, the dead slave soldiers, and the busy errand boy—offer the reader? To those Sudanese contemporaries of his or younger nationalist audiences reading Babikr in his original Arabic, such glances may have offered scenes familiar from their own youth. For scholars and former Sudanese government officials reading him soon after the first volume was translated, the flash of slaves across the pages offered details of a realistic panorama of Sudanese life during the Mahdiyya. I see people so fully absorbed in the service of others that they are barely there—it is the service they performed that holds together the tasks and resolutions of Babikr's life.

Slaves as Gifts

It is easier to see the figures of the slaves, or perceive how Babikr appraised them, when he described slaves who were exchanged to commemorate the milestones in his family's life. As Babikr became more and more adept at trading cloth and gum, first for his uncle and then for himself, he was able to purchase more slaves. In one instance, he made a profit of 114 riyals, and proud of this moment he wrote: "So I bought an old slave-woman called Umm Na'im for my wife. This Umm Na'im died long after at the age of more than 130; for she said that she was older than Sultan Husayn [the sultan of Darfur] who was crowned in 1254 (1838–9) and died in 1292 (1875–6) and she died in 1357 (1938–9). I also bought another slave-woman for my mother."[51] Because he had enough money, Babikr could bring in more help for his wife, and this slave caught his interest. Umm Na'im had a story, a long past with a history that Babikr shared. Since he knew when she died, decades after he bought her, one wonders if Umm Na'im remained in his household.

Each time Babikr made an important sale and expanded the size of his coffers, he bought slaves, increasing his status and that of his wives. The gift of a slave sometimes accompanied the closely negotiated financial exchanges that preceded Babikr's marriages. In the following example, Babikr, as he put it, "could not get out of my head this idea of marrying one of the Egyptian women who were in the Sudan" and asks a friend with an Egyptian wife if she will find someone suitable for him. The best choice, it was felt, was Nafisa, daughter of Saliha, widow of an Egyptian officer killed in Khartoum. Babikr offered forty Maria Theresa riyals for her bride price and trousseau, which he admitted was not much. The mother also thought this too little, but Babikr sent this message back with his friend: "Since I don't know anything about her daughter, forty *riyals* is enough for the time being. If when I am married I find the girl suitable, her mother can ask me for whatever she likes; but if she turns out not to be suitable, why then, forty *riyals* is not such a loss." Saliha agreed, certain that her daughter would be suitable. Nafisa did please Babikr, and when he saw her on their wedding day, her clothes and belongings also impressed him, which led him "to give a generous appearance when they asked me for anything, and to try to appear to them as a rich man."[52] Her relatives watched this in the days following the wedding and mentioned to him that while Nafisa was willing and capable of grinding corn herself, "if you think fit to lighten her tasks, you will know what to do." Babikr had thought Nafisa had a servant who was a slave, but this was not the case. So, as Babikr wrote, when the relative left him, "I went to the slave market and for sixty *riyals* bought the most beautiful slave-girl that was there and presented her to my wife."[53] Her beauty made her expensive (more expensive than the price he paid for his wife's dowry and trousseau) and therefore a more fitting gift for a much-valued wife.

Babikr began trading for his uncle Malik in 1892 but two years later went into business on his own. By 1896, he considered himself a rich man and was spending too much money on naming-parties for his babies. By 1898, however, he was considerably poorer: "I will not conceal from the reader that I was now short of money, as I had been devoting myself to the study of religion" so the naming-party for the daughter born this year was "below average."[54] He also had increasingly to confront the onerous customs collections imposed by the treasury of the Mahdiyya. One of the customs inspectors at Omdurman was an old friend; Babikr brought him gifts from his trading journeys in exchange for turning a blind eye to hidden goods he did not want to declare. This became a profitable relationship for both of them, and when his friend had a daughter, "I bought him a slave-girl to nurse her."[55]

Babikr's riches rose and fell with his personal circumstances but also as a result of the khalifa's many wars and the subsequent closing of trade routes. By the end of 1897, the price of grain had quadrupled, and those, like Babikr, who had not hoarded were in financial trouble. He complained, and the economic burden of slaves was part of his complaint:

> Our grain was finished, and I had very little money, and my household—counting my own family and slaves and guests—numbered more than forty persons. What made the mud even stickier was that al-Risala, Yusuf's wife [Babikr's

brother] gave birth to a son, Ibrahim, on the 15th of Sha'ban 1315 (9 January 1898), and I had to spend money on his naming-party and buy a slave-girl for his mother. In addition my friend Mustafa al-Tahir asked me for money for the naming-party of his son 'Umar, who was also born in Sha'ban, and I gave him all the money I had, which was only a few *riyals*.[56]

Matters worsened as the khalifa's administration weakened militarily and as merchants grew suspicious of or cheated each other. Sometimes Babikr lost his inventory of foodstuffs if it was stored in villages where people were starving (famine raged throughout parts of Sudan in the last months of the khalifa's rule).[57] Some former Mahdist leaders rebelled against the khalifa in the town of Matamma and were violently defeated. Their wives and female dependents were brought by boat to Omdurman to be distributed among loyal Mahdists as concubines. One of these women was connected to Babikr through one of her relatives with whom he had strong business connections, and Babikr hoped to obtain her release and help out some of the other captives. In his narrative, Babikr described what he thought would be a complicated scene at the treasury (*bayt al-mal*) where once-free women would be exchanged as gifts. Here is how Babikr negotiated his way through this official giving of women:

> I told you that I was intending to release Batul bint walad Dub'a, and when I reached my house I was wondering by what means I could get admission to the women, and whether access to them would be allowed, or whether they would have been put in a special enclosure, with a guard to prevent anyone coming in. But I summoned up my courage and went to the treasury, and it was open; and by God I did not find a single free woman there for me to play protector to. On the contrary, there was Shaykh Bannaqa with Ibrahim Ramadan at his side, and an auction of slaves was going on. In fact I took the opportunity to buy two slave-girls, one as a wet-nurse for my little daughter Amina, so that her mother would not need to go on suckling her, and the other for the judge Walad al-Khidr.[58]

The Proper Order of Things

Giving slaves as gifts helped Babikr and his peers maintain what they considered the proper order of rites of passage and exchange of trust. Being able to buy slaves when a birth or a wedding occurred signified Babikr's maturity, his ability to take care of his family, and in a way, his social wing-span. When Sudanese society functioned according to expected economic patterns in the last quarter of the nineteenth century, slaves themselves were the bricks on which social order was maintained. And slaves that were truly dependable could become indispensable to managing stress and life, as Babikr showed. Even with the dramatic turns taken by northern Suda-nese society during the Mahdiyya, slaves continued to perform and serve as crucial supports of normalcy. Sometimes Babikr acknowledged this de-pendence, and sometimes he admitted that he needed to be reminded.

Soon after the successful siege of Khartoum, the Mahdi died sud-denly, much to the sorrow of his committed supporters. In his memoirs, Babikr expressed the memory of his deep grief by publicly remembering a dream he had had days before the news came of the Mahdi's death. In this dream, he and the Mahdi both walked with fetters around their ankles, and suddenly the Mahdi disappeared—he vanished in broad daylight. Babikr shared this dream with others, and when the Egyptian telegraph master of Khartoum found out, he told Babikr that if the dream came true, "a tremendous and unexpected event will happen." When the news did emerge, Babikr met the telegraph master again, who asked him, "If I had told you that day that the Mahdi would soon die, what would you have done to me?" Babikr responded, "I would have sent you to death before him."[59] Clearly, the death of the Mahdi wounded Babikr deeply, but he did not say so. But the work of slaves, as noted in his text, attested to his suffering. A terrible attack of malaria felled him, and he grew so sick "that the slave-girl Bakhita had to carry me like a small child to the latrine and back."[60] The lives of many of the Mahdi's supporters were powerfully thrown off by his loss; still the slaves were there to pick them up, literally, from their sickbeds.

One of these slaves, Sabah al-Khayr, proved to be a real pillar for Babikr during these unsettled times.[61] Soon after he recovered from his bout with malaria, Babikr and a relative asked one of the Mahdi's close aides for "a slave-girl to sell, because we were very hard up." Babikr and his uncle were redirected to another official, and they traveled there on foot—"since my horse, and also my slaves" were with someone else.[62] Babikr again caught fever from the walking. They reached this official in the town of al-Masallimiyya, with Babikr very ill. Neither the official nor his uncle paid his symptoms any attention or showed any concern. Unexpectedly, Babikr's brother Musa arrived, to find Babikr alone, sick, and hungry in a nearby mosque and the uncle eating with the official. Babikr remembered:

> Musa was very angry, and calling for Sabah al-Khayr and Salim, our slaves, told them to saddle the horse and bring it round. When my uncle 'Ali heard that, he tried to propitiate Musa, who, however, would not listen to him. Then 'Ali tried to use his authority to compel him to leave the horse and the slaves, but this was no good either, because Musa had stirred Sabah al-Khayr to anger by telling him. But I knew nothing of this, because I was lying in the mosque.[63]

It is important here to notice that Musa used Sabah al-Khayr as a threat, and that Sabah al-Khayr's anger at the mistreatment of Babikr demonstrated to the family his loyalty and strength. Babikr remembered this but, in so doing, related how even such loyalty rarely alleviated the weight of social inferiority that slaves had to bear. And in his narration of this experience, he also related the lesson in generosity that his brother Musa, using Sabah al-Khayr and Salim as examples, taught him. Sabah al-Khayr and Salim came for Babikr in the mosque and put him on a horse; then they all set out for the journey back to Khartoum. As they passed through one village, they realized how hungry they were, so Musa bought millet bread for everyone, to Babikr's peevish consternation:

> We were very hungry, and Musa spent the whole of what he had left on a little of it, and gave the two slaves a share of it equal to the share he left for us, while I thought that we should have had more than the slaves. Then a beggar came along, and I thought that we might give him only a little of the food, and make up the rest with kind words, but what must Musa do but invite him to sit and share the meal with us. Then I felt mean, and admired my brother greatly.[64]

In many parts of his memoirs, Babikr presents himself as a man continually wrestling with his faith, trying to be as devout a Muslim as he could. During that terrible bout with malaria, he vividly recounted the dream he had during his fever, in which his limbs are severed one by one, but he is saved from pain by angels (*houris*) awaiting him in paradise, who even years later made him wish he had died then. But in the instance just shown of Sabah al-Khayr, whom Babikr consistently described as an exceptionally reliable slave, Babikr could not easily find in his faith a way to honor that reliability. Musa had to remind him. It is fascinating to me that Babikr made sure this image of himself, and his stinginess toward his slaves, was not forgotten.

Babikr did pay homage to the memory of Sabah al-Khayr on several occasions, and in almost all of them, Sabah al-Khayr rescued him from personal threats and indignities. In one example, during a battle with the "Turks" (as Babikr calls the Ottoman-Egyptian forces against whom the Mahdiyya rebels), Babikr and Sabah al-Khayr had to choose between wading or swimming across the Nile at a point where the river was very wide:

> I confess that while at first I grasped my horse's bridle and led him bravely, after a bit I found myself behind him, at times holding on to the cantle of the saddle, and at times sprawling on his rump, with my undaunted slave Sabah al-Khayr swimming in front and leading him. At last we landed on the island, all scattered, and if its people had been ready to fight us, they would have forced us to plunge back into the river, or would have slaughtered us by ones and twos.[65]

During this phase of the Mahdiyya, Babikr served under the leadership of Wad al-Nujumi, one of the Mahdi's earliest supporters and, after 1885, the governor of the provinces of Dongola and Berber. Wad al-Nujumi commissioned Babikr to elicit local support from the communities of these provinces. During the period in which he worked for Wad al-Nujumi, Babikr crossed many miles of territory with his family, among them young children. Babikr was able to obtain official permission from al-Nujumi's administrators to order villagers to supply him with transport or food, but sometimes it looked to the villagers as if Babikr was exploiting them. At one point, the Bedri family had reached a village and dismounted in a date grove that belonged to a merchant named Fadl Shanbu. Without being told, "Sabah al-Khayr went in to get a few dates to quieten the babies." This infuriated Fadl, who protested vigorously, even when Babikr's father cautioned him about getting angry "when the slave came in to take a few dates" for the babies, telling him al-Nujumi's armies would seize everything he possessed. Although this eventually did occur to the hapless Fadl, most of the villagers from whom Babikr had to get food were not intimidated. Babikr had to ask the mayor (*'umda*) of each village to collect food for him, and as he acknowledged, "most of them made difficulties, and had it not been for the formidable Sabah al-Khayr, we would have been in trouble."[66] On one large farm, Babikr found an untended donkey tethered to a gate. Somehow Babikr had become separated from his father and needed the donkey to catch up.

The donkey's owner had other plans:

> A tall burly man came up and told me to dismount, and when I demurred gave me a blow that knocked me out. When some time had passed and I had not reached the village, Sabah al-Khayr came back to find out what had happened to me and found me there lying on the ground. As soon as I had recovered I told him what the man had done to me, and said "Look, there is his track!" So we followed it, and found the man at his water wheel, with the donkey grazing not far off. We took the donkey, but the man saw us and caught us up at the very place where he had hit me. He snatched at the donkey, but Sabah al-Khayr gave him a blow that felled him to the ground. Then he tied his hands behind his back and drove him along with us, I riding the donkey, until we reached the house, where we tied him up with a stick under his knees, and put him out in the sun.[67]

You can see clearly here, as Babikr shows you, how easily and intimately the two worked together and how much Babikr relied on his slave for protection. In the first volume of these memoirs, Sabah al-Khayr is remembered again and again as a real and trustworthy companion. Sabah al-Khayr was a slave who rarely needed to be given orders—he seamlessly anticipated the needs of this family. When Sabah al-Khayr forgot to wait for orders, shortly after helping Babikr swim across the Nile, Babikr easily forgave him, "owing to his many and multifarious cares."[68]

Although Sabah al-Khayr was an important person in key events of Babikr's life, Babikr himself never mentioned this beloved slave's birth or death or the date or event of his being purchased. His actions were interwoven into the Bedri family's lives, but none of his autonomous experiences earned a description. Perhaps that should be expected, as Sabah al-Khayr was, after all, a slave to Babikr and never a social peer. Ultimately, perhaps, that was the saddest mark of enslavement, part of the "social death" with which Orlando Patterson characterized slavery in his study of the international trade.[69] The enslaved lost their connectedness to a shared history, or certainly to a shared genealogical history. In the second volume of *Tarikh hayati* Babikr deflected being called a slave by an Egyptian official by saying, "I count my ancestry back through twenty generations. You don't go further back than the name I know you by," in a chilling comment on what slavery obliterated (in the eyes of slave owners).[70]

Rebellion and Disorder

But if slaves rebelled against this ordering of their lives, if they asserted ties or claims to their own families, then Babikr recalled in detail their pasts. He noted their births and coexistence emotionally, as evidence of the depth of their betrayal when they turned against their owners. Their betrayal added to the upheaval and violence that followed the defeat of the khalifa and of the entire Mahdist state in 1898. When Lord Kitchener and the Egyptian army captured Omdurman, many black soldiers in the *jihadiyya* used the upheaval to reunite with enslaved members of their own families. Babikr saw these reunions as the corruption of another family network, as he described in the following event:

> Shaykh 'Abd al-Lati Waqi'allah had a slave called 'Ali, who had been born in his house and circumcised with his children, and to whom he gave a very expensive teak-wood bed, on which he had lain during the circumcision. In the year 1315 (1897–8) when this slave was twenty years old he ran away and joined the *jihadiyya*. One day 'Abd al-Latif, who was my neighbor, sent for me by one of his sons, and when I got there I found his slave 'Ali with four of the Negro Guard, demanding his mother and the teak-wood bed on which he had been circumcised. I said, "Perhaps you have a right to the bed, since you were circumcised on it; but as for your mother—the law does not allow you to take her unless you pay her price." So he took the bed and told his master he would bring the money to pay for his mother.[71]

Babikr outlines the slave's lineage very clearly as one incorporated into his master's family: he "had been born in his house and circumcised with his children." Babikr scorns 'Ali's efforts to claim his own mother, however, as being outside the law. And Babikr justifies his outrage by the "fact" of the slave breaking the bonds intimately connecting him to his own master.

Resistance breaks through the traditional, even respectable, anonymity of slaves' own family backgrounds more violently in the next excerpt. Here again, ties that Babikr considered significant were bloodily disrupted:

> That night a soldier who had been a slave of Ibrahim Bey al-Ya'qubabi came to the door of his house and called him by name. When Ibrahim came out to him he thought he had come to guard him and his family, so he welcomed him and was about to shake his hand; but the soldier shot him dead, and watched him wallowing in his blood. Then his family and the neighbors came out and found the soldier, who had been known to them since his childhood, trampling with his boots on the stomach of the corpse; and all went in again and hid themselves, fearing death; and the soldier went off.[72]

In this horrific scene, the slave's violence (an "atrocity" as Babikr called it later) smashed not only a life but a lifelong connection. Everyone was traumatized by this betrayal of Ibrahim Bey by a dependent that, Babikr strongly asserted, should have honored people who had owned him as a child.

Babikr saw with his own eyes another troubling event, one that signified to him how far his society and social traditions had been toppled:

> I and some of my relations who were my guests had left my house to visit Muhammad walad Abbashar, who had been in the Karari battle. As we reached the south-eastern corner of the market we saw a Negro soldier leading a slave-girl by the hand, coming out of the market by the gallows, (east of where the post office is now). Then we saw Ibrahim Tamim the merchant from Aswan (who seemed to be the slave-girl's master) running after them; and when he had caught them up he seized hold of the girl's hand, to take her back with him. The soldier at once loaded his rifle and shot him, and he leapt up in the air and fell to the ground—we saw it from less than 200 meters away. Then the soldier took the girl's hand again, and they went away laughing loudly. When we asked about it, we learnt that the slave-girl had been Ibrahim Tamim's concubine, and that the soldier was her brother, and that both had been born in his house.
>
> Incidents like these were atrocities of conquest by the regular army of a civilized government.[73]

This must have been a terrible incident to witness, but even though Babikr investigated this "crime" to find out its cause, his account leaves many questions open. Babikr assumed that the relationship between Ibrahim and the slave girl was one of ownership and sexual intimacy and scoffed (certainly affected by the violence of the shooting) at the almost flirtatious behavior of the soldier and the girl. Neighbors or other bystanders told Babikr that the girl and the soldier were siblings and had been born into the Tamim household as slaves.

Some doubt has been thrown on whether or not Sudanese *jihadiyya* actually did try to come back for brothers, sisters, or mothers still enslaved. As Ahmad Sikainga has presented the situation after the battle of Karari in 1898, "These soldiers ransacked Omdurman, entering houses and taking a large number of slaves under the pretext that they were siblings."[74] Why would this have been a pretext? From Salim C. Wilson's memoirs, explored in the following chapter, we know that former slaves felt strongly, sometimes violently ready for revenge, and constantly sought or hoped for reunion with their lost families. From the eyewitness accounts of military officers in Omdurman at the time, there was terrible chaos—one recounted that "for three days we pillaged the city and then order was restored."[75] I wonder what was in the hearts of the soldier and the slave girl as they wreaked revenge on a man who knew their relationship, who had owned them together, and who refused to let her go. They leave Babikr's pages reunited and laughing, but the violence of their reunion scandalized those for whom such a relationship could not represent a legal family relationship.

Babikr Bedri was deeply protective of his family's integrity and very concerned that he, his parents, his wives, and his siblings stay connected to each other through the battles of the Mahdiyya, through his growing trade networks, and even during years of exile in Upper Egypt, when he was separated from many of his relatives. The marriages of the women in his family were another means of maintaining family cohesiveness. As discussed earlier, Babikr regularly bought slaves for his own brides or for the weddings of other female relatives. Babikr's sense of custom and his understanding of religious law compelled him and his male relatives toward a strict interpretation of what kinds of marriages were appropriate for the women of his family. For this reason, the lives of the women in this family were often as abruptly uprooted or transformed as the circumstances of slaves, who could be bought or sold at any moment.

After the British-led armies had destroyed Omdurman and routed the remnants of the Mahdist forces, they imprisoned many of the fighters. Families were forcibly separated from each other or collapsed under the strain of capture and exile. In a scene reminiscent of some of the worst slavery kidnappings as narrated by former Sudanese slaves, Babikr described the breakdown of one family:

> I know of two men and their wives who abandoned their two children, since they were unable to walk farther, and their parents could not carry them because their ages were seven and ten or thereabouts. The two boys were crying out, "Mother! Father! Don't leave us! Will you get children older than us?" But the parents seemed not to hear. Upon whom rests the blame for the crime of the death of these two innocents? Who could say?[76]

Babikr and some of his brothers were sent to Upper Egypt, where he stayed for months as a prisoner of war. The British at this point, in 1899, occupied Egypt, and it was to British officials that Babikr applied for permission to return to Sudan. When this permission was granted, Babikr began to gather up his relatives in Egypt, even if this meant disentangling the women from marriages and their own small families. He insisted on bringing his sister Umm Tabul back to Sudan with him, back to their father, even though she had become happily married. Umm Tabul's husband and father-in-law begged Babikr to leave her with them, but she obeyed her brother, saying that in spite of her satisfaction with her marriage, "I won't stay away from you now, and give you pain all your life, and make you reproach yourself for having fallen short in your duty to me." Her obedience enabled him to insist that the husband divorce her so that she could return with her people to Sudan.[77]

This event repeated itself among other Sudanese families leaving Egypt, and some called on Babikr for help. Babikr was happy to help in cases where women, reluctant to leave Egypt for Sudan, had married in ways considered deeply inappropriate. One typical violation of marital norms (for women) was marriage to a slave or to a husband who could have been a slave due to his non-Muslim, non-northern origins. A friend approached Babikr and asked for his support in gathering up a sister who had married "a Negro sergeant-major" but who had promised she would return with her brother to Sudan. At the moment of departure, however, complications arose. An Egyptian policeman intervened and asked the sister if she would go with her brother and Babikr or remain with her husband. She then said to her brother, "'If it weren't that the women at home would think me an outcast because I've married a black, I'd go with you; but I couldn't stand that. So good-bye to you.' Her brother slapped her on the mouth but she laughed and went off with her sister, leaving us standing there looking foolish."[78] While Babikr presented this memory as an example of an unsuccessful attempt to reassert social norms (and, perhaps, as a cautionary note to what he, as a Mahdist, considered the corrupting influence of Egyptian society), this excerpt also illustrates one of the greatest stigmas of Sudanese slavery—the racialization of slaves' identities. Appearance, tribal affiliation, profession, and skin color identified the black officer as a slave. The self-respecting sister of Babikr's friend chose not to face the social opprobrium she felt sure to meet if she returned home with a husband whose skin color would signal to her peers that he was a slave.

G. N. Sanderson noted years ago that the solidarity of the northern Sudanese extended family "and the weight and wide ramifications of its influence—not least among the political land administrative hierarchy—can hardly escape even a casual observer." Sanderson considered that "family politics" in Sudan bore significance greater than "merely domestic relevance" but enabled families to make marriage alliances, and these alliances had the potential to create powerful political alliances.[79] Lillian Sanderson found in Babikr's memoirs important information about "the roles of individuals within the extended family, the attitude of society to women and the functions of the family as 'an old boy net.'"[80] Certainly these alliances of marriage assumed urgency under the tumultuously changing circumstances of northern Sudanese society at the turn of the century. With the Mahdiyya defeated and wiped out in 1899, families like Babikr's had to renegotiate their position in a changed society with new authorities once the British stepped in to build an administration in Sudan.

Perhaps the political implications of marriage explain the attitudes of Babikr, the wife who refused to leave her black husband on the grounds that she would be ostracized in her own community, and those who would have scorned her and rebuked such a marriage. Slavery remained a significant networking institution itself, and even in the last years of the Mahdiyya, trade in slaves grew increasingly active in regions where non-Muslim tribes lived, such as the Bahr al-Ghazal.[81] The trade enabled the development of a racial ideology by which entire geographical areas of Sudan were considered slave zones, or, as Amir Idris has described:

> The slaving area was constructed by those involved in the slave trade in terms of Islamic versus non-Islamic, Arab versus non-Arab descent, brown versus black color with each racial category giving meaning and representation to its opposite. These invented categories included terms such as *abd* or slave for Southerners or *Fallata* or *Gharaba* for western African immigrants and Western Sudanese. Consequently the importance of race in the Sudan is linked with the construction of Arab origin.[82]

As Idris concludes this discussion, "These pre-colonial processes of enslavement, indeed, imposed social meanings on social, cultural and religious differences among the people of the Sudan and served as the basis for the structuring of society."[83] But slaves in northern Sudanese society were also facing a new political day with the coming of the British, who, it could easily have been assumed, would have been eager to immediately abolish all practices of enslavement once they took power.

They were not. British officials in the new government of Sudan, the Anglo-Egyptian Condominium, were deeply reluctant to make so drastic a move. Throughout Sudan, British officials confronted a resistant population of diverse peoples and communities. They were keenly aware that thousands of northern Sudanese, under the Mahdi, had defeated the armies of Egypt scarcely a generation before. In regions where tribes were acephalous, such as the Dinka tribes of the south, the British were baffled by the fact, as it seemed to one official, that "the African seems to have little political loyalty to anything."[84] The regions of the Dinka, like those of the Nuba in the Nuba Mountains, had suffered slave raids for decades and were fierce in their resistance to armed British soldiers seeking to impose a new kind of political order. British observers could be strikingly unsympathetic to communities scarred by slavery, as exemplified by the comment of the East Africa Commission: "It should always be remembered that one of the principal curses of slavery, apart from its immoral character and its economic failures, was the production of the slave mind. A human being accustomed to slavery, when freed, seems to have lost all incentive to work."[85]

The British brought to Sudan particular ideals of "free labor," and the common belief that slaves were inherently lazy did not encourage officials toward decreeing unilateral manumission. Patrick Manning has written that these officials came to Africa with a different system of slavery, the Atlantic slave trade, embedded in their sense of history; they were "genuinely convinced that the status of the slave in Africa was not one of significant inferiority." But they also worried that "the emancipation of slaves would bring significant social upheaval." Manning charges these officials with "moral inconsistency"; their desire to "run inexpensive colonial governments and to utilize African labor cheaply further encouraged them to wink at slavery."[86] The British who came to establish a government in Sudan feared "that sudden abolition would lead to vagrancy and prostitution."[87] As they set up ministries to administer social policies, they increasingly worked closely with the groups of northern Sudanese who had owned slaves for generations. As Ahmad Sikainga has traced, these officials came to share "the slaveholders' view that without discipline the slave would be idle, mischievous and even dangerous."[88] Because of these factors, the British tampered little with slavery during the first two decades of their administration in Sudan.

The second volume of Babikr Bedri's memoirs narrates his life experiences from the beginning of the Anglo-Egyptian Condominium (1899) until the assassination of Lee Stack and the formation of the Sudanese government in 1925. His descriptions reveal his increasing interaction with British officials as he developed his own professional interest in education. It also describes his continued possession of numerous slaves throughout the twenty-five years that the volume covers. During these years, he expresses an ever-deepening sympathy for northern Sudanese Muslim women, sympathy he eventually implemented in his founding of the first secular school for girls in Sudan. Although he also cared for many of his slaves during this period, several women in particular, he offers examples showing his disapproval of people he identifies as slaves or former slaves trying to break through their social positions of inferiority. Any discussion of manumission had to be introduced by a friendly and respected British official. Only gradually and haphazardly can the reader perceive that much changed for slaves and former slaves during this period of Sudanese history and Babikr Bedri's life.

In the first pages of the second volume, Babikr recounts the continuing chaos in the defeated city of Omdurman, and one can feel how powerful traditions of enslavement remained. Although Lord Kitchener led the armies that entered and pillaged the city, many of the troops were from the *jihadiyya* regiments of the disbanded Egyptian forces, and as we have seen, these soldiers had been slaves or came from much-raided tribes such as the Dinka. Babikr witnessed the intrusion of British soldiers into his home, who took some of his possessions and attributed to them a touristic curiosity—"I think they took these merely as curios." But the behavior of the Sudanese soldiers merited more of his attention, for they were taking everything of value they could find: "copper, beads, money, ornaments and animals." As they looted his house, Babikr found an officer outside, a sergeant major, who answered Babikr's plea for help and reprimanded the soldiers immediately. It seems they had "overstepped the time limit during which the town was declared open to them, as they very well knew." But when the sergeant major interceded, the soldiers "now displayed a servile humility, very different from the brutal arrogance which they had shown on entering our house." The sergeant major even made the soldiers put everything back in Babikr's house and placed two of them as guards against further looting, even when Babikr insisted this was not necessary. Perhaps this was out of his connection to Babikr from an earlier experience—this was the same black sergeant major who had married a northern Sudanese woman, whose bride had refused to leave Egypt with her brother. So honorable was this man that Babikr remembers gratefully that "it was he who received my sword and returned it to me a couple of weeks later after the battle of Omdurman."[89]

While he tried to pull the pieces of his economic life back together, his slaves stayed with him, but his narrative gives hints that many other slaves were trying to escape forced labor. Babikr berated a wealthy chief of a village near Madani for doing little to help his people during an outbreak of meningitis, prophesying future poverty for the chief: "If your houses fall down, you won't be able to repair them because your slaves will have run off to Madani to get their freedom papers."[90] But this kind of threat does not seem to have affected Babikr, whose own slaves prove themselves loyal again and again, especially when he feared catching meningitis in this region. He became ill with stomach pains and prayed out loud, sure that death was near. But his oldest slave, Khamisa, made him tea and ministered to him, and he remembered her saying to him, "Master, I think you lost too much blood when you were cupped at Madani and that's what's given you this turn. Please let me pour some of this up your nose." Soon Babikr recovered, saved by his respectful slave.[91] In these times of illness and famine, slaves were his last currency, cited as all he had (along with two camels and worthless coins).[92] Only by hiring more slaves could Babikr make the bricks to build new shops so that he could reestablish himself as a trader.[93] While they shared his poverty, slaves formed a major part of Babikr's economic recovery plan.[94]

After several years of trying to make ends meet through trade, Babikr turned his attention to the education of northern Sudanese children. He was courted by the authorities to generate local support for secular schools and, in 1903, began to train as a teacher.[95] Many pages of the second volume detail the development of Babikr's enthusiasm for education and his negotiations with both Egyptian and British officials for how best to train young Sudanese for eventual political autonomy. When, later in 1903, Babikr helped open a school in the town of Rufa'a, he struggled to translate and teach British textbooks of mathematics while appealing for support and help from the local British administrator.[96] The graduates of the Rufa'a school did well, and Babikr made a name for himself as an educator. He eventually became close to Mr. Crowfoot, deputy director of education, although it took Babikr years to convince his friend of the importance of establishing a school for girls.[97]

When Babikr writes about his work at the school or his campaigns for more financial support for the school, there are no slaves mentioned and seemingly no slaves present. Part of his work to establish the girls' school meant trying to bridge social traditions that kept communities suspicious of educating their daughters, but these traditions also sanctioned slavery. Babikr continued to own slaves well after the end of World War I and brought his prejudices about "Blacks" and "Negroes" to his organization of schools. In the late 1920s, a British official selected a "Negro girl" named al-Risala to be a trainee teacher and brought her to Omdurman. As Babikr remembered, "This was against my advice, but he told me that we were not fair to the Negroes."[98] Soon the girl ran away. In searching for her, Babikr luckily met with "a relation of her master's" who informed him that she was at home in Khartoum because her family had decided it was time for her to marry. Although Babikr had strongly expressed his views that such a girl was not a suitable teacher, he encouraged her and her family to try to complete a year's training. She returned with him, but true to his prophecy, "al-Risala did not turn out a success as a school-teacher."[99] Babikr's lingering dismissal of al-Risala's potential would have been just one of the pressures this young woman faced in post–World War I Khartoum, as she struggled between her future as a married woman and the much more untraditional role (for a woman of her ethnic identity and economic background) of becoming a teacher.

Babikr had much kinder words for another woman, a slave named al-Rahma, whom he purchased in the 1920s (along with a donkey) and kept in his possession for five years, "until I was retired on pension, after which she left me and I sold the donkey; I am grateful to them both."[100] Soon after purchasing al-Rahma, Babikr began a tour of inspection of ten local schools in an eastern district, and a British Dr. Cruikshank accompanied him, "he and his servant on horseback and I and my slave girl on donkeys."[101] He took care of her when she was afraid during these treks (on several occasions they surprised lions),[102] and she cooked wonderful dishes for him during their travels: "I enjoyed my food just as if I had been at home; for I had al-Rahma with me and she was good at cooking all kinds of dishes—thin kisra and delicious stews of every sort."[103]

Immediately, on this page, Babikr contrasts the valuable work of al-Rahma with his discovery of a scene of women working in conditions that distressed him deeply. In al-Qirayha village, Babikr made the rounds with a clerk, Muhammad Efendi, to see how cotton was being picked.

> I found that he had about sixty women pickers, all with their hair uncovered and their *tobs* wound tightly round their loins, outlining their flanks, while the younger ones had their breasts bare. And passing to and fro among them was a young lad, only about twenty years of age, riding a colt and supervising their labors. What made matters worse was that, the cotton plants being low, they

had to stoop to pick. When I saw this offensive sight, all too likely to affront the Ja'aliyyin who are so jealous of the modesty of their womenfolk, my feelings were thoroughly roused and I called to the lad, "How much do you earn by pimping in this fashion?"[104]

Babikr protested that if a foreigner were to see these women, he would look at them lewdly, and suggested that each woman be given a headscarf, a blouse, and a basket to protect her modesty. Babikr also expressed concern over the long hours the women were forced to work.

Babikr described the work and the bodies of these sixty women with unusually vivid detail—his description of them reminds me of the photograph taken, during the same period, of the woman washing clothes shown earlier in this chapter. But the statement that they presented "an offensive sight" reveals, I think, the contradictions of sympathy and discomfort about female slavery and female labor with which Babikr wrestled in this second volume. He defends the honor of the Ja'aliyyin community, knowing the sight of immodestly dressed women will be a visual insult to them. Yet he also vocally deplores the conditions under which these women work. Babikr mentioned the wages earned by these pickers but does not mention how they were hired—if they were free laborers or slave laborers. His efforts to spare "the poor women two long walks" show his concern for their well-being and their bodies, but their seminudity made their work somewhat obscene.[105] They present a stark contrast to his wonderfully loyal, and protected, slave al-Rahma; a new form of slave labor that went against the old ways of owning slaves.

Slaves and the British

As comfortable as his relationship with al-Rahma was, Babikr could not avoid the questions of those British officials sensitive to the continuation of slavery and hopeful for the integration of former slaves into the Sudanese economy. While there seems to have been no discussion of slavery when he and Dr. Cruikshank traveled together with their slaves through villages outside Khartoum, other officials were not content to ignore Babikr's slaves. Mr. Currie, deputy director of education, had become Babikr's friend through their close work together creating a successful school for boys and trusted him to explain Sudanese customs and political situations. At some point in 1909–10 (the memoirs are not clear on the date of the following encounter), Currie asked Babikr and some other Sudanese leaders whether or not the people of the Jazira were pleased that the railway had reached their largest city, Sinnar. Babikr replied that the common people were pleased, but not the elites. Currie had understood the opposite—that the elites must have been happy with how much the government had restored their leaders to positions of authority. Currie had concluded that the common people had been most upset about the freeing of their slaves. Babikr contradicted him:

> "Compared with the deep worry of the elite, the freeing of the slave is a trifle."
>
> "What worry?" he asked with the keenest interest.
>
> "During the Mahdiyya," I answered, "I, Babikr Bedri, was a wealthy, well-to-do merchant, but on its overthrow I became a poor man. You, Your Excellency, Mr. Currie, found my salary £2 per month and doubled it to £4 and later £6 per month. It is natural that I should be loyal to you for your generosity; but the Shari'a law forbids me to love you because you are an infidel. So I am torn by a conflict of loyalties."[106]

According to Babikr, Currie did not pursue the discussion of abolition and its discontents in Sudan any further, but not long after, Babikr was forced to engage with another official, A. P. Coote, an inspector appointed to Rufa'a, for help dealing with one of his slaves. The following narrative gives a view of how complicated social negotiations between slave owners, the British, and slaves were becoming.

> Now I had a slave called 'Abdallah whose family comprised his mother, his children, wife and sisters; 'Abdallah stirred the others up to be rebellious against me. I complained about him to Mr. Coote, who sent for him, gave him a word of warning and sent him back to me. A couple of days later he sent for me and asked me if I was happy with the way he had handled the matter of 'Abdallah and his mother. I said I was very happy. He said that he, on the contrary, had not slept easy the last two nights. I asked him, "why so?" For reply he asked me a question.
>
> "If your father, or someone you loved or feared, were to say to you, 'Change a verse of the Qur'an for me,' would you do what he asked?"

"Certainly not," I replied.

"Well," he said, "with us freedom is something like that: and that is the reason why I have been suffering severe pangs of conscience."

"I will put your conscience at rest," I said: "for I will set them free, for God's sake."

He thanked me, saying, "Tonight I shall sleep the sleep of the just."[107]

Babikr freed 'Abdallah and his mother immediately. But this did not end his ownership of slaves. He continued to buy slaves for decades after this experience and to justify it to British officials.

These discussions often took place during political difficulties between the government and more nationalistic Sudanese figures like Babikr. He prefaced the following discussion he had with District Commander Huddleston in 1925 with "the first thing which the British expect from their subordinates is obedience."[108] And not long before their discussion, the governor-general of the Sudan, Sir Lee Stack, had been assassinated in Cairo, and all Egyptian professionals and military were being expelled. The British carefully watched Sudanese elites like Babikr for signs of where their loyalties lay, and expressions of obedience to British authority had taken on a political urgency. Huddleston detailed for Babikr the economic reforms that the British were trying to introduce to organize the profits of cotton cultivation. One of the most important reforms, Huddleston thought, was that tenants of farms would earn 40 percent of the profits in exchange for plowing, irrigating, and bringing the cotton to market. Babikr disagreed:

> At this I exclaimed, "Why! We used to treat our slaves better than that!"
>
> "How so?" he asked.
>
> I told him that we gave each slave a plot to cultivate for himself on one day a week and another day on which he could either rest in his own home or cultivate in his plot if he chose; and he could reap from the crop on his personal cultivation enough for his needs or to buy a beast. But his food and clothing, both for him and for his wife and family, were provided by his master throughout the year. So, I concluded, if the Government were to allow each tenant a portion of his holding, similar to that which we gave our slaves, enough to provide him with his food for the whole year, he would prefer a tenancy on that basis to the unheard-of basis which he, the Governor, had described.[109]

Huddleston changed the subject, but Babikr stipulated to his readers that being so candid was his way of serving his country. Commenting that few Sudanese would give a high British official such an honest answer, Babikr prided himself on his outspokenness: "I count myself among this minority because I want to serve my country and consider that to withhold critical advice from the authorities is a kind of betrayal. Our duty is to inform them on how we expect them to treat us, but not to try to compel them to act upon our advice."[110] What is also compelling here is Babikr's use of the past tense when he wrote, "We used to treat our slaves better than that," evidence perhaps that the current economy had eroded slave owners' ability to be so generous. But even if there is a hint of nostalgia here, there is no regret—clearly, Babikr believed an environment in which slaves could profit so well was superior to a political and economic atmosphere run by foreigners who understood little about Sudanese society. Everyone knew then how creative and effective an educator of Sudanese children Babikr Bedri was, but it is important to note how hard he worked to educate the British about Sudanese society, and in particular, about slavery. The customs, economics, and traditions of slavery formed a crucial part of the Sudanese nation that Babikr was learning to politicize, and to uphold.

.   .   .

Babikr Bedri was a man endowed with incredible sensitivities to children, one who looked back publicly on his own childhood and wrote about how his parents raised him and whether he agreed with their choices; sometimes he questioned his treatment of his own children. Babikr was a man who, as he matured, learned to appreciate the difficulties of women's lives, who fought for decades with both the British and northern Sudanese villagers to open a school for girls. He put his own daughters in school as proof of his dedication and his belief that secularly educated girls "would help prevent our educated men from marrying foreigners, a thing which would bring to naught our efforts in educating them."[111] When he encountered impoverished mothers abandoned by their husbands, he employed them and hosted them within his own household.[112] He drew on his sense of Islamic law and faith to be just to the women in his family and in his country and, by the time he was middle-aged, even challenged certain laws when they seemed to stifle women's development: he strongly protested the custom of wives staying in their mother's household even after marriage and refused to let his daughters do the same.[113]

Treating women fairly and justly was, for Babikr Bedri, a responsibility of moral and spiritual authority, as was treating his slaves well. But Babikr's immense imagination did not stretch as far when it came to changing the status of his slaves or slaves in his society. From the two volumes of his memoirs analyzed here, he continued to honor the system of enslavement, and it was difficult for him to see new positions or roles for those who bore the stigma (whether fairly or not) of slavery. Nor would he trace the pasts of his slaves. Their childhoods were absent for him, even if he had purchased them as children. If slaves like Sabah al-Khayr or al-Rahma matured, they did so only in relation to their masters. If slaves tried to seize control of their lives, without permission, Babikr criminalized it. That was an act seen as treachery to the childhoods they shared with their owners. And as much as he cared for some of his slaves, and saw them married and having children, one wonders if Babikr ever chose to see them as adults. They were never given the choice, or the chance, of education. What neither 'Ali Mubarak's *Khitat* nor Babikr Bedri can teach us, however, is what these slaves talked about in their native languages before Cairo or Khartoum became their home. We must turn to other sources to explore the struggles of slaves, contemporaries of these two men, to find a language in which to narrate their own history.

How Salim C. Wilson
Wrote His Own Enslavement

'Twas mercy brought me from my Pagan land,
Taught my benighted soul to understand
That there's a God, that there's a Saviour too:
Once I redemption neither sought nor knew.
Some view our sable race with scornful eye,
"Their color is a diabolic dye."
Remember, Christians, Negroes, black as Cain,
May be refin'd, and join the angelic train.

Phillis Wheatley (1753–84),
"On Being Brought from Africa to America"

In 1882, British armies occupied Egyptian soil, and British officials extended their control of the Egyptian treasury and the political administration of the country. In 1885, the famous British officer and abolitionist
General Charles Gordon, who had been asked by Khedive Tawfiq to protect the Egyptian armies facing the Mahdiyya, was killed in Khartoum by
the Mahdi's forces after more than a year of siege. For over a decade, the
proconsul of Egypt, Lord Cromer, refused the pleas of Egyptians anxious
to recolonize the territory, as well as the hopes of British citizens eager to
avenge Gordon's death. His successors, however, were more aggressive in
their goals for the control of Sudan, and this energy, coupled with popular
outcry in England, resulted in a British-led military campaign against the
Mahdiyya in 1898. Using the funding of the Egyptian government, British officials now assumed control of the administration of Sudan as well,
under an arrangement known as the Anglo-Egyptian Condominium.

While abolitionists in Great Britain had long been concerned with erad-
icating the slave trade in the Nile Valley, soldiers new to Sudan had little
experience with this issue. Quickly, this administration had to confront
the presence and reckon with the future of numerous slaves and former
slaves. To help make sense of it, British soldiers sometimes documented
these encounters with the help of cameras, most notably in the photograph
of British officers with two Sudanese men taken in Kordofan, in western
Sudan, in 1910. The description for the photo mentions that the officers
were talking to "Murgan, an Arabic and English-speaking Nuba man who
was sold into slavery as a child before joining a traveling company and visiting various European cities."[1] Murgan, sitting naked in front, is motion-
ing with his right arm as he describes his journeys. But we have more than
this photograph and this description.

R. V. Savile kept a diary of his travels through Kordofan and wrote this
of the encounter:

> After breakfast spent most of the morning interviewing various meks [local
> chiefs] etc. while the Camel Corps watered their camels.

Murgan with two British officers, A. L. Hadow and R. B. Black, and the *mek* Toto. Photo by
R. V. Savile, February 10, 1910. Sudan Archive, Durham, SAD-12/51.

> Hadow went exploring up the hill and met the mek Toto and with him a stark naked savage who knew Arabic. He talked to this man and showed him his glasses. When the man had looked at them he returned them with the words "thank you" in English. Hadow got a good deal of his story out of him and brought him down with the mek to see me. The man's name was Murgan and he had had a very varied existence. He had been kidnapped as a boy by a Hamrawi and sold to a slave trader who had sold him in Alexandria. Later he had joined some sort of a traveling company, representing an African village, and had gone to London, Portsmouth, Cardiff and various other English towns and eventually went to Paris. He had remained 6 years in this company, chiefly in England, and had then returned to Alexandria, where he was enlisted in the XIV Sudanese in which he served 8 years.[2]

One life's story offered in a paragraph. But this complicated paragraph demonstrates that Savile considered Murgan's story compelling enough to write it down and to photograph the man (first called "savage") in the act of telling it as well.

As I read it, Murgan announced himself to these officers by expressing an interest in the glasses that belonged to one of them and then speaking to them in English. That sparked their attention, as did his ability to converse in Arabic. He is even shown telling his story actively. What was learned of Murgan's past and his identity was that he came from the Nuba Mountains and had been enslaved several times; he had journeyed far beyond Sudan and had a sense of European cultures and at least two foreign languages.

Murgan's trajectory through slavery in Egypt, Sudan, and Europe was also theatrical. He described the remarkable experience of having spent years in Europe, most of them in England, as part of a touring company in which he was a reenactor of Nubian cultural practices in a re-created African village. I do not know if he did this as a slave or as a free man, but he was hired to provide physical authenticity to British audiences observing displays of African culture in international exhibitions. This record of him, his photograph with the officers, ended up in an archive in the north of England, perhaps not too far from one of the towns where he played at being an African. And his photograph, unlike any other photograph of a slave that I have seen, shows him talking, commanding the attention of not only the officers who lean toward him to listen intently but also of the *mek*, his social superior and perhaps his master. We do not know what autonomy Murgan had over his life in England, just as we do not know if and how he became a slave when he returned to Sudan. Perhaps he told the story of his experiences many times in Sudan to other slaves or former slaves, even to the *mek* with whom he met the British officers. But for the public, published, or archival record, it is only through the truncated notes of R. V. Savile that details of Murgan's life have been recorded.

When Murgan was in England, he and other Africans performed according to scripts designed for European audiences—he did not actually perform his own life story.[3] This chapter explores how another former slave, Salim C. Wilson (or Hatashil Masha Kathish, as he was named by his family), publicly remembered and narrated his experience of enslavement. It investigates how Salim told the story of being captured and the labor he performed as a teenage slave, of being redeemed by European officials, and of converting to Christianity. It examines how a person with such experience created a home for himself in England as an adult, as a liberated former slave. Although Salim lived much of his life differently from how Murgan lived, both men were displayed in Britain as "'real' black bodies on stage telling their 'real,' 'authentic' stories." Particularly for Salim, it was "the theater of abolition" that enabled his "moments of articulation, the moment of bearing witness."[4] This chapter then considers how he struggled for control over his narrative with his English evangelical editors and how, because of this struggle, his narrative changed through several versions published between 1881 and 1939. It raises questions about who believed Salim's story and who did not and the challenges that literacy in English created for the reception of his narrated life story. In tracing the landmarks of Salim's journey, this chapter describes the vast distances he traveled geographically, culturally, religiously, and politically before he died in northern England in 1947.

A Life Framed by Slavery

> It did not need missionaries, as often alleged in Sudan, to keep alive the
> memory of slavery—it was deeply embedded in the folk memory and in-
> evitably shaped responses to Islam and to Christian missionary endeavor
> in the Condominium period.
>
> Andrew C. Wheeler,
> "Freed Slaves and the Origins of the Sudanese Church"

I consider it true, as Andrew Wheeler wrote, that the memory of slavery
was deeply embedded in many Sudanese communities, certainly so by the
late nineteenth century. It is also true that the sense of folk memory mentioned by Wheeler was deeply important to Salim, who tried to personify
what he remembered as the collective memory of his family and village
and who relied on his sense of shared and inherited cultural perceptions
when he told the story of his childhood and his life as a slave. The discussion of slavery and the memory of losing people to the trade were widely
articulated among communities in Sudan who were vulnerable to slave
raids and kidnapping. Salim himself related that his father's brother was
ostracized by his family and village after he connived with slave traders
to replace his kidnapped wife with another, younger Dinka girl. Salim remembers how much this girl was missed.[5]

Relationships with European military officers, abolitionists, and missionaries changed the language of slavery for many Sudanese former slaves.
These relationships also transformed the public audience for the slave narrator, since narratives sponsored by Christian or abolitionist organizations
were rarely, in the nineteenth century, published in Arabic or other languages indigenous to Sudan. Without the intercession of European Christian missionaries, the memories of Salim and former slaves like him would
never have been published outside Sudan. For the slaves, this intercession
usually began accidentally, with a surprising and dramatic encounter with
soldiers or abolitionist missionaries working in Sudan. For the Europeans,
however, finding slaves like Salim was the reason for their very presence
in Sudan.

Salim had been taken far from his natal village, Amerwai, when European soldiers working under General Charles Gordon found him during
a small war in 1879.[6] By then, he was a teenager and had been a slave for
several years. Salim had been caught in a violent raid against his village
and had witnessed the killing of his father, a Gok Dinka chief, right before
Salim was seized and sold by men whom he later described as Arabs. His
first master named him Salim and treated him with kindness, but financial
circumstances forced him to sell Salim to a much harsher owner, who was
an ally of the slave merchant Sulayman Zubayr. Sulayman was the son of
the well-known trader al-Zubayr Rahman Pasha and had taken over his
famous father's monopoly of slave-trading networks in Darfur. Sulayman
ibn Zubayr mobilized against Gordon's forces that year, and Gordon hired
the Italian officer Romolo Gessi to defeat Sulayman and liberate the slaves
who had been under his control. Gessi eventually defeated killed Sulayman. During these skirmishes, Gessi arrested Salim's master, Muhammad,
and rounded up his slaves. At one of these camps, Salim met representa-
tives of the Church Missionary Society.[7] He worked as a servant for one
of these men, Charles Wilson; traveled with him to Cairo; and eventually
went to England in 1881. Salim thus left Sudan before the Mahdiyya had
overtaken the country, immediately before similar chances for liberated
slaves to flee Sudan had evaporated. In England, Salim converted to Christianity and trained to become a missionary and evangelist. He traveled to
the Congo with another missionary from the Church Missionary Society
and returned to England in 1888. He lived in the northern town of Scunthorpe, married a local woman, set up a grocery, delivered many lectures
around England, and wrote his autobiography.[8]

By the turn of the century, a small but growing group of men and women
from different, non-Muslim tribes had left enslavement with the help of foreigners, as Salim did. A number of these men and women, such as Father
Daniel Sorur and Bakhita Kwashe, were Dinka and were redeemed and
educated by Italian Catholic missionaries, notably Fathers Niccolò Olivieri
and Daniel Comboni. I discuss them at much greater length in Chapter 5,
because there were real differences in the training, treatment, and legacies
of these Catholic freed men and women and those, like Salim, who were

adopted by British Protestant evangelists. It was more common for the Italian missions to educate these former slaves in the languages of the region and, if possible, in Italian and other European languages. There they became "the raw recruits for a new campaign to evangelize 'Africa by Africans.'"[9]

Those Dinka former slaves and Christian converts found themselves in a religious cross fire in late nineteenth-century Sudan, between European missions and belief systems and the rising tide of the Mahdiyya movement. For the followers of Muhammad Ahmad, the Mahdi, the redemption of these slaves represented an illegal breach of contract and a sign that non-Muslim foreigners had co-opted the Egyptian government's administration in Sudan and contributed to its corruption. For the missionaries in the field and their constituents and backers in Europe, these redeemed slaves' lives bore witness to what they viewed as the despotism of Islamic rule and the violence of Arab slave raiders.

This struggle accelerated after 1881, when the Mahdi's movement began to attract and mobilize thousands of mostly northern Sudanese religious and tribal leaders. Many of those who joined the movement were merchants in the slave trade (*jallaba*) who had been losing money and ground to General Gordon's efforts to abolish the slave trade in Sudan. By 1883, the Mahdiyya had gained much support and strength in Kordofan and had begun closing in on Sudan's capital city, Khartoum, where General Gordon had set up headquarters. It is a rarely noted fact, clarified by Douglas H. Johnson, that at this time in its history, two-thirds of Khartoum's population were slaves. Caterina Zenab, a Dinka missionary who was trained to become a highly skilled missionary by Monsignor Comboni himself, worked energetically among these slaves, many of whom were also Dinka.[10] This was a time when, as Johnson writes, "it was this population which was amalgamating . . . a variety of spiritual beliefs and practices, some of which were incorporated into such urban spirit-possession cults as the *zar*."[11] It was therefore a time when Dinka and other slaves were finding ways to articulate the story of their enslavement and to share in spiritual development and create religious history.

It was very hard for Sudanese former slaves to create a written record of their lives and experiences; to do so required crossing vast boundaries

of education, literacy, and cultural acceptance and tolerance for their testimony. The Catholic missions demonstrated more sympathy for the autobiographical witnessing of former slaves than British officials did. Language
training, in Italian and in Arabic, was a priority for the Comboni mission
from the middle of the nineteenth century. But even after the Mahdiyya
was defeated by British-led forces in 1898, when the Church Missionary
Society began to set up schools in the parts of Khartoum and Omdurman
where Caterina Zenab had worked, the missionaries chose to teach former
slaves and the children of slaves in Arabic but written in roman letters.[12]
These children and former slaves had already learned several languages,
from their natal tongues to spoken, colloquial Arabic. Heather Sharkey describes the "educational imprint" on a student of these schools (in this case,
not a slave): "For rather than using the vocabulary, syntax and script of
literary Arabic, she wrote Sudanese colloquial Arabic in a Latin print of
mixed upper and lower cases. She was not, in other words, demonstrating
literacy by the region's common standards."[13] Sharkey shows how this particular kind of missionary, linguistic education perpetuated the social mar-
ginalization of its students from the "Arabic-literate mainstream." As she
points out, all literacy provides the power "to leave personal records or to
communicate and comprehend through fixed symbols," but literacy in missionary Arabic "had few applications, and would have made more sense to
a British expatriate than to a learned Sudanese. Moreover, since missionary
Arabic represented colloquial Arabic, and since dialects vary by region, its
forms were inherently local."[14] This language training also seems to have
left little room for instruction in English, meaning that its students would
reach only a small, particular audience of British missionaries.

Autobiographical Fragments

British colonial administrators and missionaries were often mistrustful
of the fluency of freed slaves, although they were intrigued by the experiences of these liberated men and women. This skepticism over former
slaves' mastery of English could obstruct the very telling of their story, as
the experience of Bakir Ahmed, a freed slave, can attest. Bakir Ahmed left
fifty-eight "part-typewritten, part manuscript sheets" describing his life,
sometime between 1919 and 1949. The details of his life—"written by or at

the dictation of"—were sent to the administrative journal *Sudan Notes and Records* in 1949 by a "friend of this Journal" living in the United States.[15] This journal collected the articles and memoirs of British administrators in Sudan so was intended for an audience who worked as colonial officials after the establishment of the British-led Sudanese government in 1925 and had lived or were still living in Sudan. The editors clearly considered Bakir Ahmed's life a tale worth telling but seem to have found it hard to believe his capacity for self-narration.

Immediately, the facts of Bakir Ahmed's life experiences are clouded by some doubt: "Bakir Ahmed was apparently a Kara from the southern part of Darfur born about 1865."[16] He was captured as a child by the raiders of al-Zubayr Rahman Pasha, then smuggled into a rival tribe's caravan. Sold to different owners, he was eventually adopted as the son of a translator, Ahmed Abdel Rahim, who worked on a tourist boat. This put Bakir in contact with Westerners at the approximate age of eleven. His presence on the boat caught the attention of tourists, one of whom, "Mr. (later Sir) Reginald Beauchamp, took an interest in the boy, gave money for his education in an American mission school, and 3 years later, in 1876, had him sent to England."[17] There, Bakir worked as a valet for the Beauchamp family for four years. But his patron married, and Bakir fell from favor in the house.

Despite its many obfuscations, the narrative does make clear that Bakir was a decisive young man and made his own choices. After falling out of favor with the Beauchamps, "he resented his relegation to an inferior status, and as the adoptive father in Egypt was pressing for his return, Sir Reginald seems not to have been sorry of the opportunity to get rid of him." Bakir returned to Cairo in 1881 and went to school to improve his Arabic. But when British troops arrived in Cairo the next year, at the beginning of the occupation of Egypt, Bakir's adoptive translator father thought it would be better to open a mess for the battalions quartered in front of the Egyptian royal palace. While working at the mess, Bakir "recognized a regular visitor" to the hall in England where he had worked as a valet, "and he decided that domestic service was more lucrative than a telegraph office."[18]

As the narrative describes it, "thereafter Bakir began a second installment of life in his native land." He hired himself out as a servant to a British officer and then became an interpreter for the mission sent out to relieve

General Gordon from the Mahdi's increasing pressure—the "Gordon Relief Expedition, where he had various adventures." The narrative says nothing about the complete failure of this expedition or what happened to Bakir over the next fifteen years but assumes authority over the next details of Bakir's life, although it acknowledges that Bakir said nothing about them: "It appears also, although there is no account in his notes, that Bakir was on Kitchener's successful march to Khartoum in 1898."[19] Nowhere does the *Sudan Notes and Records* article say how these biographical details were obtained.

It does return to Bakir Ahmed's own account after this, but only after warning readers that these notes contain little of interest. The article states that "the last, and longest, part of these notes consists of a day-to-day account of Bakir's travels in 1899–1901 as an interpreter to a Major Austin" on two expeditions; however, it qualifies these details by saying that "this diary, which is incomplete, contains little but the trivial details of camp life and big-game shooting, and is of little interest or value." It was known that he accompanied another Westerner on hunting trips near Khartoum, and that in 1919 "an American scientific expedition got in touch with him at Cairo and recorded these autobiographical fragments." The author of the article wants to know more about what was clearly a fascinating life. As T. H. B. Mynors writes: "It would be interesting to know what became of him thereafter, for in the first forty years of his life he had found more adventure than falls to the lot of most Sudanese."[20]

T. H. B. Mynors registers awe for Bakir Ahmed's "adventures" but maintains an almost contemptuous distance from Bakir's efforts to put this life into words. While the article presents Bakir's many transitions from servant to translator to big-game hunter as adventurous, it scorns the very language Bakir uses to tell his story, framing his authorship as a linguistic failure. This becomes particularly stark when quoting Bakir directly. The article states,

> Three extracts from the narrative of his early years will give an idea of the style and quality:
>
> In describing his origins at "Harrah [sic] south west of Sudan and next to the province of Darfur" he says:—
>
> 1) "The religions much still like the ancient heathens, believing in Demons, familiar spirits and worships at stones and C and C style of the early Egyptians

no deference they edify a large Huts for these images and kept them in by numbers and sanctuary is in centre and only the high priest enters in side and also they build up sort of Huts for convent and in it appears to them those subjects the young men girls used to go in to be converted and shut up for certain days and when they let out they do pinchs the other youngsters that never been went in, I have had a cousin use to pinch me with her nail fingers and my mother used run up and stops her for doing it, I could imagine the idea of it however she makes me cry all day when we are alone."

2) "Sporting, a foot-polo nearly same as European style only this having crooked heads of bamboo sticks and ball the same kind, the playing would be between two villages and in the middle halfway starts by two leaders but all the rest standing in good orders, all scattered about. Thus whom could drives the ball to they home will win the sport."

3) "Livings we generally secure our grain until next season of rain as before mentioned. The men perpetually roving about seeks for hunting gums what they could get, principally fishing they are abundant in the narrow river and small lakes, Hippo and crocodiles be sun everywhere the spears them or dig up holes and covered with grass, so may tumble in, the same to the Elephants. Curious way to fish from reeds made square and hollow at bottom a shape of bottle, having mouth open and about four feet in height by moving it about in water the fish will wobbles about inside so he, will put his hands through and pull them out."[21]

The English used here may be awkward for British officials, but it is vividly expressed, each extract offering a vibrant picture of religious practices, games, or hunting among Bakir's community. Perhaps this was meant to conjure for his English-speaking audience an image of the community in which he lived as a child so that they could imagine him a little differently. Perhaps it was also meant personally to help Bakir not only to remember and relive his life in childhood but to immortalize it, to show that he did not enter slavery without roots and cultural practices of his own. Yet Bakir also employs an almost ethnographic distance from the material he presents. By calling the religion he may well have once practiced "much still like the ancient heathens," Bakir echoes a missionary approach to the nonmonotheistic tribes of western and southern Sudan.

By describing the "sporting" as "a foot-polo nearly same as European style," Bakir makes a Sudanese game familiar to a British or American reader. And by the details he utilizes to describe how to take down a hippo or an elephant, Bakir shows what an excellent hunting guide he must have been to those tourists who employed him on gaming expeditions. What all of this shows to me are the many ways in which Bakir Ahmed turned himself into a translator of several cultures and several languages, with the expertise gained from years of servitude, luck, and seizure of opportunities when they arose. Although the editors at *Sudan Notes and Record* may have questioned his English, they made a note at the end of the article that Bakir's papers "are being presented to the Gordon College Library, Khartoum."[22] Placement in an archive shows some measured respect for those slaves' voices loud enough to register.

Writing Slavery Far from Home

Although Bakir Ahmed cared enough to describe the religious practices in which he was raised as a small child, neither he nor his editor focused on his spirituality as a demonstration of his growth and development from slave to free man. For the other freed slave narrators published in English or other European languages, however, evincing a deep faith in Christianity was part of the proof of their literacy. These slave narrators all found themselves in Europe, often for many years, before or if they ever returned to Sudan. But what did this make them? Where could they be considered at home? In Europe, even to those whose life work was the abolition of slavery, the redemption and religious education of these young African freed slaves alienated them from any real national or cultural identity. Monsignor Daniel Comboni, the most activist of the Catholic missionaries and perhaps the most sympathetic to Sudanese freed men and women, doubted they could be whole people in Europe:

> In Europe Africans cannot receive a complete Catholic education which enables them subsequently to be dependable, in body and soul, in promoting in their native land the propagation of the faith. This is because either they cannot live in Europe, or by the time they return to Africa, they have become unsuitable for the continent because of the European habits which have become almost second

nature to them, habits which become repugnant and harmful in the conditions of African life.[23]

Andrew Wheeler uses this comment by Comboni to explain the hardships experienced by freed Sudanese slaves who migrated to Europe: "Purchased in slave markets, conveyed to the strange cold lands of Europe and often then confined to convents and various religious institutions, one wonders whether 'emancipation' is the right word for the treatment of the several hundreds of young people who came to Europe in this way."[24] This eloquent empathy for the isolation and alienation of the freed slaves fails, however, to recognize their own process of self-transformation. It fails as well to investigate the transition these Sudanese men and women made "from a socially stratified, ethnically based identity directly tied to a specific land to an identity predicated on the concept of race."[25]

As Michael A. Gomez writes, "There were specific mechanisms in each phase of the African's experience . . . through which he was increasingly nudged toward reassessment of his identity."[26] Gomez explores the journey of "exchanging country marks" for African slaves forcibly migrated from West Africa through the Middle Passage on the Atlantic to the southern United States. In his powerful analysis of the personal trajectory this propelled the slaves to embark on, he shows how, in the late eighteenth and early nineteenth centuries, African men and women began to view themselves differently, as belonging to a new community of fellow enslaved, while still on the boats heading toward the American coast.[27] One of the strengths they did share was that they came together in large enough numbers to create a community. African Sudanese former slaves, however, arrived in Europe one by one. If, like Bakir Ahmed, they were not isolated in convents, they were connected to European families, often as the sole black servant. Some learned to adapt to the religious schools or convents in which they were cloistered. And a few, like Salim C. Wilson, struggled to make themselves part of a Christian and British culture while always looking for a way to return to their families in Sudan.

Salim arrived in England in the 1880s to a society that identified slavery as a great evil (after centuries of involvement in the trade) and that had developed "an aesthetic and polemical tradition" that intimately linked the "tortured slave body" to "Christian martyrdom."[28] What did this mean when he and other slave narrators put pen to paper, still a decidedly un-African thing to do in the late nineteenth century?[29] Although contemptuous of slavery itself, white European audiences often questioned the linguistic and literary fluency of former slaves. These same audiences also registered, as Marcus Woods discusses, some anxiety about just how Christian the physical suffering of slaves made them:

> The experiences of Christ are experiences at the heart of slavery and of the abolitionist mythology of slavery. Yet for white abolitionists the slave posed a problem. The abused and tortured body of the slave was closer to Christ's experience than were the bodies of free abolitionists. Ultimate suffering at the hands of the wicked implicitly raises the slave victim above the white audience either inflicting or contemplating the suffering. Consequently, the representation of slave suffering within Western iconography can be found to exhibit a degree of envy.[30]

Envy becomes, in Woods's analysis, the progenitor of "competitive counter-thrusts which attempt to reduce, even to erase, the superiority of the slave's suffering."[31] Thus, a slave had to choose just the right words and find just the right tack to sail through these domains. This, then, was part of the terrain through which Salim had to navigate, where abolitionists and missionaries set the terms, if you will, of his suffering. If the voice of the ex-slave was too strident, however, or even too independent, it would be muted. Church authorities were thus careful in their choice of African ex-slave missionaries.[32]

What does such "terrain do to the slave narrator"?[33] Salim came out of a society in which slavery changed his name and his language and was then redeemed and brought to England, where there was a "language about slavery that preexist[ed] the slave's telling of his or her own experience of slavery."[34] This "discursive terrain," as Dwight McBride calls it, "creates the very codes through which those who would be readers of the slave narrative understand the experience of slavery."[35] It was therefore critical in the nineteenth century to be able to hear the words of a slave or ex-slave:

> But to speak of what? It allowed for speech on one's very experience as a slave. That is, it produced the occasion for bearing witness, but to an experience that

had already been theorized and prophesied. In this way the slave serves as a kind of fulfillment of what has been told before. Before the slave ever speaks, we know the slave; we know what his or her experience is, and we know how to read that experience. Although we do not ourselves have that experience, we nevertheless know it and recognize it by its language . . . and the language that will have the greatest degree of efficacy is the language of slavery that the reader already recognizes—the very discourse that creates the situation for the slave to be able to speak to us at all. I mean this both in the theatrical sense of speaking publicly and in the written sense of the slave narratives that we still have today.[36]

How did Salim negotiate these dictates of public speaking and writing about his own enslavement? With a careful eye to the tastes of his audiences, he performed. He knew that his transformation, physical, spiritual, and linguistic, was always under scrutiny.

Salim Writes His Life Back

Salim wrote his first narrative, *Jehova-Nissi: The Life Story of Hatashil-masha-katish, of the Dinka Tribe of the Sudan,* in 1881 under the name his parents gave him at birth. The first pages of the book display two pictures of Salim, a kind of "before" and "after" viewing of the man after two decades of life with missionaries. In the second edition of this work, published in 1901, the editor, William Engledow Harbord, discusses the significance of these pictures:

> Since in the Providence of God, I was first introduced to our Friend—Mr. Hatashil Masha Kathish, I have had frequent opportunities of watching his intellectual and spiritual growth. No greater evidence of this growth can be adduced than in comparing the two Photographs given in this edition. If the reader will study the Photograph of 1881, he will observe that it is a portrait of our friend as a *Child of Nature.* The Photo specially taken for this Edition reveals the great physical and intellectual change that has come to him in the meantime. It illustrates what the grace of God can effect in the individual life of a man—while it is a reason in favor of Mr. Kathish (when the time comes) returning to them the Gospel that has so marvelously transformed and raised him to his present condition—intellectual or spiritual.[37]

Right away Salim's life experience is offered to the British reader and viewer as if on display. Salim was a willing partner in this, adding his own caption to the photographs in his own preface to this edition, saying that much had changed since 1881, when "I truly was as a child." He continued: "This Life Story was originally put into English prose by a very dear Friend. Fourteen thousand copies of which have been sold. It was written specially for Boys: but it found such a wide circulation among adults that I have been urged frequently to revise the story. I have, therefore, done so, trusting that it will not lose any of its charm to my young Friends, while it will satisfy my senior Friends throughout England."[38] But this display reveals a curious tension. Both voices, Salim's and Harbord's, speak about the heavy editing of the narrative, and both claim an intimate role in shaping the work, but Salim's use of the first person still asserts just whose story this is. Yet the story has been fashioned to please its English readers, to charm them into buying even more than fourteen thousand copies.

Salim's second book, *The Ethiopia Valley*, was also carefully framed and begins with a similar spiral of these two voices. In his preface, Salim, again signing himself as Hatashil Masha Kathish, explains that "oft-expressed wish of friends" and his love for his own "country and its People, although it is some years since I saw them," induced him to give details about his homeland. He admits that the details he describes come from memories of long ago, because slavery stole him from his culture: "I have written here of the Country and People as they were 40 or 50 years ago; the changes that have come are not altogether to the uplifting of the moral, social, educational and religious life of the nation, nor will this be accomplished until the Arabs are subdued and the country made free for the spread of Christianity with its glorious beneficial effects."[39] Again, William Engledow Harbord's preface follows this plea. As editor, he seems to try to make Salim/Hatashil and his memories sound both more authentic and sympathetic with an assertion of the rudeness of the book's language: "There is no attempt at literary excellence. It is an unvarnished story taken from the MS. and the lips of the Author, a Native of the Country." In fact he apologizes for this and hopes "that the readers will not be too critical of the style of this book, but read it as an attempt to interest and instruct them." Harbord claims that for him, as editor, this has been "a labor of love, from appreciation of the noble struggle of the Author to overcome his early disadvantages, so fully detailed in his 'Life Story,' of which 20,000 copies have been sold."[40] Both books thus introduce their author and his narrative as a work in progress. With each printing, Salim/Hatashil made his way closer toward Christian understanding, and each printing sold more copies than the last. Yet each edition was deemed to require heavy editing because the years that had passed between the first edition (1881) and *The Ethiopia Story* (1908) had not yet turned Salim into a fluid writer of English, at least in the thinking of his editor and publisher.

These excerpts help show, I think, how complex and difficult it was for former Sudanese slaves to author a text of their life experiences with such pressure put on their self-expression. Salim's names testified to claims that others had on him: Salim was the Arabic name given to him by his first Sudanese owner, and Charles Wilson was the name of his first British benefactor. At least Salim/Hatashil's narrative reads in crystal-clear English instead of being mockingly presented in a self-taught, rough creole (as happened with Bakir Ahmed). But as smoothly as *Jehova-Nissi* and *The Ethiopia Story* read, the reader knows, from William Harbord's prefaces, how much the narrative's language depended on the editor's native command of English. Somehow, Salim and Bakir Ahmed had to find a way, like so many other former slave narrators bearing witness to their experiences in North America, to "write themselves into being."[41] The generation of these authors' texts bears witness to decades of struggle with language and veracity. One way in which Salim wrote himself into being was by holding on to his natal, Dinka name, always using it as a symbol of his authorship and his belonging to another society. Salim's experience resembled that of other former slave writers writing from the eighteenth until the late nineteenth century, under pressures described by Henry Louis Gates Jr. and Charles T. Davis. By considering the relationship between literacy and its hoped-for provision of political rights (to which former slave narrators were deeply sensitive), we can "understand both the transformation of writing into a commodity and the sheer burden of cultural imperatives that both motivated the black slave to seek his text and that defined the 'frame' against which each black text would be read."[42]

Gates and Davis note that many narratives "are prefaced by ironic apologia, in which the black author transforms the convention of the au-

thor's confession of the faults of his tale, by interweaving into this statement strident denunciation of that system that limited the development of
his capacities."[43] While his texts were indeed punctuated by "ironic apologia," here Salim's experience departs from that of former slaves writing in
North America. A very different political and cultural infrastructure had
caused his enslavement and "limited the development of his capacities."
And his editor, a friend and an official in the Church Missionary Society, carefully vetted his published words. Salim must have known that he
risked being muted if his writings deviated from the conventions of his
editors or if he asserted his independence too loudly. Church authorities
chose African ex-slave narrators with extreme care, as Salim discovered
on several occasions. In one example, in 1905 the British and Foreign Bible
Society considered whether Salim could be of help in publishing a Dinka
translation of the Gospels. They consulted the vicar of Pavenham, who, as

Salim C. Wilson. Frontispiece to *I Was a Slave*. The original caption reads: "The Author
(the only freed slave in England) takes part in the Wilberforce Centenary Procession at
Hull, July 1933."

Douglas Johnson describes, had helped Salim in writing the first edition of his narrative in 1889. Although the vicar did not challenge the truth of Salim's belief in his letter to the Bible Society, he threw Salim's narrative and his character into doubt, writing that "I have done all I have been able to do for him, but he allows himself to be influenced by people of whom he knows nothing." The vicar complained that Salim fell in with a "new friend" (perhaps Harbord) who had rewritten Salim's *Life Story*. Although invited to participate, the vicar refused to be a part of this collaboration: "Of course I could do nothing of the kind, and so he just used up what had taken me a couple of months to pull out of Salim's original manuscript." Although the Bible Society eventually consulted Salim, we can see how treacherous his path to publication was.[44] It was safer to stridently denounce Arabs and their culture, as he did in his final narrative, *I Was a Slave*.[45]

The Performance of Slavery

Salim wrote during an era in which the existence of African shows in world's fairs proliferated as a result of "a world of popular entertainments increasingly shaped by the active intervention of anthropologists."[46] In the years that passed between the writing of Salim's first and second editions of his memoir, the question of how to discuss blackness, slavery, and performance arose in Chicago in 1893 during the planning of the World's Columbian Exhibition. On the opening day of the "Dahomeyan Village," no less an observer than Frederick Douglass found both beauty and outrage in the Africans' dances. No African Americans were invited to perform in, or help organize, the fair. "We come out of Dahomey into this," Douglass wrote in a speech, referring to the Columbian Exhibition.[47]

> But I need not elaborate the legal and practical definition of slavery. What I have aimed to do, has not only been to show the moral depths, darkness and destitution from which we are still emerging, but to explain the grounds of the prejudice, hate and contempt in which we are still held by the people, who for more than two hundred years doomed us to this cruel and degrading condition. So when it is asked why we are excluded from the World's Columbian Exposition, the answer is Slavery.

Outrages upon the Negro in this country will be narrated in these pages. They will seem too shocking for belief.[48]

Here is the most famous freed slave in the United States remarking on the irony between the performance of African life and the deliberate silencing of the injustices inflicted historically on African American lives. This from the author of the most well-known slave narrative in America, remorseful that dances and ceremonies of African culture were being used to negate the history of slavery. The pamphlet that he produced with Ida B. Wells and other activists sharply reflected how much the refusal of white Americans to dignify the laborers of slavery diminished the history of the slaves and their descendants in the eyes of the world.[49]

Salim saw his place in the eyes of the world very differently. Always appearing in public by himself, Salim found a literal way to join in others' performance of Africa. Salim mastered how to perform as a freed slave, while narrating how he performed as a slave. This becomes particularly clear when he describes in *I Was a Slave* how his first Arab master learned to appreciate Salim's musical gifts. He had not been enslaved for long and was still deeply traumatized from being torn from his village and family. He was just beginning to adapt to the new name, Salim, which his owner had imposed, and to Arabic, the language of his master. His master delighted in showing off his slaves, or as Salim puts it: "These Arabs were in the habit of showing off their slaves to each other, as civilized men might show off their dogs or horses."[50] One evening, Salim's master, Abdulla, was entertaining, and called out to his young slave:

> "I have heard, Salim," said my master, "that you are a good dancer and singer. I wish you to show my guests what you can do!"
>
> I felt dreadfully nervous—suffering from what an actor, I suppose, would describe as stage-fright. But I drew a deep breath and plunged right into it.
>
> My first "number" was a lively little song the Dinka children used to sing and dance to—approximating, I suppose, to what is known in England as a "nursery rhyme"—only, of course, we poor Dinkas had no nurseries.
>
> It had a lively little lilt, and I put all I knew into it, anxious to earn my master's praise. By the time I had embarked on the second verse I was glad to see

that several of the listeners' heads and hands were keeping time to the lilt, and I knew that I "had got them," as an English performer would phrase it.

At the end of the song I did the dance, with a few variations of my own, humming the tune in time to my own movements.

When I had finished, I was told to give them another one, which I did. And I finished up with as good an imitation as I could of a Dinka war-dance—which, strangely and dangerously enough, fired me with a sudden desire to attack these men who were the enemies and destroyers of my tribe. Luckily I was able to resist the inclination, or my end might have been something like that of Samson when he pulled the building down upon the Philistines. Only not so successful! It did not occur to me, either at that time or afterwards, that if the Koran had really been doing its job it would certainly have told my master how near he and his guests were to being attacked by a Dinka boy rendered suddenly murderous by singing his tribal war song.[51]

It is interesting how Salim literally sets the stage here, bridging audiences in London with the slave-owning audience in northern Sudan. This excerpt is filled with nudges and nods to his British audience (perhaps penciled in by his editor) that help them understand Salim's position: the characterization of the Arabs as "uncivilized," the mention of stage fright, the comparison with an "English performer" when he knew he had captured his audience, and the likening of himself to Samson. But even amid the push and pull of translating his feelings and actions into a moment with which his British audience can identify, Salim makes it clear that he is in complete control of his own Dinka language. No one in either audience (slave owners or English readers) speaks that but this son of a Dinka chief. And even if no one understands, the power of this language helps this dancing boy express his rage in an ironic performance that is both public and deeply private.

Salim learns Arabic songs as well and a resistance song taught him by a "Central African negro" composed in defiance of the slave owners, which he also sang in front of them:

The refrain, broadly translated, ran as follows:
Ah! . . . Ah! . . . Ah! . . .

Bird of freedom, oh . . .

You sold me—ah! Ah! Ah!

I shall haunt you . . . Oh . . . oh . . . oh!

I used to sing this song to the man who had sold and bought me, and they never knew what it was about. I used to sing it with many quaint and grotesque gestures and grimaces, and they used to think it tremendously funny. So did I, and I got much satisfaction from singing it. I remember singing it on one occasion in the hearing of an African negro slave, who understood it and his face was a study! From that time on I think he regarded me as a hero.[52]

The relationship between Salim and his editor may have complicated the telling of this memory, for there are cultural distances inserted here that do not quite ring true for a young Dinka slave boy or even a mature African adult evangelist. *I Was a Slave* states that the song Salim learned from the man from Central Africa "had been specially composed, I gathered, by some of the followers of voodoo, or black magic, which is so rife amongst certain of the negroes."[53] How can Salim write with such disengagement about "negroes" and "voodoo," as he does here and in other instances when he describes slave caravans? When he sang in front of the "African negro slave," was he not also an African negro slave? And although he did not write the song but learned it from others, this particular slave looks at Salim (or so he imagines) as a hero for singing it in front of the slave owners. Is this the perspective of his white, English editor, looking at African slaves as foreign, unequal, and degraded beings? Or is this Salim, detaching himself from those like him to better highlight the drama of his singing performances for his English Victorian audience?

I think these questions are resolved by the way telling the story of enslavement sets a stage for Salim, and so does the abolition movement of the Church Missionary Society. There are actually several performances presented on the pages Salim dictated. In one, he is the secretly but verbally defiant slave who sings for his masters in languages they do not understand, but with melodies that they love that earn him their applause. The language of the song, however, is one that ill-defined "negroes" and fellow slaves do understand, and Salim sings the defiant songs for them as well. They cannot applaud, but they look on him as a hero. Salim returns the honor by keeping them visible as the most sophisticated members of his audience: they understand the irony of the songs without any need for translation, while Salim's English readers are never even told in what language that song is sung. And in having this scene written down, Salim puts himself in the middle of the stage. His written English may not have been strong enough for him to write his own book, but he presents himself as the only one in the book, or reading the book, who understands all the languages involved. He transcends the subordination of his enslavement and attempts, in this remarkable passage, to suborn the framework of his editors. At least on these pages, Salim achieves mastery.

Slavery's Languages

What did it mean to the African to hear and at some point repeat words associated with his captors? What did it signify to the African to be ex-pected to learn and embrace concepts which further concretized his con-dition of social death? . . . The enslaved had several matters to consider. To be sure, new words were necessary. But the degree to which the African chose to ever utter these words was very much an individual choice. The fact that she may have spoken "broken" or "bad" English does not at all mean that she did not understand the language. Although it is obvious that some would have picked up the rudiments with ease and would have spoken the tongue with facility, others may have simply refused to speak it, or to speak it very much, out of a conscious decision to resist their op-pression. As Caliban used Prospero's words to curse him (and Miranda), the African may have cursed the words themselves.

Michael A. Gomez, *Exchanging Our Country Marks*

Michael Gomez's questions about African slaves choosing to speak the language of their masters, and hearing themselves speak in these lan-guages, are extremely important for African slave narrators from the Nile Valley. Former slaves whose lives made it into print had to be trilingual, confronting and interacting in even more languages than Africans forc-ibly migrated to the southern United States. Salim, for example, was a native Dinka speaker who had to learn Arabic, the language associated with his captors. Later, as an adult, he had to learn English, the language associated with his liberators. Slavery was as much a journey through languages as it was a transformation of identity, as attested by Salim's many public names. Each acquisition of a new language was difficult for him, but the first—Arabic—turned Salim into Caliban, using Arabic words to curse Prospero.

In *I Was a Slave*, Salim relates the process by which he learned Arabic as if he were going to war with both the language and the Qur'an. It begins after his capture, when he and other kidnapped Dinka are brought to the compound (*zariba*) before their sale. Salim the narrator looks back on himself in his youth, on the sad boy only recently traumatized by the murder of his father and the loss of the rest of his family, as a savage, "like the young wild animal he really is," because he recovered rapidly. The slave raiders are preparing the new slaves, feeding them and getting them used to Arabic: "Our food was served to us by other slaves, under the direction and supervision of the guards, of course. These slaves were of all nations, and it was part of their business to talk to us and to teach us elementary Arabic, for a slave must understand the orders of his master before he can obey them."[54] Other slaves warn Salim not to even think about running away because the punishments were terrible and because nothing, not even the thoughts of a slave, could be kept secret from the magic book of the Muslims. An older Dinka slave "mentor" (as Salim calls him) warns him that there is no chance for success in escaping, that the Arabs will track him, hunt him down, and leave him to die. Their abilities to do so are presented as otherworldly:

> Moreover, they have a wonderful thing called a book, which is magic. It is called Koran, and it will tell its masters all sorts of things: amongst others, when a slave is planning to escape. And so, my young friend, it is better that you do not even think about escaping.
>
> I completely believed this story about the Koran, and the first time I heard an Arab reading from the book to a number of attentive listeners, I quite believed that the book was *speaking to him*, and that he was translating the words for the benefit of his audience! Such was the condition of ignorance I, and practically all my fellow-slaves, were then in, and you may believe that the Arabs did not hesitate to take advantage of that ignorance, and to play upon our fears and

superstitions for their own advantage. It was, indeed, one of their most power-ful weapons to *"keep the wretch in order."*[55]

Salim's first master, Abdulla, reenacts this warning several pages later, af-ter asking Salim if he has thought about escaping (this conversation pres-ents Salim as having mastered Arabic very quickly). As if following the script set by Salim's Dinka mentor, Abdulla warns Salim that if he escapes, he will be caught and beaten on the soles of his feet until he dies.

> "See here . . ." He went into his tent and returned carrying what was to me a strange-looking object which he handled with the greatest reverence.
>
> "Behold!" said he. "I have the Great Book—the Koran, which is the word of Allah, the All-Powerful. Now, should you ever even think of escaping this Book will tell me so. Should you plan any other sort of evil, then this Book will also tell me. Therefore, be careful! Do you understand?"
>
> And, shivering in awe at this most magical Book, and at the proof that what my Dinka friend of the compound had told me was true, I replied:
>
> "Yes, Master!"[56]

These passages perform several functions for their Victorian-era readers. They equate Islam with idolatry, with Muslim slave owners cynically using the Qur'an as an idol with which to deceive the unlettered, nonmonothe-istic Dinka slaves. They identify Arabic as the language of despotism, a language in which slaves answer orders or sing cheerful songs but never one in which the slave's true past and identity can be articulated. And these passages also link Salim to an earlier generation of narratives by freed slaves who wrote about their masters' similar manipulations of English and the Bible in the late eighteenth century. Charles T. Davis and Henry Louis Gates Jr. note that the "figure of the voice in the text" constituted, in the nar-ratives of men such as "James Gronniosaw in 1770, John Marrant in 1785, Ottobah Cugoano in 1787, Olaudah Equiano in 1789 and John Jea in 1815," vital "scenes of instruction" in the slave's path toward freedom. Being lib-erated from their bonds was not enough—these former slaves were truly free only when they could tell the story of their enslavement fluently in the language of their former masters. This testimony, to Davis and Gates, dem-onstrated the transformation "through which the African would become the European, the slave become the ex-slave, the brute animal become the human being."[57] They include a passage from Gronniosaw's narrative, one in which the similarities to Salim's are clear:

> My master used to read prayers in public to the ship's crew every Sabbath day; and when I first saw him read, I was never so surprised in my life, as when I saw the book talk to my master, for I thought it did, as I observed him to look upon it, and move his lips. I wished it would do so with me. As soon as my master had done reading, I followed him to the place where he put the book, being mightily delighted with it, and when nobody saw me, I opened it, and put my ear down close upon it, in great hope it would say something to me; but I was very sorry, and greatly disappointed, when I found that it would not speak. This thought immediately presented itself to me, that every body and every thing despised me because I was black.[58]

Once he became literate, Gronniosaw was able to speak back to the book that earlier would not have him. Perhaps he converted to Christianity and learned to believe in the words of the Bible. Salim also learned to speak back, but the Qur'an remained his lifelong enemy.

As he told it, Salim's Arabic certainly improved. The more used to slavery he became, the stronger his communication skills in Arabic. In *I Was a Slave*, he relates how he was increasingly able to understand and communicate with his first master, Abdulla. This greater fluency did not help him with his second and far crueler master, Muhammad, who was uninterested in hearing or watching Salim sing and dance in any language. Muhammad, in fact, tried to turn Salim back into brutishness, making him perform but silently, as a fighter. Usually afraid not to win because he would be harshly beaten, Salim turned out to be a decent boxer. In one scene, Muhammad has arranged yet another fight for Salim with another slave, to be conducted in front of "several other of his countrymen, who all looked nearly as desperate and evil as himself."[59]

> There was also a grinning negro lad, who must have been at least two years older and was certainly a great deal bigger and stronger than I was.
>
> "Now, Salim, my hero of a hundred fights," announced Muhammad, smacking his lips and grinning evilly. "I have here an opponent worthy of your steel at last. Let us see what you can do with him!"

I looked at my proposed adversary with a sinking heart once more—but this time the reason was quite a different one.

For he was a big, brawny fellow, at least half a head taller than I was, and proportionately broader. As he moved I could see the muscles rippling under his skin, and the length of his arms and the width of his shoulders spoke of very considerable strength. He stood there looking at me with a ferocious grin that told me he was not only sure to beat me but that he felt he was going to enjoy doing it too!

"Now, Bimbo," said Muhammad, addressing the negro, "let us see if you can beat this young fighting cock of mine! I don't fancy you will, but if you can I will see to it that you have extra rations all to-morrow!"

At which the negro grinned and nodded, and then looked at me and licked his lips in a very disconcerting manner.[60]

Both of the slaves, Bimbo and Salim, understand and respond to these orders in Arabic. Neither of them ever speaks to the other; they communicate only through increasingly fierce blows to the head. By narrating the dialogue that precedes the vicious fighting, Salim serves his readers as a translator, using his comprehension of Arabic to illustrate the imperious mind-set of Muhammad the slave owner (and Muhammad was known to have been a confederate of the infamous al-Zubayr Rahman Pasha). Salim's narration of this scene does not, however, offer sympathy for both slave fighters. Only Salim seems to be sensitive to Muhammad's misuse of authority and sarcastic language. Bimbo, on the other hand, comes across as insensate, a "grinning negro lad" who answers Muhammad's orders by licking his lips at Salim in a pseudo-cannibalistic way. Bimbo's described behavior sets him apart from Salim and fulfills a Victorian stereotype of the unfeeling, lascivious, and brutal African man.

Salim had mastered Arabic by the time he was liberated and could speak freely in front of white European soldiers who were closing in on Al-Zubayr's son and his fellow slave merchants. In the late 1870s, Romolo Gessi Pasha and other officers hired by General Charles Gordon confronted Muhammad Ahmad, whose entourage of slaves had raised their suspicions. Although Muhammad tried to convince Gessi of his loyalty by mobilizing his cohort and his slaves to fight other slave raiders, Gessi began to ask questions about the slaves themselves. Eventually, Salim

was brought before a commanding officer, informed that he was now a
free young man, and asked to tell the story of his relationship to Muhammad, then under the officers' custody. Other slaves also testified about
how they were treated, but none gave details about their mistreatment at
the hands of their master as Salim did.[61] This officer then informed Salim
that Muhammad would have to be set free and solicited Salim's help in
giving Muhammad some kind of punishment before he could escape. He
handed Salim his whip and led him to a courtyard, where Muhammad
was stripped to the waist and tied to a post:

> "Why, Salim—my good Salim—you are surely not going to turn against me
> in the hour of my desolation and misfortune? You, who I have fed and clothed,
> and to whom I have always been kind—and merciful, even in your most wicked
> moments! Surely you would not humiliate me now?"
>
> I grinned at him, and cracked the whip loudly. At the sound he let out a yelp
> of fear. On one side of the courtyard were drawn up a lot of slaves, watching
> eagerly, and on the other a number of Gordon's soldiers. They all laughed as my
> late master yelled his fear.
>
> Then I answered him. I said:
>
> "Muhammad, I will be just as merciful to you as you have been to me! Per-
> haps more so, because I do not think they will let me cut you with a razor!" Here
> I tapped my scarred cheeks, and he shut his eyes and moaned. The spectators
> laughed and applauded my speech loudly. I went on:
>
> "A short time ago, Muhammad, I was your dog—you used to call me an
> infidel dog. But now the wheel has turned and it is *you* who are the dog. *Dog of
> a Muslim . . . !*"[62]

Salim brutalized his former master until he collapsed, then handed the
whip back to the officer. The whip, remembered Salim, "was clotted with
the blood of Muhammad," and Salim offered to clean it for the officer. But
the latter refused, saying to Salim, "My servant will do that. But I can see
that you have been a good slave—better than that dog deserved . . . !"[63]
Shouting in angry fluency, Salim summons his best Arabic to publicly
insult his former master, calling him a Muslim dog for the benefit of the
slaves and officers watching the spectacle.

No longer is Salim any different from the other "negro" slaves who have stood mutely and stereotypically in the background of his book. The narration of this scene, with its detailed description of a bleeding and humiliated slave owner, also displays Salim's own savagery. His fluency in Arabic, his triumph over the language of his oppressors, led him headlong into violence and barbarity. Salim wrestled with this a few pages later:

> I was a little ashamed of the way I had flogged my helpless master in sheer revenge—and you must remember that in those days I was still a savage, with no glimmer of the Light to break up the darkness of my soul. I have, of course, felt even more ashamed of it since I have become a Christian and have learned from the Greatest of all Teachers how one should "love your enemies, bless those that curse you, and do good to them that hate you!" But even today I cannot, in all justice, feel that my master suffered one whit more than he deserved.[64]

I see the Salim that whipped his master brutally as a young and traumatized teenage boy whom a British officer actually goaded into a public performance of violence. Salim did not cede this authority outright in his memory of the moment, but that guiding hand cannot be hidden. And in what language did the two engage each other?

Salim in English

Even though his relationship to Arabic had been both forced and violent, when Salim was freed, he found himself dependent on Arabic speakers to explain his new circumstances. When the soldiers of Gessi Pasha freed Salim and the other slaves, he was delivered to Church Missionary Society sponsors, Charles Wilson and his colleague Dr. Felkin, for whom Salim began work as a servant. He observed Wilson and Felkin praying but was confused by their addressing God as "Father." Salim remembered, "This was the only word I understood—an Arab who had a smattering of English had explained what it meant to me." This unnamed Arab also told Salim about the concept of heaven. He told Salim that "it was a place 'up there' where the white men went when they died," and Salim believed him.[65] Salim had come, religiously and linguistically, full circle. Arabic was introduced to him in the form of a menacing Qur'an, and he left the Nile Valley curious about Christianity, whose basics had been translated to him in Arabic.

His dependence on Arabic speakers only increased when he traveled to London because he understood no English and white people frightened him. He arrived there in 1881, a scared teenager who stuck closely to Charles Wilson, the missionary who was also his mentor and employer. They stayed first in a hotel, and one day Wilson left, without telling Salim, to visit friends. Salim ran out looking for his mentor and soon lost his way. He began to cry, and Londoners crowded around him. A policeman approached to investigate the scene: "I did my best to explain, but as I only knew about a dozen words in English (such as 'God,' 'Heaven,' 'water,' 'food,' 'bed,' and so on), none of which was really applicable to the situation, and as the policeman knew even less of either Arabic or Dinka, we did not get very far." Luckily, one of the boys surrounding him recognized him (Salim mentions that he was "a matter of considerable curiosity, especially to boys") and told the policeman his details. Taken back to the hotel, a maid there also recognized him and found a guest who spoke Arabic. Salim remembered the moment: "Goodness! How wonderful it was to hear that familiar language—the language of my slavery though it had been—and to find someone I could understand and make understand in my turn."[66]

As he accustomed himself to life in England, Salim had two sets of teachers for English. His mentors, the Wilson family, instructed him both in English and in the beliefs of Christianity and sent him to school in the village of Pavenham (where they moved Salim after his stay in London). But it was the boys in the village, particularly those who picked on him for his obvious differences in skin color and culture, whom Salim credited as being his best teachers. Although they picked on him for fun, "they were very useful to me, and helped me a lot in increasing my knowledge of the English language." In many ways, the English boys' mocking of Salim's efforts summed up his relationship to the English language—always trying, constantly writing, but always with his fluency being challenged, as we have seen in regard to his editors. Salim continually maintained his gratitude and his dignity, as shown in his appreciation of his rough playmates: "They would find a lot of pleasure in showing me an object and making me repeat, in my clumsy, broken accents, the name of it. This would make them laugh hugely—but it also taught me quite a lot."[67] He refused to be made the "other," using their mockery to join them, and the reader, in their language.

Salim's journey toward literacy in English took him to Nottingham, where he converted to Christianity. It was then decided, as Salim remembered, that he should go on to missionary training in Derbyshire, where he would also be groomed for public speaking. Other young Africans joined Salim in this training, and they were presented at meetings where the audiences numbered "seven or eight hundred people." Such publicity exerted great pressure on Salim: "I felt dreadfully nervous when called upon to say a few words to what seemed to me in those days a vast audience, but I managed to survive the ordeal quite well, and felt very pleased with myself afterwards that I had not broken down."[68]

It is at this point in his text that Salim begins to assert, in a quiet and interesting way, his equal standing with his British mentors. We have seen how Salim, writing about his days as a slave, deliberately disengaged his own identity from that of the other "negroes" around him, even to the point where his narrative evoked some of the worst stereotypes about African men. But as he became increasingly expressive as a public speaker and as he committed himself more deeply to Christianity, he asserted a new kind of professionalism. When Charles Wilson was appointed to a position in Palestine, Salim joined him. There he was introduced to General Charles Gordon and had the chance to speak with him at some length. Gordon was a great hero to Salim, and Salim used this reverence to make an interesting and ironic point: "Even the most ignorant negroes knew perfectly well that the average white came amongst them only for his own gain or profit in some form or another—but they knew equally well that Gordon had only *their* interests at heart, and they loved him for it."[69] Never before had Salim qualified or judged white Europeans, but here, talking comfortably and privately with Gordon, his view had changed. Nowhere does it say what language the two men conversed in, but Salim portrays Gordon as the best judge of Salim's character:

> As we walked though the streets of Jaffa he became more confidential, and questioned me, with great interest, about my faith. I dare say he wondered whether any conversion, as is the case with a number of coloured people, was just a piece of hypocrisy designed to further my own material means. He said:
>
> "Why are you a Christian? Why would not Mohammedanism satisfy you?"

I answered—I think—without hesitation:

"Because the religion of the Lord Jesus Christ is a religion of love—the religion of Mohammed is not!"

He did not comment on that, and I added:

"The Lord Jesus Christ laid down his life for sinners, but the Mohammedan religion makes those who believe in it take away the lives of other men."

"That," he said, more warmly than he had spoken to me yet, "is a very satisfactory reason. Hold fast by the religion of the Lord Jesus, and you shall have everything that will be good for you."[70]

This acknowledgment by Gordon was the best recommendation Salim could find. In his own account, at least, he passed the test that Gordon had set for him.

Salim's manipulation of Gordon's opinion of him is also important because he struggled with his status among the missionaries during the rest of his trip to Palestine. The self-confidence he exuded in his encounter with Gordon seemed to have been difficult for church authorities to accept. In Palestine, he found himself in a difficult situation, as Johnson describes: "Salim Wilson found himself a servant among other local Arab servants; an ex-slave speaking slave Arabic among persons who would be contemptuous of his race and his slave background."[71] I wish we knew more about how this struck Salim, thrust into an Arabic-speaking society again as a servant, finding out that the Arabic he spoke was considered the language of the servile. There is not one word about this situation in *I Was a Slave*, only the redemption of his private conversation with General Gordon.

On Salim's return to England (and Gordon's to Khartoum), the struggle between the forces of the Mahdi and the Egyptian army, led by Gordon, had turned into the siege of Khartoum. Salim went to work on the public lecture circuit, now as a representative of Sudanese society, enrobed in a costume made to resemble that of a Dinka chief. In public speaking engagements and performances, Salim once again performed as a Dinka:

> The main part of my help was on somewhat novel lines, for I used to appear on the platforms in a leopard-skin *karnass* and, as far as it could be managed, all the panoply of a Dinka chief. So I was made to remember my name of Hatashil and what it meant—"the Continuer." Well, I was continuing, and, by every right of

heredity, I was in truth a chief of the Dinkas. But, alas, chief over what? Where now were my father, my mother, my sisters and brothers, and my tribe? These thoughts made me very sad. Still, I felt that if my appearance in public in this guise did anything to stay the activities of the Arabs, who had brought all my troubles upon me, then the effort was worth the while.[72]

This excerpt is reminiscent of the younger Salim's performance of Dinka war songs for his first owner. Each performance turned him into a character, showing him off in the bare bones of his royal past and his culture. For Salim it was a public reenactment of his sorrow but also an assertion of his very clear identity. Such assertions began to aggravate his relationship with the Church Missionary Society.

Throughout all three of his narratives, Salim reiterates how much he hoped to return to his people in southern Sudan. He could only afford to do so under the auspices of his missionary sponsors, so when Graham Wilmot Brooke invited him to join a "gospel tour of the Dark Continent," Salim could not contain his delight.[73] But as the journey, which began in the Congo, continued, Brooke was not able to see Salim as an equal. In Brooke's letters home, "Salim emerges as a caricature and something of a figure of fun."[74] Brooke considered Salim intemperate in his zeal for the church and turned him increasingly into a "native assistant." And Salim had lost the taste for service. Ultimately, it was the issue of language that broke apart these two men. As "native assistant," Salim was to translate for Brooke, who knew little of the linguistic complexity of Central Africa. His ignorance made him arrogant, however, in Johnson's account of their trip:

> Brooke was critical of Salim's "imperfect" knowledge of Arabic after he had difficulty communicating through the medium of Sudanese slave-Arabic to Zanzibar traders who spoke only Swahili or Omani Arabic. While Brooke arranged for their supplies, Salim was sent ahead to Equatoria Station on a traders' steamer. Salim recorded that, bereft of the protection of his English companion, he was treated like any other "Congo native," and the journey was not a pleasant one.[75]

It is important to imagine Salim's dilemma. Salim had been employed because of his skills in Arabic, but here, trading with Zanzibari merchants, even the most fluent and formal literacy would not equate with Swahili or

Omani Arabic. Salim's Arabic was a Sudanese dialect, one that might have translated well a few miles farther, since Equatoria Station was in Sudan and much closer to his old home than he had been in years. Yet without Brooke, Salim had no status, few resources, and no way to differentiate himself from the other "Congo natives." Shortly thereafter, the trip ended, and Salim returned to England.

Part of the linguistic strife between Brooke and Salim lay also in the language of religion. Salim hoped to bring the Gospel directly to his fellow Dinka, in a manner not dissimilar to Caterina Zenab's work with slaves and former slaves in Khartoum at the same time. But this desire ran counter to the policies of the Church Missionary Society, which by the 1880s had turned its work among Africans to do "practical 'civilizing' work along the lines of 'industrial education.'" As Johnson summarizes the situation, "Within the restricted missionary code of the CMS and the Sudan, there was no place for an English-educated, Christian Dinka evangelist. It was not that he would not go; it was that they would not have him."[76]

Salim in Dinka

Interestingly, Salim Wilson's narratives do not resonate with protest against British Protestant missionaries' construction of racial and religious hierarchies. Instead, a self-conscious ethnography emerges, with Salim as the primary object of cultural scrutiny. But he is not displayed as an anthropological specimen; he appoints himself both guide and teacher, to both his readers and the world from which he came. In all of his narratives, he observes within himself his heritage as a Dinka man, son of a Dinka chief, and legatee of Dinka traditions. From the 1901 edition of *Jehovah-Nissi* to the 1939 publication of *I Was a Slave*, Salim (and his editors) presented examples of the customs and beliefs of the Dinka. Most of *The Ethiopia Valley* (1909) summarizes Dinka life rather than Salim's experiences as a slave in the Nile Valley. Although we have seen many examples of the tensions over authorial control in his texts, Salim's command over the details of his culture seem to me to go unchallenged.

Many chapters of *The Ethiopia Valley* read as if they are ethnographies: the typical houses, labors, and habits of the Dinka are described and illustrated by photographs of both Salim and other Dinka (the photographer is unnamed in this edition). For example, chapter 4, "The Inhabitants of Dinka Country," explores the divisions of the tribes and the origins of their languages; chapter 7, "Occupations and Customs," goes so far as to characterize certain habits as "curious customs": "The Dinka ladies are not particular on the whole, as these dark-skinned ladies would allow their hair to receive no attention for a month at a time. To look after it then was quite hard work, as it took a day-and-a-half in some cases to get the hair smooth again."[77] This voice adopts an attitude of distance and skepticism, remarking rather archly how differently women in northern England would treat their own hair and hygiene.

Even though he seems to side with a British audience on the "curiosity" of his own people's customs, Salim also challenges other European ethnographic assumptions about the Dinka, especially their beliefs. He refutes the German scientist Georg Schweinfurth's 1874 book, *The Heart of Africa*, and its statement that "whatever religion the Dinka has, centers in an institution called 'Cogyoor,' which embraces a society of necromancers and jugglers."[78] In scholarly fashion, Salim asserts that the Dinka have the spiritual sense to condemn the unscrupulous and the superstitious "necromancers" and "jugglers." While they may be heathens, he sees in their religious rites "a mixture of the Hebrew faith with the Egyptian beliefs and teachings."[79] They believe in a trio of beings: a God who created and rules the universe, a Man "who is addressed as 'a Man of Eternity in Sacrifices,' and a holy spirit 'the cause of life.'" As he asserts these deep spiritual beliefs, Salim inserts himself into the community: "This Holy Spirit existed in the air, which we drink in and breathe."[80] In *I Was a Slave*, Salim affirms similar monotheistic affinities between the Dinka and Jews, giving the Dinka a different place in history than that usually allotted them by Victorian anthropologists and thus attributing to the Dinka the creation of a real civilization. Salim states that though he speaks of the Dinka as a tribe, "I suppose I should really have described them as a nation."[81]

All along, in all of his narratives, in his struggles with fluency and his effort to be heard, Salim expresses his determination to adopt Christianity on his own terms. Salim was not just anybody's convert; his recognition of Christianity came through his Dinka identity and his culture's martyrdom to slavery. It was through Christian symbolism that Salim was able to

finally own his memories of his family, particularly his much-missed father, but Europeans did not originate this idea for him—he had been born
into it. It is when he asserts these very strongly and personally held beliefs
that Salim exerts full control over his life and narrative, even in a language
not his own:

> His supreme self-confidence that Jesus was his personal saviour and that he
> could speak forth the word of the Lord, even in a foreign tongue, to those who
> might otherwise take the credit for bringing him to the Lord was a product [as]
> much of his experience as a Dinka as of his Christian faith. The personal pedi-
> gree which he asserted, linking him to the God of Abraham, made some of his
> religious teachers—in a land where pedigrees are highly valued and jealously
> guarded—feel distinctly uneasy.[82]

A Black Man in England

Salim never returned to Sudan. Although his final narrative ends with
sadness about his isolation from his Dinka nation, he lived a full life in
Scunthorpe, marrying into the community, lecturing, and becoming a
popular member of the all-white town where he made his home. Altogether, Salim spent more than fifty years in England, a life that spanned
decades of use of blacks as entertaining, living displays of African life;
race riots in England's larger cities immediately after the end of World
War I; and growth of the Pan-African movement among young black
intellectuals in London in the 1920s and 1930s.[83] By the time Salim had
published *I Was a Slave* in 1939, "Black political traditions were meeting
and uniting towards a more Pan-African style consciousness." In this consciousness, "Black Englishness became less about 'good character' and
more about this marriage of social and political visions with the intent to
'correct [and to educate] . . . the errant motherland.'"[84] Salim said nothing
in his last narrative about how this affected him, and as I have read them,
his published accounts of his life do not appear to speak to other black
communities in the United Kingdom. I am unsure about how a man who
identified himself as "the only freed slave in England" connected himself
to intellectuals like George Padmore.[85] He was honored in Hull during the
centenary celebration of the renowned abolitionist William Wilberforce,

but "his speech and voice are still variously described as being like that of Paul Robeson or Uncle Remus."[86]

But his hopes to reconnect with other Dinka were uniquely, if posthumously, respected. In 1961, Godfrey Lienhardt, a Cambridge anthropologist who studied the Dinka, honored the works of "Hatashil Masha (really Macar) Kathish" in his own study of Dinka spirituality by citing his work as proof of certain Dinka beliefs. Lienhardt wrote, in a footnote to his long citation of *The Ethiopia Valley*, that "despite a tendency to idealize his people before their contact with foreigners, Kathish refers to some features of Dinka life which have not changed to this day."[87] And Salim's memories of his people were not only honored as anthropologically accurate. Shortly after Salim's death in 1947, Church Missionary Society connections found a British commissioner in Sudan who was able to locate relatives of Salim's father. A substantial portion of his estate was given to them, in his honor.[88]

Huda and Halide and the
Slaves at Bedtime

I used to imagine that I was not my mother's daughter—that my real mother was a slave girl who had died, and the truth was being withheld from me. Firmly convinced of this, I suffered all the more. I could keep everything suppressed until nightfall but as soon as I laid my head on the pillow, I was overcome by anxieties and frightening thoughts moved me to tears.

Huda Sha'rawi

The woman whom she calls "mother" is lying in semi-darkness beside her, in a large bed, clad in her white gown. There are those long silky plaits which seem to coil with the life of some mysterious coiling animals, and that small, pale face with its unusually long, curly black lashes resting on the sickly pallor of the drawn cheeks. This mother is a thing of mystery and uneasiness to the little girl. She is afraid of her, she is drawn to her, and yet that thing called affection has not taken shape in her heart; there is only a painful sense of dependence on this mother who is quietly fading out from the background of her life.

Halide Edib Adivar

By the time Huda Sha'rawi described how haunted she had been as a child by the idea that her imagined slave mother had died, she was a powerful figure in the Egyptian nationalist movement, a middle-aged woman with her own grown children and an internationally recognized leader of the women's rights movement in Egypt.[1] Her strong political and nationalist voice made her a figure that for decades dominated articles in the Egyptian press. By the time Halide Edib Adivar wrote down her memories of her sickly mother, whose chronic illnesses left her daughter to be nursed by slave wet nurses, she, too, was a powerful figure in the Turkish nationalist movement that would eventually and successfully replace the Ottoman government after World War I.[2] When she wrote her memoirs in 1926, Halide was a self-exiled, twice-married mother of three and best-selling novelist who had been an activist spokesperson for the Young Turk Revolution nationalist politicians and who eventually would become a member of the Turkish parliament.[3] Both women were born into highly privileged families during a period in the late nineteenth century in which massive political and cultural change would alter the traditions that shaped women's education, marriages, and public lives. Slaves were an integral and intimate part of their childhoods, and the many vivid experiences that both Halide and Huda remembered about the slaves with whom they had grown up shaped their vision of what maturity and independence should mean for themselves and the women of their countries.

Motherhood, Childhood, and Slaves

Huda Sha'rawi was famous enough by the 1920s that photographs, even caricatures, of her image were published in many newspapers. As Beth Baron has shown, increasingly vocal and politicized Egyptian women leaders struggled for control of their images in the press, and Huda was arguably the most famous and visible of all.[4] Given the sensitivity to slavery that she later revealed in her memoirs, it is interesting to see Huda caricatured in the popular political magazine *Al-Kashkul*. The Arabic title of the cartoon is "Where Is Independence?" and refers to a fraught political confrontation over Egypt's nominal independence between Egyptian nationalist politicians and the British. The caption, placed at the feet of Huda Hanim Sha'rawi and al-Bash Ağa, begins with his asking, in colloquial Egyptian Arabic, "My lady, if there is no independence for those men, what will they do?" Huda answers, "Listen, oh Bash Agha, as long as there is a nation that wants independence, don't be afraid. You're more of a man than all of them!"

The joke here, as *Al-Kashkul*'s readers would have immediately understood, is that al-Bash Ağa was a eunuch and had been a slave in the

household in which Huda grew up. Beth Baron points us toward the emas-
culating irony with which the caricatured Huda states that this eunuch is
more of a man than the leading politicians of Egypt's Wafd Party. But the
cartoon reveals another, perhaps less intentional irony as well. Under the
title stands a remarkably outspoken Egyptian woman with the slave who
had been part of her household since childhood, who had, as this chapter
discusses in more depth, helped raise Huda since her infancy and stood
with her, was satirized alongside her, well into her adulthood. Sa'id Aǧa,
as she called him in her memoirs, played a pivotal role in her observations about slavery in Egyptian society yet remained with her as she matured into a national political figure. We can assume that his role in her life

Caricature of Huda Sha'rawi and al-Bash Aǧa. *Al-Kashkul*, January 21, 1926.

changed after her marriage and the birth of her children, but his connection
to her household did not. How does this slave, this companion, accompany
the dramatic trajectory of this groundbreaking woman's life? Could he do
so independently? How did this leader of the Egyptian women's movement negotiate the distance between childhood nightmares of a mother's
enslavement and the constant, loyal service of a slave her entire life?

Although by the turn of the century Egypt and the wider Ottoman Empire were no longer as united politically or economically as they had been
a century earlier, the domestic cultures of the two regions were deeply
connected and in massive flux. As they moved up the socioeconomic
ladder of opportunities created by the secular schools and institutions of
Muhammad 'Ali, a generation of men with the ambition of 'Ali Mubarak
Pasha or Huda Sha'rawi's father often chose to marry Ottoman women
or to purchase Circassian women as concubines, a practice they shared
with their Turkish-speaking elite counterparts in cities like Istanbul. In the
late nineteenth century, when the children of these unions were born, this
"upper-class Ottoman-Egyptian household—one of the most important
social formations—unraveled." Harem slavery dwindled dramatically, in
part as a consequence of abolition but arguably more likely as a consequence of the rise of nationalism and the powerful idea that, as Beth Baron
writes, "foreign-born slave mothers could not be entrusted with raising
good patriots."[5] She continues:

> The new nation could not be built on households that included harem slaves
> from the Caucasus, retainers from Central Asia, concubines from Ethiopia, eu-
> nuchs from Africa, and patriarchs from Anatolia or the Balkans. The Circassian
> slaves and their descendants would be absorbed into the new elite, and the new
> nation would be constructed around bourgeois families—Muslim, Copt, and
> Jewish—grounded in Egyptian territory. The transition from empire to nation-
> state was reflected on the micro level as large, multi-ethnic households were
> reconstituted as models for the nation.[6]

As men like Muhammad Sultan Pasha, Huda's father, merged with the
Ottoman-Egyptian elite through marriage and concubinage, Ottoman-
Egyptians also merged with a changing Egyptian political landscape in
which leaders by 1881 spoke eloquently of "Egypt for the Egyptians!"[7]

Huda Sha'rawi was thus not only the daughter of an immensely privileged family but also a figure who bridged this very transition from the multiethnic Ottoman-Egyptian household to the bourgeois and monogamous family. Although the political and historical significance of the transition of the Egyptian family is clearly shown by Beth Baron's careful research and analysis, this transition was difficult, often polarizing, and always deeply felt. Nor was it always definitive, as the *Kashkul* caricature of Huda Sha'rawi shows; this symbol of the activist, modern Egyptian woman could never quite escape her close connection to slavery. In many ways, this transition also occurred in the late Ottoman Empire, where a growing politicized awareness of Turkish identity also studied carefully the position of women in marriage and the family. Halide, like Huda, was positioned directly on this cultural fault line and wrote about it.

Both women share with Babikr Bedri childhoods intimately structured by slaves and the rituals of the slave trade. Though much wealthier than Babikr Bedri, both Huda and Halide grew up as he did in environments where the presence and work of slaves were as elemental and comfortable as furniture and helped define and articulate these elites' sense of home, not only its physical structure but also the traditions of family structure that bound their Sudanese servants to them. But it is important to note that Huda Sha'rawi and Halide Edib internalized this relationship with slavery differently than Babikr Bedri. The trade in slaves punctuated the women's lives as it did for Babikr, but they were connected to an even broader network of slaves than that available to him. Within the system in which Babikr grew up, all slaves came from other parts of Sudan or Ethiopia. His was a system that enabled him to take pride, repeatedly in his memoirs, that none of his ancestors were slaves. This was not the case for Huda, whose childhood household was made up of slaves and servants from Sudan and the Caucasus and whose own mother came from a group of people intimately connected with Circassian slavery. Nor was it similar to Halide's upbringing. As we shall see, she was constantly anxious and defiant when being told she looked like a slave or that her personality came from blood ties to slaves. Babikr's confidence about his genealogy protected him from that kind of anxiety.

Both Huda and Halide collaborated in a genre of fiction and memoir writing in which upper-class individuals, most but not all of them Ottoman women, carefully described the physical and psychological dimensions of the harems in which they grew up. One of the first of these to be both published and translated into French and English was *Thirty Years in the Harem: or, The Autobiography of Melek-Hanum (Wife of H. H. Kibrizli-Mehmet Pasha)* in 1872. Even its title shows how bonded, and gendered, autobiography and harem life was for Ottoman women. Through 1920–21, Leila Saz Hanum published her memoirs in Turkish newspapers; the memoirs were translated into French and published in 1926 as *Souvenirs de Leila Hanoum*.[8] Halide wrote her memoirs soon after, which were published in English in 1926. In 1936, Ahmad Shafiq Pasha published his *Mudhakirat fi nisf al-qarn* (My memoirs over half a century) in Cairo, in Arabic, in which he shared in close detail the slave origins of both his mother and his wife. Huda's memoirs were published posthumously but certainly written during this period.[9]

This chapter compares Huda's famous and unfinished memoir, *Mudhakirat*, with Halide's *Memoirs* regarding what they heard about or from the slaves in their fathers' houses.[10] It also compares both memoirs to those of other famous elite Egyptians and Ottomans regarding their memories of family connections to slavery. Unlike Babikr Bedri, whom, as we have seen, scholars consider unique in his personal presentation of the cultural and social history of Sudan, Huda and Halide were but two among well-known men and women writing about their personal experiences in the harem and with slaves. Their relationships to the slaves of their households, most of whom they remembered with tenderness, exemplify the close personal ties and intimacy with which many Egyptians and Ottomans of their age viewed those who served them. What is important here is whether, in telling their stories, they could really hear the voices of their slaves. Could they move with Huda and Halide into adulthood—not only into their masters' maturity but also their own? Could they make the transition with their masters into modernity?

Was My Real Mother a Slave?

As we have seen, Huda was haunted by the fantasy that she was not the daughter of the mother she knew but of a slave girl who had died. What circumstances could have frightened this privileged little girl into such a sad dream? In 1879, Huda was born into the wealthiest stratum of Egyptian society and, consequently, into a social network in which Circassian slave women were often concubines, wives, and mothers to very affluent children. These parts of Egyptian society were intimately connected to the elites of Ottoman society; as Ehud Toledano has written about Cairo and Istanbul in the mid-nineteenth century, "members of the prominent households in both cities were linked to one another by family relations or through social networking."[11] The children of these communities, especially those born in the same years as Huda, shared many connections of ethnicity through genealogical inheritances from Ottoman, Circassian, and Sudanese slavery. As Beth Baron noted about Huda's female and political contemporaries,

> Huda's mother was Circassian and Munira's [Thabit] was Turkish; Fatima's [Ruz al-Yusif] parents were Syrian and Esther's [Wissa] were Copts. Their own family backgrounds and political trajectories show the transition from Ottoman households—with slaves and ex-slaves—to Egyptian families. Huda's mother was a concubine and a Sudanese eunuch presided over the harem; Esther grew up in a household run by a Sudanese ex-slave, daughter of a chieftain.[12]

A generation earlier, thousands of young women the age of Huda's mother were brought from the regions of the Caucasus to the largest cities of the Ottoman Empire as slaves to be sold. If these young women were fortunate enough to be sold to wealthy families, they stood the chance to be educated and well maintained. If they bore children to their masters / husbands, their position was enhanced legally and they could be manumitted and gain rights toward inheritance. Their lives in the harem—the rooms in the households where they were segregated from unrelated men—intrigued Western travelers and readers in the nineteenth century, who romanticized the daily lives of these white Circassian women much more than they did the drudgery of African slaves working in these same chambers. But often there was little romance to the challenges faced by these women, in a time when they could exert very little control over their sexual and reproductive lives.

Ehud Toledano has unearthed documents that describe the sadness of many of these teenagers' lives. He explored the difficulties such young slave women had in controlling their physical circumstances when he published the testimony of Şemsigül, a young girl born either in the late 1830s or early 1840s in the Caucasus. At that time, this region (now encompassing Armenia, Georgia, Azerbaijan, and parts of southeastern Russia, such as Chechnya) was divided among the Ottomans, the Qajars, and the Russians, but large parts were fully absorbed into the Russian Empire as it expanded into Muslim territory on either side of the Caspian Sea. This political turmoil added to the poverty of the region and in the early decades of the nineteenth century exacerbated the practice of parents selling their children to slave dealers. "Parents who did so," Toledano has noted, "believed that they were thus improving the chance of their offspring to attain better living conditions and, possibly, gain entry into the Ottoman elite."[13] Şemsigül was one of these children, sold as a teenager in Istanbul to a slave dealer, Deli Mehmet, who brought her to Cairo in 1852. On their journey, he forced her into sexual relations and impregnated her.

Two years later, Şemsigül appeared before Cairo police who were investigating her assertion that Deli Mehmet and his wife had sold her illegally and caused her to lose her baby. Perhaps Şemsigül was an unusually brave and vocal young woman; it is certainly unusual to have nine pages, written in Ottoman Turkish, of a young bonded woman's narrative.[14] The police took her narrative very seriously, for her accusations meant that Deli Mehmet had committed several serious crimes. The first was not that he had forced her into sexual relations before selling her but that he had sold her when she was pregnant, thus presenting to her buyer (a son of Muhammad 'Ali Pasha) a slave diminished in value. When the buyer returned her because it was clear that she was pregnant, Deli Mehmet and his wife committed another crime by trying to forcibly abort her baby, force-feeding her dangerous liquids, and beating her repeatedly. A peasant woman who lived next door took pity on Şemsigül and rescued her from this mistreatment by telling Deli Mehmet and his wife that she would bring the girl to the home of a nearby notable for a proper abortion. Şemsigül found refuge in this house, but when she was ready to give birth to her son, Deli Mehmet's wife came "and stood at the bedside. As he was born, she took the child to another room and passed him through her shirt to mark that she was adopting him. To me, she said that he had died."[15]

Şemsigül saw her baby again briefly when the notable's wife brought him secretly to her, but only that one time and then never again. She returned to the household of Deli Mehmet, who continued to try to sell her but without success. At the time of her testimony to the police, Şemsigül was a slave of unclear status who could not be sold because too many in the community of slave traders knew that Deli Mehmet had broken the laws of the slave trade guild. Toledano's research leads no further into what happened to Şemsigül, although he did discover that her baby was never returned to her. He maintains hopefulness that a girl of such clear resolve was manumitted and found her way, perhaps by seeking patronage in the house of the notable who had been so kind before.

> We do know that she was courageous enough to state her case and stick to it despite the pressures that were undoubtedly put on her. We also know that during her pregnancy, when she was most vulnerable and virtually defense-less, most women with whom she came into contact showed her compassion. And, not least important, although as a woman and a slave she belonged to a doubly underprivileged social group, Şemsigül did ultimately receive justice in the courts, although her baby was not returned to her. Given these propitious circumstances, there are grounds for cautious optimism that Şemsigül's story ended well.[16]

As a fellow researcher into the lives and voices of slaves in the Ottoman Empire, Egypt, and Sudan, I share Ehud Toledano's admiration for the re-sourcefulness of those slaves whose lives have left some visible traces. But Şemsigül's story leaves me with much less optimism, simply because she was forced to give up her child, a child she clearly and tenaciously had tried to keep. I find more persuasive Toledano's subsequent presentation that rape reinforced the female slave's status as slave.[17] Even the place of her purchase was decided by where she was on her sexual journey: a young Circassian virgin would be sold privately within the homes of the dealers or the potential buyers, but a young mother like Şemsigül was often sold openly in the tent markets of Tanta, in Lower Egypt, as her asking price would have been lowered. Şemsigül's story brings home more clearly how much of maternity was lost to the rules of enslavement, and the tragedy of seeing her baby seized emerges in her narrative as clearly as Salim C. Wilson's cries for his father at the moment of his enslavement do in his story. Toledano concludes, "Without wishing to argue that Şemsigül's story was

typical of most *harem* slaves, I do maintain that her experience was familiar to many of the women whose lives spanned the spectrum of poverty
in childhood, uprooting in adolescence, and *harem* realities in youth and
adulthood."[18]

Whispers among the Women: Şemsigül's Shared History

A child at the time that Şemsigül told her story to the Cairo police, Huda
Sha'rawi's mother, Iqbal, would have understood this. In fact, as Huda
wrote, her mother confronted sorrow and depression through much of her
adult life. Although her pregnancies were not disrupted like Şemsigül's,
she, too, was forced to make a difficult and traumatizing trek from the Caucasus, where she was born, to Egypt during her adolescence. The decade
between 1854 and 1864 marked a period of political terror and economic di-
saster for many of the ethnic groups of the Caucasus. This vast multiethnic
region had long been a major provider of slaves for the Ottoman Empire,
and as Liubov Derluguian writes, "the Caucasus was the world-renowned
source of male and female slaves, employed for concubinage and sexual services."[19] Huda Sha'rawi's mother came from a politically important family
in the Caucasus so would undoubtedly have been familiar with a world in
which, economically, slaves "were also a universal measure of exchange."
This was a system in which there were different kinds of slaves: those kept
in the household who eventually achieved a form of belonging and acceptance into the family, and those who had "virtually no status or identity,"
were probably prisoners of war, and were strangers to the family and the
society of the family.[20] Huda's mother may have been aware, as a young
child, of the raids that many nobles of the Caucasus launched against one
another with devastating results for many villages;[21] certainly she was an
eyewitness as well to the more serious wars that broke out between ethnic groups in the region toward the mid-1850s. During this period, Russia
began to exert more control over the region, sometimes as a force of abolition and often as an expansionist empire. Torn between affinities with the
Ottoman Empire and the promises of political strength extended by Russia, the nobility of the Caucasus found itself under increasing political and
economic pressure, until some broke out in a full-fledged rebellion against

Russian attempts to solidify its control. Huda's grandfather, her mother's father, was a leader in these revolts.

As the details she painstakingly included in her memoirs show, it was important to Huda to understand her mother's origins in the Caucasus and how her mother ended up in Egypt. What we know of Iqbal's journey came to Huda from her maternal uncle, Yusuf, who told her of the war that erupted between Russia and the Caucasus in 1860, in which his and Iqbal's grandfather (Huda's great-grandfather) fought against the Russians but lost his regiment and was taken prisoner. The grandfather's nemesis, the more famous anti-Russian rebel Shaykh Shamil, spread rumors that the grandfather had joined the Russian side. Local, pro-Shamil authorities took then sixteen-year-old Yusuf prisoner, holding him as a hostage for ransom and threatening him with execution if he did not deliver his own father to them. The family, however, gathered armed allies who freed the boy.[22]

After this brief success, Russian soldiers killed many members of Yusuf's family, most traumatically Huda's great-grandfather.[23] The continued turmoil was destroying the family, and Huda's grandmother (Yusuf's mother) fled the Caucasus with her five children, following thousands of other émigrés on well-worn paths to Istanbul. Hungry and anxious, they waited at the border for months as the overwhelmed Ottoman authorities sorted out their status (and took their property and money, according to Uncle Yusuf). During the long wait, the two youngest children died of illness, and Huda's grandmother, fearing for the life of her remaining daughter, arranged to send Iqbal to Egypt to live with her uncle. The family entrusted Iqbal's delivery to her uncle to a friend also on his way to Egypt, but when the pair arrived in Cairo, they discovered that the uncle was in Sudan, fighting against the Mahdiyya, and the uncle's wife refused to claim any connection to this Circassian refugee. Iqbal, a beautiful, young, unmarried woman, was placed in the household of another elite officer to wait for her uncle's arrival. Here her situation soon became difficult; her position, it was felt, made her too competitive for the attention of the men, and as Huda writes, "It was good fortune that my father chose her to be his wife."[24]

There is actually no proof that Muhammad Sultan Pasha, Huda's father, married Iqbal, and most historians of Huda's life consider Iqbal to have been his concubine, a status that often meant the woman had been purchased. Huda's memoirs contain many details about the difficult passage of her Circassian relatives from the Caucasus, but none about the possibility that her own mother had been sold to her father in Cairo. Instead, she paints a picture of a husband doting on his melancholy wife:[25]

> One day, she [Iqbal] was helping my father put on his clothes, and it just so happened that she was standing by the window, looking out on the park, and she began to weep. My father asked what caused her to cry. She responded that among the visitors waiting in the reception room there was one who resembled her brother Yusuf, and she couldn't keep herself from crying. Huda's father asked her about her family and kinsfolk. When she told him her story, he sent right away to the household of Ali Bey Raghab [where Iqbal had stayed upon first arriving in Cairo] to get the address of her family. And fortunately there were relatives present in Egypt. My father prepared the funds to send for the family. He brought them. This meeting was a great joy and deeply affected my mother, who moved into the first house in his compound. [Huda's uncle Yusuf and other relatives soon followed.] . . . And my mother returned again to her family and her relations.[26]

Huda's narrative reveals several possibilities about her mother's status in the Sultan household. Had she been Muhammad Sultan's social or economic equal, with a strong family of her own in Egypt, the details of her family and her relatives would have been made well known to him during negotiations for the marriage. He does not discover these details until after she has become a member of his house, intimate enough to help him with his clothes but without a status strong enough to deserve her own rooms in the compound, as a wife of greater standing would (and Huda's father did have a wife, known lovingly to Huda as al-Umm al-Kabira, the "first wife," who did have her own apartments). But once Sultan Pasha learned of Iqbal's forced separation from her family, and the story is proven true, she does rise in status. Certainly in the memory of her little girl, Huda, already worried by the fear that her real mother had been a slave, Iqbal succeeded in erasing any traces of slavery or concubinage. Perhaps this work of erasure helped assuage Huda's bad dreams about slavery. Perhaps these evasive silences protected the social position of Huda's children. Or perhaps these inferences helped Huda to "own" her mother.

Bearing Witness to Circassian Slavery

Slavery in the Caucasus remains an understudied topic in the fields of Middle Eastern history or slavery studies, one too large to explore in great detail here. But I linger over its nearness to Huda's family because, from the 1860s to the end of the nineteenth century, so many writers, in Europe and in the Middle East, bore witness to a forced migration endured by thousands of people from the Caucasus, many of whom ended up as slaves in Egypt and the Ottoman Empire. Huda herself spends pages describing the privations of her mother's family. Foreign observers, notably British journalists and missionaries, began reporting on the "Circassian Exodus" in 1859, and as the editor of the *Levant Herald* wrote in an urgently worded appeal to the *Times of London*, this exodus quickly developed into an international humanitarian crisis.

In his letter to the *Times*, the *Levant Herald* editor explained that "for months past, as you are aware, a tide of immigration has set in from the banks of the Konban and other parts of Circassia into Turkey. For probably excellent reasons, the Russian Government, it is said, has given the Mussulman population of those parts a choice of removal to Siberia or emigration hither. They have chosen the latter."[27] Paying about four dollars per person for "passage to Constantinople," they arrived on often decrepit, ill-equipped boats:

> The result is that the vessels are crammed to suffocation with the exiles, who endure on the voyage to the Bosphorus all the horrors of another "middle passage." During the past stormy season in the Black Sea above a dozen wrecks of these emigrant vessels occurred, hurrying many hundreds of these miserable creatures to death. Of those who made good the passage, thousands landed in every stage of disease and physical suffering, without a dollar to supply even their most immediate wants, and dependent entirely on the charity of the Government. To do the Porte justice, this was neither laggingly nor stingily given.[28]

Later reports described a worsening situation. Over five years, as the Russian government expanded into the Eastern Caucasus, the "Circassian Exodus" grew into an international humanitarian controversy. Newspaper correspondents increasingly remarked on the destitution of the immigrants as they reached Cyprus, Samsun, or Istanbul. One reporter followed a group of recent arrivals who were under Ottoman quarantine as "a shocking sight—men, women and children nothing but skin and bone dying at the rate of 20 a day and an eye-witness counted 15 dead bodies in one heap at the beach." The article reported that to help them, Turkish officials "have taken some as servants, and the rest are being sent into the interior daily to work on the farms."[29]

Soon, the servants seemed to have been transformed into slaves, as these immigrants continued to pour into Ottoman cities until the late 1870s. Foreign descriptions of their "middle passage" changed into depictions of widespread domestic enslavement. Although terms like "middle passage" were repeatedly used, implicitly comparing the trek of the Circassian refugees to the transatlantic traumatizing voyages of African slaves, Western observers were somewhat ambivalent in their judgment of this burgeoning network of slavery. Magazines such as *Harper's Weekly* began to circulate images of strikingly pale and beautiful Caucasian women fleeing the despotism of Russian imperialism across the mountains into Turkey.

Circassian captives. The original caption reads: "The captives—young Christian girls captured by Bashi Bouzouks (Turkish irregulars) on their way to Constantinople to be sold." *Harper's Weekly*, November 7, 1874.

Other Kinds of Slaves

Circassian concubines and the sales of young women into slavery in the 1860s and 1870s excited a great deal of attention, both locally and internationally, because of the tragedy of the refugees' circumstances. International pressure also caused the trade in African slaves to be made illegal in 1874. Slavery itself, however, was not outlawed, and African slaves continued to make up significant parts of the domestic labor force, particularly in wealthy homes like Huda Sha'rawi's. Writers like Leila Saz Hanum described in great detail the atrocities and the complexities of the "middle passages" made by both Circassian and African slaves in her account of the imperial harems of the mid- to late nineteenth-century Ottoman Empire. In Leila Hanum's memoirs, there were important differences among the various groups of women. Circassian women, she noted, particularly young ones who strayed too far from their homes, were subject to raids by slave traders. Hoping to achieve great riches and status in Istanbul, others sold themselves voluntarily. The saddest, most odious situation of all, wrote Leila Hanum, was "predestined slavery," in which the children of Circassian slaves were sold by their masters.[30] Some slaves were priced high for their beauty, but the absence of even one tooth, or flat feet, could send a slave girl's price down.[31] But even with all the suffering that Circassian slaves endured in becoming slaves, they at least had a certain awareness of the world and expectations of how they would be treated in the households in Istanbul or other Ottoman cities. This was not the case, Leila Hanum explained, for "les négresses," African women and girls who knew nothing of the world except for "their desert and their oasis: For these beings so completely ignorant, everything was a subject of astonishment and terror. The question of language was for them yet another cause of difficulty because they could never find anyone who could understand their dialect. Besides, they had no hope of becoming the wives or concubines of some great figure and were thus fatally condemned to the most difficult of household work."[32] And even though Leila Hanum wrote that they usually had difficult personalities, especially if they fell under the influence of other, more experienced African slave women, they generally took to their work well.[33]

Interestingly, Leila Hanum felt she had to stick up for the African slave women, whom she found generally very intelligent, against the racial prejudice of many, including her own father, who did not like to have them in his house.[34] When, through the network of slave traders, she found one who pleased her, she followed the custom of her household in which the prospective slave was always asked if "we pleased her and if she herself wanted to enter into our service." A particular slave, whom the family would name Yasemin, responded, "You may buy me; I would like to belong to you."[35] Leila Hanum felt strongly a self-imposed responsibility to teach these young African women to read and write Turkish, especially urgent in the face of the racial discrimination they suffered from the Circassian slaves. She developed a strong personal relationship with a young Sudanese slave named Yekta who had been purchased by Leila's sister. This young girl proved so adept at both managing household work and sewing and embroidery that Leila Hanum began regular lessons with her, teaching her the alphabet and how to write words. When Leila's father was transferred to Crete to become the Ottoman governor, these studies were interrupted. It was thus a great surprise for Leila Hanum when Yekta wrote her a letter:

> However, after some time, I found in a letter which I received from my sister a little piece of paper written in a rather bizarre fashion: it was a letter from Yekta. In Turkish writing, most of the letters which compose a word are attached to each other and change their form according to whether they are placed at the beginning, the middle, or the end of the word; this is obviously a source of complication and of difficulty for those who are beginning to study the language. Yekta, with a natural aptitude, had overcome this difficulty and applied to the Turkish calligraphy a simplification which certain people—among whom was Enver Pasha—have already tried to introduce in recent days; she wrote it placing the letters simply side by side in their primitive form, without attaching them or changing them, and then separated the words by a larger interval. In spite of the difficulty I had in reading this at first glance, I soon could understand what she was trying to say: she expressed her sadness in being separated from me and she said she was crying continually and that she was looking for me everywhere since my departure. Ever since I had left she worked all night long in order to bring her writing to perfection so that she could write me this letter.[36]

Touched by "this fidelity," Leila sent Yekta corrections of her letters. They wrote to each other regularly, with Leila teaching her through corrections, and Yekta making steady progress. And while she was learning to write proper Turkish, Yekta also learned how to swim and enjoyed swimming through the Bosphorus every night. Leila and her sister worried about the dangerous current and feared Yekta would drown. Instead it was pneumonia, brought about by the constant swimming, that killed her: "Thus ended the life of this unhappy little black girl whose intelligence and refinement were equal in every way to that of the little Circassians—her comrades."[37]

Leila also wrote with some sympathy about male slaves, particularly the African eunuchs (known as ağas) who, in the mid- to late nineteenth century, made up one of the most elite contingents of Ottoman slaves. As children, she wrote, they "were captured in the depths of Africa by men without heart or pity, who then emasculated them between the ages of 8 and 12 years, sold them secretly to Arab slave traders who, in turn, sold them secretly to others with considerable profit. They were then secretly to Istanbul." There they were educated in basic hygiene, reading and writing, praying, and mathematics.[38] Although she names a few notable ağas, only one merits more than a sentence:

> But the most remarkable among the eunuchs I knew was certainly Muhterem Ağa who was in the service of Sultane. Before entering the Serail, Muhterem Ağa had received an excellent education and an extensive upbringing in the house of Fuad Pasha where he had grown up. He became even more refined and educated in the service of the brilliant Sultane, his mistress.
>
> Muhterem Ağa fully understood Turkish, Arabic, Persian and he spoke a very correct French, as well as a little bit of Greek; he was really remarkable for his intelligence and his spirit.[39]

Always on the lookout for the intelligence of slaves, Leila Hanum was one of the few chroniclers of enslavement who recorded the intellectual work and study of those employed in her household or in the homes she visited. Their intelligence inspired her to ally with her black female slaves (particularly the ones whose education she oversaw). Yet while evincing sympathy for the difficult beginnings of enslavement for eunuchs, and maintaining a clear respect for the intellectual leaders among them, Leila Hanum did not enjoy the same intimacy of relationship with them. They do not seem to have shaped her sense of herself as an increasingly political Ottoman woman.

Huda Sha'rawi expressed the depths of her relationship with the eunuchs of her childhood household differently and in profound ways. In her remembrances of her childhood, Sa'id Ağa, an intimate guardian, figures prominently. There are other Sudanese slaves as well who wander through her past life. Almost all of them disappear as her memoirs narrate her adult life—only a passing reference to Sa'id Ağa lets her readers know he accompanied her into adulthood. But he was one of her most challenging teachers while she was growing up and taught her lessons about both education and authority that she would never forget.

The saddest and most pivotal lesson Huda learned from her childhood was about the inequality of status between boys and girls in Egyptian society. This was literally brought home to her in the disparity of treatment she and her brother received when each of them was sick. While her father, long dead, and her much-loved brother are never represented as discriminating against her, Huda cites the women and the dependents of the house as being unequal in their love and treatment of her. Mama al-Kabira explained this to her:

> I remember I asked her one day, she writes, to explain to me why my brother was preferred over me. She replied with her sweet smile, "Do you not feel now the difference between you and him?" I said, "Yes, but I am the elder and first; my share should be larger than his, and my place above his." She said, "But you're a girl and he's a boy . . . and not only that but also you're not the only girl and he's the only boy, whose responsibility it will be to perpetuate the family name."[40]

As Leila Ahmed describes in her account of this moment in Huda's development, "This response briefly assuages the child's anguish over the matter, and she finds herself comprehending now that her brother will keep alive her 'beloved father's name,' loving the brother all the more for it."[41] Although she also loves Sa'id Ağa, Huda memorializes her fury at him for his own collusion in the preferential treatment of her brother. Only a page after Mama al-Kabira explained the rules of gender, Huda described how much refuge she took in studying. She and her brother took lessons in French, Arabic, and Turkish, and Huda found herself particularly enthralled by Arabic. Sa'id Ağa supervised every lesson: "He was the master and last word over all of the servants and our tutors" (*kan sahib al-amr wa'l-nahi 'ala al-khudum wa'ala mu'alamina*). Huda was frustrated by her inability to read the Qur'an correctly and was informed by her teacher that this was so because she was not studying Arabic grammar. Huda was eager to learn the rules of grammar, so her tutor brought the correct books the next day. Sa'id Aǧa asked him "with arrogance and haughtiness [*bi 'azama wa kibriya*], 'What are those books?'" The tutor responded, "Grammar books." As Huda remembered the scene, "The aǧa chuckled and then said to the tutor: take your books, there is no need for them because she is not ever going to become a lawyer! This incident affected me very deeply. Despair penetrated my heart and bitterness seized me, to the point where I neglected my studies. I began to hate my femininity because it deprived me of the joys of studying, or engaging in the sports that I loved so much, just like it would impede the freedom for which I so yearned."[42]

Sa'id Aǧa becomes, on this much-quoted page from Huda's famous life, the embodiment of authority that kept women inferior and unfulfilled in Egyptian society. It seemed to Huda that he ruled over everything. If Huda and her brother committed any infraction, their nurses would complain to Sa'id Aǧa, who would make the siblings go into the yard, get branches from a tree, and bring them back so that he could beat their palms and leave them crying. "But then," Huda writes, "he would take the handkerchiefs out of our pockets and wipe away our tears. Then he would say, 'You have each made restitution but beware of doing what you did again. If you do, the punishment will be worse.'" And then "he would become a child, like us." Sa'id Aǧa played with them, ran with them, and chased them. Huda would forget his severity in the face of his playfulness, but her brother could not. As Huda remembered, her brother would return to the house after such disciplining and "climb up the stairs and hurry to my mother to tell her the news, complaining to her, while overwhelmed with tears, what the aǧa had done, saying, 'That slave hit me!' [*darabni hatha-l-'abid*]." Sa'id Aǧa would explain to the mother why the children had deserved punishment, and she would calm her son down, explaining that "he is your guardian and he only does it to keep you in check [*lisalahak*]."[43]

It took Huda awhile to understand the constraints of Sa'id Aǧa's life and the limits of his authority, but she remembered that her mother felt a special sympathy for him that she tried to explain. Sa'id Aǧa was very proud to serve in the Sha'rawi household, and Iqbal understood the source of this pride. It was not only because this was an important and wealthy family but also because Muhammad Sultan Pasha had concerned himself with little Sa'id's intellectual development, even enrolling him in school. As Huda described,

> Lala Sa'id was proud and disdainful, haughty in his behavior [*mu'tidan binafsihi*] and very proud to belong to our household. My mother was tender and sympathetic toward him because my father had bought him when he was very young and had concerned himself with his upbringing and his education in school. He loved my father to the point of worship. When he grew up, he directed that love toward us. My mother appreciated this love for my father and for us later. I also appreciated him and recognized the benefit of his raising us. It had a tremendous influence on me.[44]

Huda also appreciated how well run the household was under Sa'id Ağa's watch. She recognized a rhythm of efficiency and loyalty and described the household's laborers in terms that were often idyllic. Mohja Kahf has taken a particularly careful look at the following scene remembered by Huda:

> I recall, for example, our grand house with its spacious apartments and vast parlor, and how it used to teem with slave girls and bondsmen. They were well trained to work, sincere in performing their duties, sensitive to the responsibilities placed on their shoulders, respectful of their employers, careful with the things in their hands and loving towards the children of their employers who were born in their hands. Each one would rise to his task in the best manner and would accompany us for better or for worse, and would never reach his hand toward anything, no matter how costly, and would not covet a single thing but the pleasure of those who had authority over him. And we reciprocated this love with them, and appreciated in them this loyalty.[45]

Kahf pays close attention to Sha'rawi's wording here and the difference between certain nouns in Arabic and those in the popular English translation of her memoirs, *Harem Years*. It is Kahf's sense that in the English version, *Mudhakirat*'s vocabulary hides how nostalgic Huda was for the class arrangements of her childhood; for example, it does not include in the previous passage the terms *jariyat* (slave women) or *mamalik* (enslaved men).

What is also interesting is that Huda voiced how much she missed this economic order, "especially when I am confronted with some of the modern customs, which make me long to return to the past, and all it contains of custom and manners."[46]

At this point in my research, I have found no details about the date of Sa'id Aǧa's death and whether or not he predeceased Huda, who died in 1947. Therefore, I do not know whether he was still in her household when she dictated this nostalgia for customs of the past to her secretary. We may be able to assume from the *Kashkul* caricature of 1936 that he was still in her employ. His presence is most detailed and vivid in the first volume of *Mudhakirat*, in which Huda describes her coming-of-age. But even though his presence is less clear the further she moves into her adult and then her public, political life in her memoirs, Sa'id Aǧa stayed with her well into her adulthood, guiding her through difficult points in her life and representing a close, dependable link to the days of her past.

When Huda was about fourteen years old, she was engaged to her much older cousin Ali Sha'rawi, who had acted as family guardian in the years since her father's death. The negotiations for the engagement were made between Ali and Iqbal without Huda's knowledge. As she recounted, had she paid more attention to the murmurs of the slaves in the household when her cousin came to visit, she would have noticed more: "I remembered what I had heard from the slaves and the governesses when my aunt's son came to visit. They would say then, 'Here comes your groom; go and surrender to him.'"[47] But these comments and the many preparations being made by the slaves and servants to celebrate the engagement went unnoticed, until finally Huda was confronted with wedding guests. She dashed upstairs to her room, deeply upset, and "Sa'id Aǧa came to me and whispered in my ear: 'Do you wish to upset the spirit of your father and risk the condemnation of your sick mother? She in her room, collapsed on her bed sick and sobbing. Perhaps she cannot bear the shock if you refuse!' These words hit me in my weak spot."[48] And Huda received yet another important life lesson at the hands of Sa'id Aǧa—how to submit to the arrangements of authority.

While guarding his newly married charge's acquiescence to authority, Sa'id also supervised her negotiations with the public world. Once married, Huda insisted that she be allowed to shop in the new department stores in

the city of Alexandria. Shocked, her mother and Sa'id Ağa made Huda
wrap herself so that her clothes and her hair could not be seen, and Huda
described a situation in which she and her entourage look as if they come
from another place and time: "When we entered the store, the employees
and shoppers were surprised by our unusual appearance, especially when
they looked at Sa'id Ağa staring at them with his hard expression, as if daring them to look at us."[49] When they find a section just for women, as Sa'id
Ağa has demanded, and sit down, "one of the younger saleswomen could
not stop herself from asking the ağa from which country and which family did we come. He stared at her angrily, then complained to the department store director about her impudence. The director would have fired
this salesgirl if I had not implored him not to. I was extremely ashamed
by such behavior."[50] Here is Huda at a cultural and social crossroads, with
Sa'id Ağa as gatekeeper between her traditional, segregated, elite past and
her future as a modern consumer. In this memory, she is angry with him
for his harshness; he has embarrassed her, as has the spectacle they present
to more modern-seeming shoppers. Not very old herself when this scene
takes place, Huda is sensitive to the questions of the salesgirl, to whom the
eunuch and the heavily veiled women he guards look like travelers.[51] It
is Sa'id Ağa's body, his skin color, and his harsh and protective stare that
mark him the most clearly as belonging to an older tradition of slavery.
Huda, too, is part of this (manifested so clearly through her dress and her
entourage), although at this moment it brings her shame. She does convince her mother, however, that by going out and buying their own neces-
sities, they will save money.

In Huda's memoirs, we hear Sa'id Ağa speak in only two tones: ar-
rogantly giving orders to the children or servants in the household or to
social inferiors outside the house; or gently urging Huda to accept her
fate and accept the social rules that govern her marriage contract. Somehow Huda's mother knows that he had been sold to the family when very
young, and for this she shares a deep empathy with him. But this most
prominent slave is never recorded offering any detail of himself or his past
life. Interestingly, female slaves spoke more freely of their past. The governesses, maids, and wet nurses who took care of Huda and her brother
had been with the family since before the children's birth and knew the

history of all the household's members. In a beautifully described tableau, Huda remembers tender evenings of storytelling: "As for our nighttimes, we used to spend most of them sitting in little groups around a large lantern, because electricity was not widely spread yet in Cairo. Our wet nurses would tell us their stories, how they were enslaved, what their countries of origin had been like, what the customs of their people were like, until we grew sleepy, and they would carry us to our beds."[52] Huda and her brother knew, then, that these slaves were not indigenous to Egypt, but they had been there so long, had been in the household so long, that the pain of separation from their own families and the memories of their own childhoods had become candlelight stories, told and remembered like lullaby folktales.

The voices of the slaves in Huda's childhood home are just whispers, intended to put her to sleep and not meant to be remembered as important stories themselves. They were not part of the family lore. The bonds that tied the slaves to Huda were indeed intimate but had been forced; they were not stories that imparted a shared cultural past. While I marvel at the very human desire of the Sudanese slaves to voice their stories while putting little Huda to bed, I do not read Huda as attributing meaning to their narratives. Mohja Kahf sees in this reticence of Huda's almost a competitive censuring of the slaves.

> [Huda] subordinates that potential discursive plurality to her unified voice by evading their direct discourse and keeping their characters half-acknowledged on the margins of the story. She does not, for example, allow the recital of the servants' nightly life stories, with which they fascinated the children, to enter the narrative as direct discourse, although her own manner of storytelling, particularly her thrilling manner with dramatic incidents, surely owes much to the servants. She repeats only fragments of the servants' speech so that its charm cannot attract the reader; enough that the wet nurse's sentence is still ringing in her ear.[53]

Kahf is right: Huda did learn to tell stories from the narrative gifts of her servants. She admits this when she describes how Sitt al-Zahra, the woman who sold rosewater and perfume to the house, entertained them.

> She was tall, with a wide body and round face with dignified features. She always wore white clothes and on her head a white scarf. We loved her a great deal and

looked forward to her visits, waiting eagerly to hear her entertaining stories. Because of how much we loved her, we encouraged her to stay as late as possible.
We would spend the evening listening while she told in her loud voice her de-
lightful stories. We sat around her, all of our eyes wide and ears open. She went
from story to story . . . and the salon on those evenings was filled with the entire
household, who formed a large circle that overflowed out the door. On these
nights, sleepiness would sneak under our eyelids and we were forced against our
wills to sleep. Afterward, we'd fall into bed, dreaming the stories that she'd told,
entering the world of imagination. I think now it is because of this gifted woman
that our imaginations had life.[54]

Again, Huda Sha'rawi does not share those tales with her readers but, instead, the sense of intoxication that the tales induced. Sitt al-Zahra may
have been a former slave or servant but certainly was a peddler. Along
with the slaves who put Huda to bed as a child, she taught Huda how to
tell stories or, rather, how to tell her own story. Huda's memories of the
slaves' voices set the stage for her own repressed childhood, a truly important story, but one in which the others' narratives are only a background.

The Slaves of Halide's Bedtime

Halide Edib also grew up in a household with a male servant who was
a eunuch, and her presentation of him and what he meant to her shows
the strong similarities she shared with Huda. Sometimes in these memoirs,
written in English in 1926, Halide describes her younger self in the third
person, as noticeable in this passage, where the servant's body forms the
boundaries of her life:

Ali is the man-servant who takes care of her; he is her *lala*, that indispensable
personage in every old Turkish household, for which no English, no European
equivalent can exist, for it arose from roots wholly foreign to them, wholly Oriental. The *lala* was the natural outcome of the marked separation between the
indoor and outdoor life of that day and world. Indoors was the delicate, intimate rule of women; out of doors was the realm of men. They could play there
their proper role of protector, and one felt happy and secure in their presence.
As a child, and as a child only, one could share to the full the freedom of the
two worlds, and one's *lala* was one's natural companion into all the open-air

places of experience. Then too he brings with him into memory that *je ne sais quoi* of the old-world service—devotion, attachment, pride, possession even—which the modern Turkish world has forgotten but which made so much of the warmth and color of the old household life.[55]

Here, too, is that mourning for the past's courtesies, based on old patterns of domestic labor. Halide would have understood Huda well and why she would have seen Sa'id Ağa's place as natural in Huda's adult life.

Like Huda Sha'rawi, Halide remembered that as a child, she also feared that she was somehow related to slaves, although she does not perform the same obfuscation with her mother's past as Huda does. But one could inherit a taint of slave status in ways other than through direct parentage, as Halide describes:

> The accusation of having Gipsy milk and mixed milk was a common one in those days. As my mother had been too delicate, father had hired wet-nurses for me. It was believed that the milk a baby drinks affects its character, making it like the woman who nurses it. My first milk-mother, as we call a foster mother, was an Albanian, and my sullen moods were put down to her. Granny would say, "Now it is the milk of that cross Albanian which is working in thee." The next was the wife of an onion-seller, a supposed Gipsy. Hence anything in me different from a conventional Turkish child was her fault. For three months fortunately a good and beloved person had nursed me, and this gave the explanation of certain good traits. Whenever I was docile, gentle, or unselfish, it was attributed to my Nevres Badji [Badji is the appellation for a Negro nurse], a black slave of my granny's who had married in Istamboul. In spite of her black face she had a milk-white heart and had really nice manners. She had a respected position, and granny visited her often and allowed her to take us one at a time to her house for long visits in Ramazan. This holy month was a wonderful time in those days.[56]

And as Halide remembers it, she was not the only one for whom "slave" was an insult and epithet. She had unruly hair, and a visitor to the house teased her about it, but she refused to laugh. "When the man saw that he could not tease me about my hair, he called me a little slave girl and swore that he had actually seen me bought from a slave dealer, and actually knew the price that was paid for me, although he kept a mysterious silence on this point." Taking a step back from her childhood, Halide contextualizes the situation and writes: "This was the identical nonsense with which every little girl was teased in Turkey in those days. Yet every little girl minded it terribly, and some stupid ones, like me, almost believed it."[57]

This memory, shared with all former little Turkish girls of a certain age (and class), offers a profound insight into the ways in which enslavement entered the lexicon of gender and mothering. The insult here is about value—he "actually knew the price that was paid for me, although he kept a mysterious silence on this point." And that Halide did not consider it ridiculous, although her adult narrating self wishes that she had, speaks to the power of this epithet. And in the next memory, Halide literally has to work her way through a sense of threat and terror when an elite eunuch (of one-time slave status) has some fun with her:

There in father's room, in front of his writing-table and sitting in his chair, was a eunuch. As these people were familiar sights in the palace, the circumstance was not in itself strange, but this eunuch was different from the stately black men I was accustomed to. His face was a light milk and coffee color; his features were more regular than my own; his eyes were big and of the troubling kind—sad, humorous and very beautiful. His large handsome head was set on a crippled body with an enormous hunch on the back. I began walking around him in order to get a good view of the hunch, and then I stood and stared at him fascinated. I believe there was the curve of a smile, in fact there were many smile-curves, in the corners of his mouth, but he kept them under control and returned my gaze seriously for a time. Then he sighed and rolled his eyes, his face taking on an extraordinary look of real suffering.

"Ah, I am waiting for my father!"

"Who is thy father?"

"My father?" He looked astonished. "My father is Edib Bey, of course."

"He is my father."

"Well, I'm talking of Edib Bey too, but he is *my* father. At least he was. I was his son, his first-born, and thou, a black foundling from the streets, came and bewitched both of us. I became crippled and black and thou white and took my place, and I was turned into the street."

His face crumpled into lines; his voice sobbed, his eyes became full of tears, yet watched me furtively. I have never been torn between so many different

sensations: belief in my own wicked witchery, fear lest I might be found out
and sent into the streets and become a negress once more, pity for his miserable
fate, and hatred toward him for making me feel all this. . . . I was trying hard to
swallow the painful lump in my throat to hold back the tears that already stood
on my lashes. I needed the strength of a dozen buffaloes to keep my mouth from
trembling in ever so many directions.

   He crawled toward me, gazed at me, and tried to kiss me.

   "Thou dear black witch," he said as father entered the room.

   "What tricks are you playing on my little girl, Aga?" he said.

   "Telling her not to steal the fathers of such poor orphans as I," he answered.

   Father laughed and took me on his knees, but did not trouble to explain
what seemed a tragic dilemma to me. I carried a misgiving in my heart about
this until its absurdity gradually made itself apparent to me.[58]

Racial identity is horrifyingly fluid to the little girl Halide, and the possibility of not being her father's white child, terrifying to her. It is also interesting to see how this joke unites Edib Bey and the ağa, clearly someone close
to him (though the memoirs never reveal how the ağa was related to her
father)—it makes both of them laugh. It is also clear that Halide gave a lot
of thought to constructions of race in her childhood when writing as an
adult, in ways not imagined by Huda Sha'rawi.[59]

   In her *Mudhakirat*, Huda Sha'rawi shared the closeness of slaves in her
life without sharing their stories (with the possible exception of Sa'id Ağa).
Halide also expressed, in a different way, that the stories of slaves were
not terribly interesting to her, as she does here when she describes a servant, Fikryar, being happy to have someone to talk to: "She started each
time from the very beginning, telling me about her childhood, Caucasia,
the great emigration, the settlement in Adabazar, and how the chief of her
clan sold her in Constantinople to an Egyptian palace. Her adventures I
hardly listened to, but she always ended up with the Circassian youth, my
father's protégé."[60] But even if Fikryar did little to excite Halide's imagination, the experience of other slaves did. She represented slaves not only
as companions, servants, and nurses but also as having been bought for
her. There is no secrecy about their purchase; in fact, Halide documents
what it felt like to receive a new slave, from her perspective and that of the

slave, when she and her older sister received two Abyssinian girls bought in Yemen as gifts.

As Halide described, the little girl bought for her sister "was not an interesting creature, but Reshe, the one bought for me, was as pretty as an Abyssinian girl could be. As a rule, I believe colored people have sad dispositions, but when they arrive in a foreign country as slaves, hardly speaking a word of its language, they must feel sad indeed. Granny used to say that Turkish chickens and Abyssinian children are the most delicate creatures in the world, and I thought of it as I saw Reshe blinking at us and looking around with what seemed more like fear than curiosity."[61] Halide remembered very clearly Reshe's first night in the household and the image of her little sister, Nilufer, and Reshe staring at each other. Nilufer was frightened that Reshe would eat her: "'Art thou sure she is not a cannibal?' We were told a great many stories of cannibals, and their characteristics according to our information were two canine teeth sharper than other people's and a tail." Halide looked over at Reshe, who smiled strangely—Halide remembered it as a grimace more than a smile. Still, she reassured her little sister that Reshe was not a cannibal.[62] Years later, Halide remembered, when Reshe learned Turkish "enough to talk, it was most amusing to hear her impressions of the first night in my room." Reshe had heard in Yemen that the white people of Constantinople "were in the habit of eating Abyssinians."[63]

Halide also remembered Reshe's beautiful dancing, the song she would sing when she was happy, and the song she would sing when sad. Halide loved it:

> I never learned what this wonderful song meant, for by the time she learned Turkish she had forgotten her own Abyssinian. But it had infinite pathos and longing. From it I caught a glimpse of the misery of her past days before she was able to tell me about the way she had been stolen with her little brother from a wonderful Abyssinian forest and made to walk for months under the lash of slave-dealers. There was that in her song, especially in the way she sang it, which made one guess the dreary suffering through the meaningless words. Whenever the oppression and weariness of life settled on my heart too heavily, I used to ask her to come to my room and sing me that song.[64]

Though we cannot hear the song, Halide hums a little of Reshe's story. Then Halide borrows the melody, and the singer, to help express her own feelings.

In a sort of conclusion to this story, Halide promised Reshe she would grant Reshe's heart's desire, which was to dress exactly as Halide did. Halide promised her "that when I was grown up and married and had a house of my own, I would see that she should have the same dresses as I did, as well as a servant and a nice room to herself. At the same time, I wrote her a 'liberating paper,' worded exactly as Granny told me she had written the liberating papers for her slaves, so that Reshe no longer technically belonged to me. I gave her this paper and told her to keep it in order to insure her freedom in case I died and anyone else tried to sell her as if she were still a slave."[65]

Although free, Reshe remained in the household with Halide, and when Halide married, moved with her to her new home. As a young married woman with babies of her own, Halide observed that Reshe "had developed into a fine colored lady, dressed in the latest fashion, proud of the attention she attracted and always taking care to wear a thick veil and gloves, which caused her to be taken for a white woman with a beautiful figure."[66] They grew into women together, and Halide kept her promise about the clothes. One wonders what Huda would have thought—even more, what Sa'id Ağa would have said.[67]

Slaves and Their Own Families

The traces of the images and voices of slaves remain those written by Huda and Halide, for whom they helped define the meaning of family. Unfortunately, these accounts cannot fully answer how men and women like Sa'id and Reshe situated themselves in kinship with the families that owned them. Where would they have had such discussions, and with whom? Sa'id Ağa could not have children, and we do not know from Halide's account whether Reshe ever did. We therefore do not know what legacies they may have left to others, to people they could claim as their own children, sisters, brothers, mothers, fathers, and cousins. How were freed slaves in pre–World War I Egypt or the Ottoman Empire remembered by their own families or by other slaves?

In large cities like Istanbul, Hakan Erdem tells us, the intermarriage of slaves with their owners brought increased racial mixing among freed slave communities. But in other smaller cities throughout the empire, where the last Ottoman governments established Homes for Freed Slaves or provided small pensions and parcels of land, former slaves could marry each other, which "preserved a homogeneity among the African community of that region."[68] Mustafa Olpak, the grandchild of African-Ottoman slaves, described the history and memories of slavery and its impact on the structure of his family in *Biographie d'une famille d'esclaves: Kenya—Crete—Istanbul*. Olpak does not deny that the bonds between owners and slaves could be meaningful, but his memory of these connections reveals a very different relationship to the past among the communities of slaves than those imagined by Huda Sha'rawi and Halide Edib Adivar.

Just as Halide's memoirs offer a picture of Ottoman domestic life before it was destroyed by World War I, so does Olpak's account take us to the end of empire. Later volumes of Huda's *Mudhakirat* seldom refer to the slaves in her own, adult household, with the exception of a single mention (and cartoon) of Sa'id Aǧa. But Olpak introduces us to his relatives (and that word itself comes with complications) just as they were captured in Kenya and sold, as a couple with an infant, by slave traders, perhaps from Libya.[69] An Ottoman-Turkish family bought them in Crete and took them to a farm in Resmo. They adapted to their circumstances, but as he grew, that infant, Ahmet, could not. His frequent escape attempts provoked his owners to punish him by locking him in an iron cage. The couple had other children, also all born as slaves, and all were left in a precarious position when the father died. The Ottoman family that owned them solved this in 1912 by having the teenage Ahmet marry Nuriye, his stepmother, thus keeping them all together.

Mustafa Olpak's horror at this kind of manipulation echoes Huda's outrage at being married to her cousin and Halide's anger over her first husband's polygamy. All are shocked by the lack of individual choices offered, especially to women. But Olpak holds Ottoman culture responsible a bit differently: "In fact, they envisaged marrying Nuriye and Ahmet, who from then on had to call 'my wife' the same woman whom he considered to be his mother. It's unimaginable, but that is what happened. For them, the masters, it was a way of avoiding the family's dispersal, even a kindness [*une bonne oeuvre quoi . . .*]."[70] A few years later in 1918, when the empire was in deep crisis, the Ottoman family frayed their slaves' ties again. They sold Nuriye, who was then forty-eight, to a wealthy Istanbul family who frequented the Ottoman royal court. Nuriye would work as a cook and keep only her youngest child with her. Olpak wrote, paraphrasing the emotions of his relatives: "The children would remain without a mother and Ahmet without a wife? The lamentations, supplications, and vociferations had no influence on the decision. The masters changed nothing in their decision taken on the subject of their family."[71]

As Olpak's account shows, this begins a warp in the marriage that would leave terrible bitterness and shame between Nuriye and Ahmet, and between Ahmet, his children, and his grandchildren. Claiming them as grandparents, Olpak relates that "my grandfather and my grandmother [*Ahmet le corsair et Tété Nuriye*] lived their lives after their liberation in places near to each other. Nevertheless, in spite of their geographic proximity, they took particular care to not see each other. That is to say, we have never seen them under one roof or on the same street. They behaved as if their marriage never took place."[72] Olpak attributes two reasons for this bitterness. The first is Nuriye's resentment at Ahmet for not preventing her sale. But the second and more surprising reason is the real source of sorrow. Nuriye arranged for her sisters to care for her youngest children. But the Ottoman family had another idea, and when Nuriye was gone, resolved to marry Ahmet to one of the sisters, Sadiye. "Ahmet was obliged to marry she whom he had previously called 'sister-in-law,' that is to say, Sadiye. Of course, just as the last time, he had no right to oppose this, to say 'I do not want to.' They married."[73] When Nuriye found out later, in Istanbul, she never forgave him. Neither did some of their children.

Dispersed in so unnatural a way, this family of slaves also found themselves caught, with their owners, in a different kind of forced migration once the war ended. As international treaties decided the new borders of the former Ottoman Empire, populations throughout the empire had to move—Greeks out of Turkey, Turks out of Greece—quickly and, for the slaves, haphazardly. At this precarious moment in history, in 1925, Ahmet's owners liberated him after thirty-seven years of service. Being let go now pained this old man, who in his youth had tried so hard to escape. As his grandson stated,

> It does not suffice to say "you are free" to make the deal complete. He had devoted his childhood, his youth, his entire life to this farm. He had married because his owners had decided so, and this he did two times. He even had children from these marriages. Hardly two years before he had consented to the sale of one of his daughters in order to avoid the rupture of his family. In spite of all of his sacrifice, now they lured him with a semblance of liberty and the right to leave when he wished. Yes, but why?[74]

Through the rest of this narrative, Mustafa Olpak relates his struggle to piece together his family's history and the difficulties in even raising questions about their past. Through records lost in earthquakes to misspelled identity cards (due to his grandfather's terrible Turkish), through trails that ended in undelivered postcards, Olpak continued his research into what had happened to his family. Often his own relatives did not want to delve into the past because their sense of betrayal was too deep, because Ahmet's inability to protect any of his family had scarred them too much. Curious about the background of his family from the time he had been a boy, Mustafa and his cousins learned when and how to broach the subject of her origins with their grandmother, Nuriye. Their own mothers, her daughters, could never be present in the room. And Nuriye herself "would become irritated when we posed our questions in front of our mothers. Not only her but our mothers as well. In truth, they were not angry but experienced shame and sorrow that looked like distrust. What could they tell us? That our grandparents were slaves in Crete, thus telling us: 'You are the grandchildren of slaves'?"[75]

This poses a strong contrast to the slave women who volunteered the stories of their origins and their preslavery families to Halide and Huda when they were little girls. Yet there is a sad and ironic similarity in how difficult it was for all of these people—Huda, Halide, the children of Ahmet and Nuriye—to define and believe in the identities of their parents. Dreams of a lost mother troubled Huda's childhood, while Halide wrestled with crises of racial identity and the relationships within her own family. Iqbal held Sa'id Ağa in a special place in her heart, empathetic with what may have resembled the loss of her own parents. As easy as it may have seemed, slaves like Reshe and Sa'id Ağa worked equally as hard to find a place for themselves within the households of their owners. And Mustafa Olpak's grandparents and parents remained haunted and embittered by the forced marriages imposed on them by the Ottoman family that owned them. Through their own efforts and the monumental research of this son, pieces of this family were reunited, uneasily but incontestably.

Black Mothers and Fathers, Sanctified by Slavery

Even if it was difficult for them to talk about slavery, Mustafa Olpak's relatives found ways to hold on to each other, as fraught as their relationships were. This hard work of family restitution was simply impossible for the majority of Sudanese slaves and ex-slaves, who learned, through the intercession of the Catholic Church, to seek a different kind of kinship through spirituality. This chapter explores the journeys and narratives of a talented group of men and women for whom Catholicism offered education, freedom, and family. It also examines how they, like Salim C. Wilson, negotiated the telling of their story through the acquisition of many languages and the struggle to be recognized as Christian intellectuals.

As mentioned earlier in the discussion of Salim C. Wilson's life, a Catholic school had been established in Khartoum in 1842 and a vicariate founded in that same city in 1846.[1] In the early 1850s, Father Nicola Mazza created the Mazza Institute in Verona to train African missionaries for expeditions of evangelical work in Sudan. This missionary effort had difficult beginnings because potential investors were dismissive of Africans' capacity for monotheistic belief and many of the Italian missionaries were dying of illness in Sudan. Those most committed to this work then shifted their emphasis: instead of investing only in priests and nuns traveling from Italy to Africa, they would train Sudanese people to be missionaries themselves. By the late 1850s, another priest, Father Niccolò Olivieri, had joined Father Mazza in the realization of a program to redeem (*riscatto*) Sudanese slaves. Once purchased and liberated, the younger former slaves were examined and the brightest sent to Italy or Egypt. Deeply influenced by Mazza and Olivieri, Father Daniel Comboni joined this missionary movement.

Father Comboni's Choices

Comboni faced many logistical difficulties in sending African teenagers to Mazza's institute in Italy and in establishing his own foundation in Cairo. After more than a decade of effort, Comboni had established the Institute for Blacks (Istituto di neri) in Cairo in 1867, which became the headquarters of his missions in Sudan.[2] As shown in the voluminous correspondence between them, Mazza worked quite closely with Comboni in negotiating obstacles, and these challenges went some way toward shaping which individuals to bring. Along with the mistrust and misgivings of Catholic officials in Italy, Comboni wrestled with the British surveillance of ships and smaller boats on the Red Sea, the Nile, and the Mediterranean suspected of carrying slaves into Egypt, Istanbul, Aden, Arabia, and other regions on the Indian Ocean. Such close surveillance had ground Father Olivieri's efforts to a complete halt in 1861, when three African girls, all redeemed slaves traveling with the priest to Europe, were arrested at the Cairo railway station and imprisoned.[3]

European officials hired by Khedive Isma'il to combat the trade in slaves that his predecessor had outlawed (thus providing a counter to the mounting pressure of abolitionary movements in Britain and France) confronted claims by slave traders that the African women, often slaves, accompanying them were wives.[4] If these slaves carried documents, they were manumission papers or, more rarely, marriage contracts, but they were never passports or proof of citizenship. European officials often had no way of determining the origins of these travelers. Nor was it easy for the traveling slaves to articulate their origins to their interlocutors, and arrests of women like the three with Father Olivieri were not infrequent.

Having witnessed the confusion over citizenship that blocked Olivieri's efforts to bring redeemed slaves to Italy for religious education, Comboni reasoned that greater care had to be taken with consular officials from Great Britain, France, and Austria, as well as more careful diplomacy conducted with the Ottoman sultan's authorities and Egyptian governors. His success in creating the Institute for Blacks in Cairo was due, in part, to his deliberate cultivation of a network of many hierarchies of officials and businessmen, up to ministries of foreign affairs.[5]

Added to the politically fraught circumstances that surrounded the redemption, liberation, and education of Sudanese slaves was the demand for their spiritual and personal suitability; Comboni and his counterparts did not consider all those they redeemed to be either ready for or worthy of higher linguistic or religious education. Here is how he introduced to Father Mazza a young woman named Zenab whom he thought had proven her capabilities (she was one of the few African women he encouraged who had not been enslaved):

> I now want to add that the pro-vicar has just brought a few African young women to Cairo on the Stella Mattutina from Fr Beltrame in Holy Cross. Among them there is a certain Zenab of the Dinka tribe whom I know very well. She has a good knowledge of Arabic and Dinka and it was she who, after an African called Kachwal, helped at Holy Cross and especially helped Fr Beltrame to compile the Dinka dictionary and grammar. This young African woman has great talents and a very good heart. Now with reference to the Plan that you devised for the African Missions, this young Zenab could be extremely useful in our African Institute in Verona to teach the Dinka language and its true pronunciation. Although the pro-vicar is somewhat opposed to sending Africans to Verona, I am nevertheless certain that if he had a letter from you, he would spontaneously do anything you wished. Therefore, in my opinion, Fr Superior, you should write to the pro-vicar in Cairo begging him to let you have the good young Zenab for the good of your Institute in Verona, promising that at the end of her education she would be available for the Mission.[6]

And for years, Caterina Zenab, as she became known in both Italy and Sudan, did fulfill the very high hopes that Comboni held for her. She became, in his words, "una grande missionaria abilissima" (a highly skilled missionary). In Verona, she achieved fluency in Arabic and in Italian and, as Comboni mentioned, helped Italian missionaries learn the Dinka language. She also taught in Cairo at the Missionary Institutes, established in the mid-1860s. Caterina Zenab returned to Sudan and grew popular as a charismatic evangelist.[7]

She married an Italian carpenter in 1874, and they had a daughter, but Caterina was saddened by her husband's death in 1875 and then devastated by her daughter's death in 1878. She remained an important and revered figure for church officials until she chose to live, unmarried, with an Italian explorer in 1880, with whom she had a son. The explorer, Ernst Marno, died in 1883, leaving Caterina with her child to face a rapidly changing political and religious situation in Sudan, as the influence and forces of the Mahdi increased across the country. But Caterina survived the Mahdiyya. She returned to work as a translator for missionaries in Cairo in 1898 and in Khartoum in 1902 (at a time when Italian Catholic missionaries were returning to Sudan). But many of the Catholic missionaries she knew, already disappointed by her living out of wedlock with the explorer, believed rumors that she had renounced the Catholic faith under the Mahdiyya; although the church was willing to "take her on its work in Sudan," Caterina Zenab finished her life living on a grant from the Egyptian government.[8]

Comboni was one of those most disappointed with her, as other missionaries related.[9] Perhaps it was difficult for him to empathize with the cultural and religious struggles she may have faced; perhaps, with all of her linguistic brilliance, she could not explain to him the depth of her loneliness after the loss of her first family. One wonders at the depth of the mutual heartbreak involved. But early on, Comboni was clear that the former slaves he would consider suitable for the kind of training that Caterina Zenab received were those that seemed tractable and compliant (skills learned during the duties of enslavement). Here is his description of how best to sort potential students from slaves:

> Today I visited seven of those that are here and there; and although I intend to examine them in two months' time, during which period I shall study their character and intelligence, I can already estimate that I am morally certain that I will be taking at least six. But rest assured, Fr Superior, that I will show the greatest care in selecting them according to your criteria, specifically insisting on docility. I can say nothing for the time being of the African girls nor of an older boy or girl that could serve as a guide for the others. The six I have my eye on are all male.[10]

Although I explore later the first-person account of Comboni's great prodigy, Comboni's own words demonstrate the careful ways in which he watched young African slaves. This was not done without love or concern, but such examination did amount to a certain evaluation of those under consideration for particular kinds of characteristics. Of course, Italian men and women hoping to be priests or nuns had to prove their suitability and were also carefully examined, but the intensity of scrutiny of the Africans was different. They had to be mirrors of the evangelist in different ways. Their spiritual journey was thought to be much harder. And sometimes the pressure on the young Africans could be immense, as the day that Caterina Zenab and other young girls were brought by Father Comboni before one of his patrons, King Ludwig I of Bavaria, at the king's palace in Rome. In Comboni's own words, the event was spectacular:

> He even deigned to talk at length with the African girls, to ask each several questions, to show them the famous date palm that towers so majestically in his garden, and to tell them about his trip to Algeria. Good Caterina Zenab, the daughter of a chieftain, that is, a small African king, had the honor to be asked by this distinguished celebrity about her background. But the poor girl, overcome by shyness because of the old monarch's dignity and nobility, did not answer several of his questions. This was a beautiful day for the poor African creatures, who one day when they have returned to their peaceful, modest huts, will still talk at length of the majestic impressions of the lovely days they spent in the Eternal City. In Rome lives a noble person whose name is blessed by the poor and by a great number of religious institutes.[11]

Later that evening, Pope Pius IX agreed to escort "the new African colony" around the gardens of the Vatican. In preparation, Comboni wrote, "We arranged the African girls in a row on the lovely avenue reaching along the Vatican library." Even Comboni was a little overwhelmed: "Our hearts were beating, excited at the thought of the happiness that divine bounty was enabling us to share." And then the pope arrived "at 5 o'clock on the dot," and a fascinating exchange began, to which the little girls listened:

> We knelt on the ground before him to kiss his feet that like those of the divine Saviour walk only to do good and to save. But in his extraordinary kindness, he raised us, gave us his hand to kiss, and blessed us. After giving Conte Vimercati a friendly greeting, he turned his gaze to the black caravan, who awaited him, kneeling, and asked us: "But is this the interesting caravan? . . . I am most pleased to see it. . . . Are these the African girls educated in Verona? . . . Well, well! Have all responded successfully to the education that was offered to them?" "Yes, Holy Father," Msgr Castellacci replied. "I put all my hope in them," the Holy

Father continued; "I am exceedingly pleased that with these girls it was not all a waste of time, because generally the more good that is done for an African, the more ungrateful he becomes. . . . In my youth in America we once came across three Africans; we were well supplied with provisions; we lacked nothing and treated our black servants well. But for gratitude they would always rob us, they were ungrateful, they lied, they were capable of telling us that green is white and red, black, so that for a long time we could never be too careful with them, despite all the good we had always done them; but this, as the saying goes, is 'washing the donkey's head.' They were very ungrateful. In Central Africa, are the Africans thieves, liars and as ungrateful as they are in America?"[12]

What did the girls think when hearing this? What images came to mind for Caterina Zenab, daughter of a chieftain? It was Comboni who first responded, in an attempt to equalize the two cultures:

"Holy Father," I replied, "we are all human. Not only Africans have faults, white men would be ungrateful, thieves, liars and wicked if they found themselves in the sad condition of slavery, like the latter, who seem to exist only to serve the thousand pretexts and often the cruel and bizarre whims of their wicked masters. If Africans were to receive from childhood the education given to white people, they might perhaps profit even more; only with great patience, love, and a sound Catholic education can one obtain what one desires from these children." . . . As we talked, we reached the place where the African girls were waiting on their knees. With deep interest he turned his gaze, full of kindness and grace, on these black creatures whose souls with Holy Baptism have become whiter than snow. "Welcome, my dear daughters," he said; "I am happy to see you; how many are you?" "Twelve," they all replied in chorus. "Come near me," he continued.[13]

And now the girls showed the depth of their training and their abilities to navigate the racial perceptions under which they walked in Rome, with their own responses to the pope:

The Pope sat on a great armchair, which had been prepared for him while he was speaking to the African girls. . . . "Stand up, dear daughters; get ready and line up. Like that; are you all there now? One, two three, four, etc., . . . twelve. . . . Good! So you want to return to your villages in Africa! . . . But why do you want to go back to your homeland?" Two or three of the African girls answered as follows: "To teach our compatriots the faith of Jesus Christ and to show them the ways of heaven. . . . We want to share the good things we received in Europe with our sisters." "You want to make them white, don't you?" the Holy Father continued. "Yes, Sir," the African girls replied. "But how will you do this if you yourselves are so black?" the Holy Father went on. Maria Zarea answered on behalf of all: "We want to make their souls white." "Quite right, quite right," the Holy Father said, "white in soul, as you are. . . . You are half white . . . and how many of your sisters' souls does each of you think you will gain for the Redeemer and guide to heaven? A dozen?" "More than twelve," I said, speaking again, "far more, Holy Father." "Far more," the African girls repeated all together. "Good, good," Pius IX added. "But what will you tell your sisters over there? Will you tell them of all you have seen in Europe, of the beautiful churches and palaces, the lovely buildings and big cities?" "Yes," answered Maria Zarea, "we will tell them every-thing, and we will also introduce them to our Lord and Saviour, Jesus Christ."[14]

And that is exactly what many of them tried to do.

Among the twelve girls kneeling at the feet of Pope Pius IX was a young former slave named Bakhita Kwashe (or Fortunata Quasce, as Comboni identifies her). She remained Comboni's student and a companion of Caterina Zenab and the ten other girls over the next few years as they grew into young women. They were given a rigorous education under a curriculum that included the study of the Old and New Testaments, the basics of Arabic literature, Arabic and Italian grammar, mathematics, geography, and the arts of sewing and embroidery.[15] All were given, as Terence Walz writes, "a special name in Italian, *moretta/moretto* [black mother], perhaps suggesting a higher degree of civilization than *Africana/Africano* or *neri/nero* [black], but certainly a distinction from ordinary Africans."[16] As highly educated as the young women were becoming—and Comboni noted that Caterina Zenab usually took first place among her peers—he was anxious about their na-tures, as he lamented: "But our African adult women, however good and devout they may be, do not possess the docility they showed when they were little girls. They must be guided with greater sagacity and be forgiven some shortcomings. However, for the moment we are satisfied with their progress. That is all I can tell you of my Africans for the moment."[17] Walz wonders, in his article about Bakhita Kwashe, what docility she failed to display. I share that question and also wonder what their transition from teenagers to young women meant for Father Comboni. At a time in Italian history and culture when little was known about African cultures, but much was speculated about the unbridled sexuality of African women, this passage from girlhood to womanhood for the few Africans in Italian Catholic institutes must have been very difficult and, for all parties, uncomfortable.[18] The docility may also have been homesickness, which strongly affected all of the young women.[19]

What was the experience like for Bakhita Kwashe, young former slave now turned devout Catholic scholar? What did it mean to be a *moretta* in Italian society of the early 1860s, a time of great political tumult for the new Italian state, the Vatican, and a Catholic Church that felt under increasing attack? What did this mean for the other African sisters with whom she studied and the white Italian nuns with whom she also lived? And how did Bakhita Kwashe, so gifted in languages, translate the vast differences and distances of culture that she learned to encompass? As one thoughtful

Pope Pius IX, Daniele Comboni, and liberated slave girls. From Comboni Institute, *Daniel Comboni*, p. 16.

historian has written about Caterina Zenab, with whom Bakhita Kwashe would surely have empathized,

> An intelligent, multi-lingual woman who combined the influences of several cultures, Caterina was also aware of the contradictions of European Christianity. Here she bears similarities with later Dinka converts who, having grown up in the rarefied environment of mission schools, returned to their own peoples to confront conflicting expectations surrounding culture, race and faith. Certainly, her life reveals deficiencies in the "work of stupendous charity" as Comboni termed the work of bringing young Africans to Europe for education and spiritual formation.[20]

Bakhita Kwashe's Life

Sister Bakhita Kwashe did not leave a manuscript of her life, so I am continuing in the tradition of piecing together her biography from information other historians have gleaned from what she told her fellow sisters and from what Father Comboni and the priest Geremia da Livorno, who redeemed her in Cairo, knew of her circumstances. One aspect of her identity no one seems to know is her original name—Bakhita was the name that slave raiders commonly gave to recently enslaved girls. As Terence Walz has noted, "We do not know the name that Fortunata was given by her family, nor do we know the names of any of her family members. If she ever disclosed this information to her fellow sisters later in life, it was not remembered. Her name could have been a variant on the name Kwashe/ Kwache, since the Italians, who adopted her, tended to preserve at least one of the African names of people who came within their orbit."[21] She did remember where she was born, Tongojo in the Nuba Mountains in southern Kordofan province, circa 1841, and raiders enslaved her when she was about ten years old. She eventually reached one of the slave markets in Cairo. Father Livorno, on instruction from Father Nicola Mazza, "went to the slave market looking for bright and intelligent-looking African children to buy" for possible enrollment in Mazza's institute in Verona.[22]

By the age of twelve, Bakhita Kwashe had crossed a huge expanse of Sudan on foot, from the Nuba Mountains along a trade route used by the *jallaba* to the Nile and Cairo. From that city, she moved with Father Livorno to Alexandria, and then by another but much larger boat across the Mediterranean, and eventually to Verona. Who traveled so far in the middle of the nineteenth century, in Europe, the Middle East, or Africa? The uppermost echelons of Ottoman and Egyptian officials, European consular officers, missionaries, traders, sailors and merchants, armies and slaves. The only other group to move so far was explorers, who achieved great fame for the distances they traveled. Bakhita and her eleven other counterparts were children. Where did they think they were going?

Although Father Comboni did not consider her initially as outstanding in her studies as he did Caterina Zenab, she did well, and later, in the year after Bakhita and others had met Pope Pius IX, he took sixteen of these *morette* with him to Cairo to open the Institute for Blacks. Bakhita, who by now had been trained for eleven years and was a young woman in her early twenties, was one of the institute's first teachers.[23] She and her peers were responsible for teaching freed slaves who were poor and needed housing and food, and as one sister described, "they took special care of the sick, and offered to watch over them and tend to them, while at the same time initiating them into the true faith."[24] Bakhita and the other Sudanese teachers were by now very well educated, yet she left little behind in writing. So it is interesting that, as Terence Walz notes, "this was a beginning of Bakhita's new life to evangelize Africans by dint of her own life, using herself as a model that her fellow Sudanese could accept and follow."[25] Her memoir could only be in how her fellow sisters remembered her, and how the freed and redeemed slaves who were lucky enough to find her remembered her. What was their experience of her? Did her excellent Arabic and her fluent Italian surprise them? Could they talk to her in her natal language? A world of shared history lived between this missionary and her students. What mastery it must have taken to bring that out. Comboni saw her gifts and identified her, in letters, as "outstanding."[26]

In 1872, the church appointed Father Comboni pro-vicar of Central Africa, thus making him responsible for the apostolate in Khartoum and Catholic missionary work in Sudan. Comboni traveled in a caravan from Alexandria to Khartoum with Italian nuns and priests and three of the Sudanese "adepts," including Bakhita Kwashe, who had moved back to Sudan twenty years after having migrated on foot from the Nuba Mountains to

Egypt. The mission was established, with a school and garden, and its teachers found themselves in a city half of whose population were slaves. How did these different groups of slaves, freed slaves, Christians, and others look at each other? Walz, in his article about Bakhita Kwashe, includes a fascinating quote by Licurgo Santoni, a contemporary Italian observer and a friend of Father Comboni, as he witnessed the presence of black converts within the mission's walls. Describing their European ways of dressing and their devotion in hearing Mass, this observer imagined them to be "proud of finding themselves free while viewing outside their compatriots who are scarcely dressed and filthy slaves."[27]

Did Bakhita Kwashe's many years of religious training enable her to look differently at the enslaved people working so close to the mission's walls? Had she internalized a European view of citizenship or of "compatriots" that would have made her proud, or did she, from her previous experience as a slave herself, respond with empathy or helplessness? Comboni valued her work in Khartoum greatly, enough for him to select her and another young woman, Domitilla Bakhita, who had also trained in Verona, to accompany him in 1873 to Sudan's second-largest city at the time, El Obeid. His decision to bring Bakhita and Domitilla came at a time when he shared his doubts about the future of training African girls in Europe for missionary work:

> Sister Giuseppina and I, together with all the missionaries and our sisters, have established that we will no longer receive African girls who have been to Europe. They are the ruin of the missions and the death of the sisters. The journey from Cairo to Khartoum cost me 22,000 francs, and there were 28 of us. On this journey each African girl costs me 800 francs: for that amount, we can redeem six of them. Then the food, the clothing, etc., of one African girl in Cairo costs a lot, and we get no profit from it. These African girls from Europe think of nothing else but getting married and take up the time and resources we should dedicate to the mission.[28]

It is fascinating that Comboni attributed a new kind of nationality to these girls, an "African-European" mentality and sensibility that seemingly ruined them for inclusion in his missionary community and denaturalized them from the very Sudanese culture from which he had hoped to save them. Despite his many years of work with African women, his observations, made here to a French nun, were similar to Santoni's in that he distanced these women from what he considered their "native" culture.

Shortly after writing this letter, Comboni was able to arrange for European sisters of the order of Saint Joseph to help teach in El Obeid in 1874. A few years later, sisters from another female order founded by Comboni, the Pious Mothers of Nigrizia, also came to El Obeid. Through the relationships that she established with these different sisters, Bakhita decided to become a religious herself, and in 1879 she began the two years of preparation required to become a nun. Her movement along this important spiritual path meant that she would not accompany Comboni as he founded a new missionary outpost in the Nuba Mountains in Dilling (or Delen). Had she gone there, she would have found herself among the communities from which she had been forcibly removed, and as Walz rather wistfully writes, "grave, dignified and inwardly thinking, she must have embraced the idea of returning to her native land as the logical consequence of her special training."[29] As thoughtful a person as she was, perhaps Bakhita had sensed in El Obeid how difficult it might be to go home again and that she

Bakhita Kwashe, now Sister Fortunata Quasce. From Walz, "Bakhita Kwashe."

would be truer to herself and to the belief system in which she had participated for so long if she joined it on a far deeper level. Becoming a nun gave
her a truer passport into the Catholic community. Bakhita Kwashe became
Sister Fortunata Quasce (the Italian translation of her name) in 1882, in the
order of the Pious Mothers of Nigrizia, "the only one among all the Africans sent to Europe during this century" to join this order.[30]

In October 1881, months before Sister Bakhita joined the order as a nun,
Father Daniel Comboni died at the age of fifty. As both worked toward
the fulfillment of their respective spiritual goals, the Islamic movement of
the Mahdi was gaining ground quickly, especially in the areas near Khartoum and El Obeid. In 1883, the Mahdi's forces captured the new sister,
along with her sister nuns, other Catholic priests, and all of the members
of the mission who had been liberated or redeemed. All of them were considered slaves of the Mahdi. When asked by the Mahdi's successor, Khalifa
Abdullahi, if she would convert to Islam, she reportedly refused. Apparently
the khalifa thought she would be easily persuaded:

> He questioned her by herself: "Do you see your fellow country women? They
> were ignorant like you and did not know the truth, but now after learning and
> being enlightened they believe very fervently in our religion. Come along, if
> you agree, you can be happy like them and stay with me."
>
> "No," replied Fortunata firmly, "I will remain faithful to the Christian reli-
> gion. I have received much and found the truth."
>
> At this reply, the Caliph became very angry and ordered the slaves to tie
> her by her wrists and beat her. They lashed her seventy times and left her half-
> dead. Some men stood around her with swords. "If you do not pronounce the
> formula, we shall kill you." "To die for my God is the sweetest thing that could
> happen to me," she answered.[31]

This conversation has been published as an example of Bakhita Kwashe's religious courage, and it is difficult to argue with that. Nor is it hard to imagine
how important a figure Bakhita Kwashe became in the religious and ideolog-
ical war between devout Muslims and devout Catholics in Sudan at this time.

What is most intriguing, however, is that this alleged conversation, perhaps overheard by Bakhita's fellow nuns (who would have been trained
in Arabic so may well have understood the khalifa), contains elements of

national identity that Bakhita herself may never have claimed. Here is the khalifa, remembered as pointing out her "fellow country women" as exemplars of the power of Islamic conversion. What makes them her fellow country women to him, or to the European nuns who may have overheard or to whom she may have related this anecdote? Is it the presumption of premonotheistic ignorance that is attributed to former slave women from the equatorial regions or the Nuba Mountains? Bakhita was invited into a community who looked like her—was she to relate to them racially, according to the Sudanese traditions of racial identification created by the slave trade? Bakhita found that she had quickly to negotiate a careful path through the racial stereotypes thrown at her from different cultures.

After Bakhita's violent encounter with the khalifa, her fellow sisters agreed that life for Bakhita would be particularly dangerous in the camps of the Mahdiyya and that she was to escape with another sister, Maria Caprini. In early October 1885, the two nuns fled, with Bakhita posing as Sister Caprini's slave woman. The escape was successful, and the two sisters reached Aswan later that month after weeks of walking. As Walz has concluded, their success was in large part attributable to "Bakhita being Sudanese and therefore assumed to be a slave."[32] I have not yet discovered any record left behind either by Sister Bakhita or Sister Maria about their experiences or any role-playing they were forced to perform, but given the many checkpoints looking for slaves on the Egyptian-Sudanese border, the two sisters must have repeatedly stated that one was the owner and the other, the slave.

After that reenactment of enslavement, Sisters Bakhita and Maria returned to the Institute for Blacks in Cairo. As a response to the numerous slaves and former slaves fleeing the Mahdists' Sudan, the Egyptian government emancipated many who were then drawn to Comboni's institutions. So many slaves came that Khedive Tawfiq granted the Comboni orders a tract of land on the island of Zamalek, "large enough to support a substantial community, with enough land on which to construct housing for the priests, nuns, and adepts, and land that could be tilled." Bakhita worked on this new institute, the Colonia antischiavista Leone XIII, teaching catechism.[33] This was a calm juncture of Bakhita's life. Her expertise was valued, and it was clear that she had trained for years to do this work.

These were again years in which her presence as a nun and multilingual teacher made her an important symbol not only to her colleagues—the other priests and nuns—but also to the former slaves or recently emancipated slaves who were her students. She was honored by an appointment to teach at a new Comboni institute established in Aswan in 1896. But there the students were different. These were not slaves or refugees from Sudan but children of Egyptians. They were as unfamiliar to her as students as she was to them in her role as teacher. A year after she arrived, parents of Bakhita's Egyptian students "protested to the school authorities about the suitability of an African woman teaching their children." A group removed their children from the institute and enrolled them in American mission schools, "where the instruction was primarily by white women." Bakhita fought back and protested, especially after being removed and sent back to Cairo by the vicar in response to the parents' protests.[34] Here the parents used her race to deny her expertise, at a time in Egyptian cultural history when changing educational curricula relied heavily on European expertise. Bakhita had also mastered many subjects taught in European curricula, but either her skin color or her status as a former slave stood in the way of the parents' being able to see her as a role model for their children. And with Comboni dead, the organization that had trained her failed to stand up for her seniority. Bakhita moved back to Cairo, to Zamalek, and died there suddenly on October 12, 1899, her feast day, while being honored as one of the first *morette*.[35]

A Sister's Troubles in Italy

Sister Mary Josephine Zeinab was another formidable migrant whose travels began with enslavement and eventually led her to Italy. Like Bakhita Kwashe, Zeinab was redeemed by an Italian priest who brought her to Italy when she was very young, but unlike her contemporary, Zeinab remained and built a religious career there. Zeinab was also a gifted language learner, like Caterina Zenab and Bakhita Kwashe, and, like them, she left no manuscript of her life experience. The only narrative of her life that I have found in English begins with a paraphrase of her voice and represents perhaps what she told her fellow nuns, the keepers of her history:

The young girl's father was called Alif, a village chief, who was known by all as an affectionate father of his three children. She could not remember her mother's name any more and kept referring to her as "Mama." While she remembered her parents and the life she had spent with them in the village, tears fell in abundance. Zeinab, the girl's name, still had clear in mind how "Mama" used to toil to provide the family with enough food, plenty of water and toys to play with. She knew how to cuddle her children before going to bed, telling them stories before saying evening prayers.[36]

Born around 1846 in the Nuba Mountains, Zeinab remembered a family practicing Christian or Muslim rituals, and a father with an Arabic-sounding name. The narrative implies that Zeinab was her given name, not the name given to her by slave traders. Did she mean to relate, as Salim C. Wilson did in his narratives, that her family already had an understanding of monotheism? Or did she imply that when the raiders seized her and her brother and sister (raiders whom she identified as from the Baggara tribe), they had taken Muslims as slaves, an illegal practice in mid-nineteenth century Sudan?

Very quickly her siblings disappeared, and Zeinab continued the sad, long trek across Sudan alone with the traders and other traumatized new slaves. Once they reached a market, all of the slaves were placed in a room where they waited to be sold. From the narrative it seems Zeinab was about seven years old when she began to be purchased and sold, by different masters, for approximately a year. Then, in 1854, Father Niccolò Olivieri, one of Comboni's mentors, redeemed her. The narrative tries to imagine what Zeinab must have felt:

One evening as she was closing the windows of the house, she saw a white man and some young girls standing in front of the building across the street. It was not the first time she noticed him. He had even waved at her, but she did not reply, afraid as she was of falling into the hands of another slave owner. Nevertheless the man did not give up and eventually walked into her master's house. He said to her, "I am Abuna Nicholas Olivieri. What is your name?" She answered, "I am Zeinab." He showed her some signs of kindness, like patting her head and caressing her malnourished cheeks. It had been a long time since she had received human affection and attention. Abuna was giving her what she had been suddenly deprived of. He seemed to be a trustful person and gentle as her own father was.

"Would you like to come and stay with us?" he asked her. Zeinab replied that she would but wanted to know what type of work he would make her do. "You will go to school and learn how to read and write. You will live with us and with the other girls and we will be like a happy family."[37]

I imagine that this memory of Zeinab's and Olivieri's first encounter was quilted together from what Zeinab shared with her Italian sisters and what Father Olivieri perhaps wrote in a letter or related when he returned with her to Italy. It is striking how the priest simply walked into the master's house and immediately (as related here) touched the little girl, patting her head. This gesture is imagined as summoning up Zeinab's intimate memories of her lost family, yet she never lost sight of the transactional nature of the encounter. Months of enslavement had taught this little girl to ask about the kind of work she would be required to do.

After haggling with her master, Olivieri paid 350 francs for Zeinab and, with seven other African girls, traveled from Sudan to Cairo to Alexandria, and from there to Marseille. The narrative does not mention her impressions of these cities, only that "no doubt the group members kept to each other, praying together and sharing past experiences as well as discussing the unknown future, which was to unfold before them shortly. They learned the basic notions of European living, some Italian grammar and the fundamentals of the environment they were soon to become a part of" over the six-month journey.[38]

Apparently that was not enough time to prepare Zeinab, who was at that point about eleven years old, for the 200–year-old monastery of the Sisters of Saint Claire in Belvedere. The problem of docility emerged, as it did with Caterina Zenab and Bakhita Kwashe. The issue of obedience seems to have become a code with which religious authorities, after making themselves responsible for young African former slaves, interpreted the culture shock the girls must have experienced at yet another juncture in their lives. Zeinab was warmly received but "somehow, due to the exuberance of her and accustomed to open spaces and plenty of greenery, the walls of the monastery began to be too much for her. She began feeling depressed and started searching for holes in the fence so as to squeeze through and escape. She would take out her frustrations on her schoolmates who could not clearly figure out what was in the mind of their African friend."[39] How difficult it must have been. A century later, even writers sympathetic to Zeinab attributed her sadness and restlessness to her African-ness, to her being used to "open spaces" and "greenery," even after years of forced labor in northern Sudan—the nuns who watched this girl climb through holes in the fence to escape had no idea where she came from, what had traumatized her, and what her strengths were.

One older nun, however, reached out to Zeinab as a mentor, offering friendship and faith as tools of cultural transition. By the fall of 1856, Zeinab had been baptized as Mary Josephine Zeinab and was becoming increasingly engaged with Catholicism. She "expressed to the Sisters her desire to become one of them, but they thought it to be the fruit of youthful enthusiasm and felt it was better for her to receive some professional training, which would enable her to become productive and financially independent." Eager now to stay at the monastery, she followed this advice and learned to play the organ, soon showing herself to be quite skilled musically. In 1860, the monastery named her second organist. As Ratti's narrative of her life describes, Mary Josephine Zeinab's musical talents attracted people to the monastery's chapel. In Italy, "people used to dismiss her as an oddity," but now she became personally popular.[40]

She continued to play, using music to integrate herself into the monastery, and continued to pray that the monastery would allow her to become a nun. She sent a letter to Father Olivieri in 1863 in which she stated in clear terms that "Jesus is the only one who has set the world free from all evil and did it by putting his life on the line. I like his kindness to the poor and the sinners. When I read the gospel I want to belong to him for ever."[41] She seems to have mastered the kind of modest, docile behavior expected of a devout Catholic woman, yet by then the obstacles before her were not only racial and cultural intolerance but much more broadly political. Mary Josephine Zeinab was trying to commit herself to religious traditions during a historical moment in which the church's relationship to Italian society was under tremendous and sometimes violent strain.

Father Olivieri had brought Zeinab and the other girls to a land of fragmented political states. In 1856, when the girls first arrived, Italy was divided into seven parts: six sovereign states and the region of Lombardy and

Venetia, which was part of the Austrian Empire. Mary Josephine Zeinab was placed in the small village of Belvedere, in Ancona, part of the Marches province that belonged to the Papal States in central Italy. What she had learned from Olivieri about "the basic notions of European living" was, in 1859, sharply challenged by the political movement for national unity of the Italian states led by the king of Piedmont-Sardinia, Victor Emanuel II. Victor Emanuel defeated the Austrian Empire and gained possession of Lombardy in 1859 while a series of revolutions erupted in central Italy around the Papal States, very close to Zeinab's monastery.[42] In 1860, the charismatic leader Giuseppe Garibaldi defeated the kingdoms of Naples and Sicily and joined with Victor Emanuel and his political movement. By 1861, the majority of Italy was united as a kingdom, and the Papal States were diminished to the Vatican's estates in Rome.[43]

This strikingly quick and successful movement grew out of the reactions of the Italian ruling classes to the political changes and revolutions throughout Europe, particularly in France. In the years before Zeinab's arrival, the word *Italy* had little political meaning for the uneducated, but the upper economic and political classes were reevaluating great social changes in neighboring countries, imagining for themselves a different kind of state and, even more important, reconsidering their relationship to the Catholic Church. The Risorgimento pushed for a parliamentary constitution for the new state, directly challenging the pope's temporal jurisdiction in Italian society. The forces of the Risorgimento also demanded a breakup of the Papal States' landholdings and properties. Pope Pius IX (the same pope who would sit before the kneeling figures of Caterina Zenab and Bakhita Kwashe in the Vatican gardens) vehemently opposed the new state, for it had "usurped" a great deal of papal territory in 1860 and had "repeatedly expressed the intention of depriving him of whatever temporal power he had managed to retain." Pope Pius responded in 1864 with the "Syllabus of Errors," a proclamation that denounced the secular nature of the new state and the liberalism of political trends in Europe and defiantly reasserted the concept of papal infallibility. To Pope Pius, the times demanded that

> We, owing to the Apostolic office with which God has entrusted us in spite of Our insufficient merit, protest against laws which have produced such great

evils and make one fear even greater ones; and as far as we are able to do so with the sacred authority of divine law, We vindicate for the Church the freedom which has been trodden underfoot with sacrilegious violence. That is why by this letter we intend to do Our duty by announcing openly to all those whom this matter concerns and to the whole Catholic world, that these laws are null and void because they are absolutely contrary to the divine constitution of the Church. In fact, with respect to matters which concern the holy ministry, Our Lord did not put the mighty of this century in charge, but Saint Peter, whom he entrusted not only with feeding his sheep, but also the goats; therefore no power in the world, however great it may be, can deprive of the pastoral office those whom the Holy Ghost has made Bishops in order to feed the Church of God.[44]

The pope vigorously opposed the Risorgimento for seizure of Vatican holdings themselves but also for the closing of hundreds of religious institutions throughout Italy. As his opposition grew more pitched over the 1860s, so, too, did the new Italian government's pressure on the institutions where the pope's authority reached all classes of the population: "No less severe was the government's treatment of monastic orders. Laws enacted in 1866 and 1867 and inspired in no small degree by financial considerations had proclaimed the suppression of all religious corporations in Italy."[45] Pope Pius protested vehemently and tried to summon support from Catholics all over the world, but

the pope, however, was pleading a lost cause. Sentiment in favor of legislative action against the monastic orders in Rome continued to grow. The clamor of the anti-clericals showed no sign of abating. The drafting of an appropriate measure was pushed and there was greater readiness in authoritative circles to make its terms rather severe. The temper of the country was accurately conveyed by one writer who declared that modern society, which found the religious corporations incompatible with its own ends, would reap important economic and moral advantages from their suppression.[46]

The second article of the bill did allow the heads of these condemned orders to remain in them, until their time in office expired. The bill passed in 1873.[47]

This suppression of membership in religious orders sharply limited the ability of the monastery of the Sisters of Saint Claire, where Mary Josephine

Zeinab lived, from accepting her as a novice. But the sisters found ways to keep her living there, giving her duties that became more critical. She worked as an organist but also as a nurse. Her role as an affiliate, but not as a cloistered nun, also enabled her to communicate with the world outside and negotiate with the village authorities. It is interesting that at this point in her biography the sisters now deeply valued the advantages gained from "her firm personality."[48] Their hopes for her now included leaving the order that might soon be disbanded and settling down in marriage. But she would not and persisted in her decision to join as a nun. After years of waiting, Mary Josephine Zeinab was granted permission to become a novice in 1874, at the height of the church's vigorous struggle with the government. During this time, she considered joining Daniel Comboni's Congregation of Sisters and returning with them to Sudan, but her spiritual director, Father Ferri, assured her that she was called "for a contemplative life-style, there where the Lord had brought her many years before."[49] In 1876, she was admitted as a nun to the monastery.

By that time, the bill passed by the Italian parliament had drastically cut the funding for the Sisters of Saint Claire, who appealed to Pope Leo XII for financial help. So intense was the pressure to suppress this and other religious institutions that when former congregants who supported the Italian state discovered that Sister Mary Josephine Zeinab had become a full-fledged nun, they reported it to civil authorities. Sister Mary Josephine had to hide her religious habit and pretend, by continuing the duties and services she had performed as a laywoman, that she was not a nun.[50] Others who loved her worried that she, having escaped slavery as a child, had become "the slave of these old nuns."[51] But her growing abilities to heal other sisters deepened her commitment to her vocation, and she was an even more forceful nun when laws relaxed in the 1880s and she was again able to wear her habit in public. The order to which she belonged, however, had been losing sisters, and the worsening situation called for merging with another order. It was Zeinab who encouraged the nuns to merge into one community by comparing their journey to the ones she had made in childhood: "I left my country on the back of a slave trader's camel. We can certainly leave this town and survive. I see better days coming."[52] The merger was successful, and in 1900, the new monastery was beginning to expand and adding new novices.

Sister Mary Josephine's participation in Italian Catholic institutions was rare for an African woman, but her success as a nun also reflected how the Risorgimento's pressure on the church actually opened opportunities for women religious in late nineteenth-century Italian society. The anticlericalism of the Risorgimento forced Pope Pius IX and his successors to reach out to those elements in society still available to them. As Lucetta Scaraffia has written, "To restore its historical autonomy [the church] chose an active form of social resistance, relying for this purpose on its base among the people"—the poor and women.[53] More women founded religious institutions after 1850, enabling them to participate in the establishment of "the recognition of sanctity" and opening the candidacy for sainthood to a wider spectrum of women. Before this "irruption" of women into religious life, "only 14 out of 125 saints created by papal authority were women, and of 981 saints chosen by various churches, only 209 women were saints." The beatification of women also increased geometrically.[54] Women saints were no longer canonized only for their martyrdom or self-denial but also for the good works they accomplished:

> This contrast in models of sanctity probably derived in part from the different opinion groups that supported the canonization proceedings. Supporting the active and joyous models, which fought sickness with concrete activities, were the new women's congregations; and supporting the women's mystical or martyr model, which offered its sufferings for the redemption of the world—as with Gemma Galgani or Maria Goretti, both laywomen—were the more traditional Catholic organizations, such as the Passionist fathers.[55]

This remarkable empowerment extended directly, as Scaraffia states, from the repression of the Risorgimento. The suppression of religious orders that began in Sardinia in 1855 and continued throughout Italy from 1866 to 1873 "spared only those religious institutions that performed some useful function in society, thus pushing nuns to a more active social role."[56] And it vastly changed the terms and ambitions for those who chose to become women religious: "Many other instances could be adduced to show that in the nineteenth century becoming a sister in one of the new congregations offered travel, social mobility, education, or at least a professional skill, the possibility of managing substantial capital and above all an escape from the power of family and the opportunity to feel that being unmarried and working was not something inferior."[57] Sister Mary Josephine was one of these transformative women, who led her cloistered community toward interaction with surrounding communities. She rose up the ladder of authority as well; she became the assistant to the abbess in 1901 and abbess of the monastery itself in 1910. The little girl who had tried to run away, disappointing her superiors with her inability to adapt, became a strong and respected religious leader. Blind in the last years of her life, she stepped down from the office of mother superior but continued to work. She died of pneumonia on April 24, 1926, after collapsing while singing the *Magnificat* with her sisters.

A New Type of Christian Man

When a young Dinka boy then named Sorur Pharim Deng walked to the Central African Mission in El Obeid and knocked on the mission gate, he asked to see the mission's master.[58] Daniel Comboni walked over to him, to find his spiritual son. The young boy Sorur had escaped from his master, despite his terror at the idea that the missionaries would murder and eat him, and had pushed through his fear toward that door. His memory of how he got there can be found in almost all of the many testimonials and narratives about his life. He described what happened after he jumped over the wall of his master's house.

> Two powers seemed to fight within me; the one seemed to compel me to leave the town, the other seemed to keep me back, and I almost seemed to hear it whispered in my ear: "Go to the house of the Christians!" I did not know what to do. I halted and pondered, leaning against a wall, while my interior struggle went on. Finally I got to the conclusion: "I shall go to the Christians. It is better to die at once and to be consumed, than to die slowly under the cuts of the korbatch [*corbaj*]." To have made this resolution and to feel quite tranquil again, seemed to be but one thing.
>
> I had to pass along the wall of my master's property. From the open windows I could hear a deafening vociferation, and I could catch repeated threats of death against my poor self. That made me run for the rest of the way.[59]

Comboni had studied the Dinka language with the help of Caterina Zenab's dictionary of terms and spoke Arabic fluently. Sorur Pharim Deng's native language was Dinka, but also being linguistically gifted, he had absorbed Arabic in the house of his Baggara master. Their following exchange seems to have been easy for both to understand:

> "Whose slave are you?" Comboni asked.
>
> "A camel-driver's."
>
> "Where is your master's house?"
>
> "Far from here."
>
> "And who has sent you hither?"
>
> Farim who hitherto had heard little enough about God simply answered: "Allah."
>
> This unexpected reply provoked Comboni and another missionary who was present, to smile, and the two white men exchanged a few words in a tongue unintelligible to Farim. Then he was conducted to the boys' dormitory.[60]

Sorur Pharim Deng would become a prodigy and dear friend of Monsignor Comboni for the rest of Comboni's life. When Pharim was baptized a short time later, Comboni gave him his own name, Daniel. Although he shared many qualities with other Comboni protégés—the intellectual intensity of Caterina Zenab and the piety and linguistic talents of Bakhita Kwashe and Mary Josephine Zeinab—this young man's brilliance and assertiveness (rarely valued in his female predecessors) made him the perfect embodiment of the new type of Christian man Comboni so deeply wanted to develop and introduce to the world.[61] Comboni would keep his promise, and like his fellow former slaves, Daniel Sorur Pharim Deng would travel thousands of miles through Africa, the Middle East, and Europe. Unlike them, however, he wrote the narrative of his life, as well as sermons and scholarly articles, in fluent Italian. He became a priest, highly esteemed by Catholic peers, but his writings have also earned him the respect of critical readings and analysis by Italian scholars. People appreciated the accomplished voice it took him years to perfect.

The New Christian Man Looks Back

Daniel Sorur Pharim Deng's narrative does not evoke the same kind of editorial challenges that confronted Salim C. Wilson, nor does it present the same process of dictation implied by the life narratives of Sister Mary

Josephine and Saint Josephine Bakhita, who could read and write only a little. Daniel Sorur's narratives demand instead that his reader join him in facing the uniqueness of his enslavement trauma, his profoundly sad relationship with his mother, and his clear-eyed navigation of the many cultures through which he sailed and into which he was trained. Daniel Sorur takes his readers through the many experiences of multicultural racism he experienced and his careful, faith-based analysis of the bases of racial discrimination.

Daniel Sorur Pharim remembered many of the details of his origins. Born in 1859, he lost his father before he was twelve, the age at which he, his mother, and his sisters were abducted from their village in southern Sudan. He quickly lost sight of his sisters, whom he never saw again, but he and his mother, Aquid, remained together during the trek of the slave caravan to El Obeid. They were able to remain together when sold to a camel merchant, Abdullah wad Dafa'ala, and both worked as slaves in his home for two years. Sorur escaped to the mission in 1873 and was imme-

Daniel Sorur Pharim Deng. Archivio Comboniani Roma.

diately accepted. Dafa'ala must have realized how intelligent the teenage boy was, because he persisted for years in trying to retrieve him from the mission, even using Aquid to try to persuade Daniel to come "home." But both Comboni and Daniel refused, and Daniel completed his catechetical training in December 1873 and was baptized in 1874.[62]

After he left El Obeid, Daniel attended school in Khartoum, where he began his studies in Italian and Arabic. By this time, Comboni also used his influence, his many missions, and the most talented of his Sudanese protégés to staunchly defend Pope Pius IX in his struggle against the Risorgimento for papal infallibility, and in return he received financial help and political support from the pontiff. In 1875, Pope Pius IX offered to enroll two Sudanese young men in the Collegio di propaganda in Rome, after more training for them in Verona. When the monsignor left for Italy, he took Daniel and another man, Arturo Morzal, with him. This first international journey took them from Khartoum to Cairo to Trieste, and they reached Verona in the spring of 1876. Comboni even took Daniel with him to visit Comboni's father in Limone sul Garda. Daniel returned to Verona and continued his studies for a year; then he and Arturo rejoined Comboni in Rome.[63] Pope Pius admitted both him and Arturo into the elite missionary seminar of the urban College of the Propaganda Fide, and invited the two for an audience. Comboni's pride and care come through clearly in this letter addressed to both young men:

My Dear Sons, Arturo and Daniele!

After the grace of the gift of faith God gave you in Africa, the greatest gift God has offered you is certainly the one he is offering you now, which is your acceptance by the Holy Father Pius IX into the most sublime institute in the world, the Pontifical Urban College of Propaganda Fide, to be trained for the Apostolate of Central Africa. Here in Rome, under the influence of the Holy Apostolic See, you will drink in that spirit that must form you as true apostles of your brethren who lie in their millions in darkness and in the shadow of death.

I therefore invite you with all my heart to be equal to such marked graces by leading a holy life, by studying what is prescribed for you diligently, and by abiding by the holy rules of the famous college that are the fruit of the experience of more than two centuries and were conceived by many supreme pontiffs.

You will therefore come to Rome next week, in accordance with the orders of your Rector, Fr Antonio. You will attend my Episcopal consecration and enter the holy Institute of Propaganda filled with the desire to become holy, subsequently to sanctify and save from death your brothers and sisters in Central Africa.

In the meantime I bless you with all my heart,

Your most affectionate Father[64]

Daniel studied in Rome for six years and then attended the Jesuit University in Beirut from 1883 to 1886, where he taught the languages in which he had become fluent, French and Italian. He returned to Cairo, where he also taught African men at the institute of the mission and where he was ordained as a priest. Crowds celebrated his ordination, the first of a black man in Cairo.[65] Unfortunately, Comboni did not live to see this moment. His death in 1881 was deeply mourned by many, especially Daniel, who became physically ill with grief.[66]

Father Daniel returned to Sudan in 1888, where he taught and personally confronted the forces of the Mahdiyya.[67] When the situation grew insupportable, Father Daniel left for Europe on a speaking tour with another priest, P. Geyer, that was intended to raise funds for the Comboni missions in Africa and the Middle East. For two years, until 1891, the two men lectured throughout Austria-Hungary, Germany, and Switzerland. The next years of his life Father Daniel spent in Helwan, near Cairo, where he dedicated himself "in particular to the teaching of young black men." Long afflicted with respiratory illnesses, Father Daniel had tuberculosis by the end of the decade. That his fellow priests arranged for him to be sent to Austria for a cure is testimony to their respect and affection, although ironic, because Helwan itself contained a famous sanatorium for those suffering from respiratory ailments. He died in Austria on January 11, 1900, in the arms of another famous priest, Father Ohrwalder, who had been a prisoner of the Mahdi for years.[68]

Daniel Sorur Pharim Deng, gifted with skills in language, learning, and friendship, crossed more geographic boundaries than any of the other slaves encountered in this book. While amazing his students, colleagues, and audiences, Father Daniel bore the psychological weight of the trauma of his enslavement and escape and the physical toll of respiratory difficulties; many letters about him expressed worries over his weak health, even when he was still a boy.[69] But he never stopped writing. He invested deeply in the importance of setting down his own record, not only of who he was or where he came from but also what it meant and felt like to be a black Catholic priest and in how lonely a place he often found himself.

Lose Your Mother

In his years of teaching freed slaves, Father Daniel heard the testimonies and narratives of how others were enslaved, how they said during the moments of the raid family members were murdered or dragged off never to be seen again (thus I borrow the phrase "lose your mother" from Saidiya Hartman).[70] "I have heard various testimonies like this, and it is nearly impossible for anyone with a shred of human compassion not to feel such horrible agony," he wrote. "How can I hear this story without crying? I recounted only those parts that touched me the most, even though there are ones a hundred times more sorrowful, having myself seen the miseries of the wretched children of Ham."[71] Although this passion is expressed in the terms of a well-trained missionary, Father Daniel made clear he was not some distant observer but a fellow victim who had also experienced the violence, or worse, remembered by other freed slaves.

Daniel Sorur remembered his mother, Aquid, with particular pain. With tragic irony, it was not slavery that tore them apart from each other but his escape and liberation. When the raiders seized them, he and his sisters remained with their mother. And when the *jallaba* began trading members of his family, his mother's shrewd assessment of their circumstances kept them together:

> I have been a witness to such events, having seen my three sisters sold to a Ba-gara, and then most likely, subsequently separated from each other. Following that, I would have been separated from my mother if not for her cleverness. See-ing how the Jalaba [slave dealers] separated family members, my mother asked me not to indicate her as my mother; otherwise we would have been separated. I indicated an elderly woman whom the Jalaba did not seem to take as much of an interest in as my mother. Our plan worked, and we were not separated. Even though we did not have the same masters, there was still hope to see each other

a little and exchange signs and gestures, as deaf people do, since our respective masters were good friends.[72]

As he remembered the sad, deep, strong connection with his mother, Daniel could also remember the joy of another former slave in the El Obeid mission who was separated as a child from his mother, only to rediscover her many years later with other slaves:

> He was separated from his mother because the Jalaba feared their escape since he was young, robust, and strong. He was given to one Jalaba, and she was given to another. The Jalaba who took the young man thought of selling him when they reached Obeid, the capital city of Kordofan. Yet, he escaped to the mission, and the destiny for which he was born was finally fulfilled. He was bought from the wicked Jalaba, and that young man lived many years without ever running into his mother or receiving any news of her. Yet, one day when he was about performing a task for the mission that brought him to the city center, he encountered his mother among other slaves, all carrying water for their master. Can you imagine, dear reader, the emotions of that unfortunate mother who for so long had not seen her son? Consider also the tears of joy that flooded the heart of that fortunate young man after finally finding his beloved mother. He immediately informed the mission and led them to the home of his mother's master. She was bought by the missionaries and became a Christian just like her son.
>
> How lucky this young man was to find his mother, but I was unfortunate for never having found my sisters.[73]

Father Daniel expressed both personal pain and empathy in this passage, which also shows how often stories of enslavement were shared among the liberated (and, as we have seen, between slaves and their masters' children). He shares here the void his long-separated sisters had left in his heart and the pride he felt as a grown man in his mother's cleverness in keeping him close to her. What he does not share here is how he lost her, too.

Daniel Sorur's former master, Ahmad wad Dafa'ala, did not give him up to Monsignor Comboni very easily. Another of his slaves passed by the mission a few weeks after Daniel had escaped and told Dafa'ala where he was. Dafa'ala repeatedly visited the mission, insisting that his slave be given back to him, promising better treatment and often higher and higher prices for the boy. None of these appeals persuaded Daniel or the mission-aries. Finally, Ahmad wad Dafa'ala brought Aquid, Daniel's mother, to the mission to see her son. This is how Daniel's biographer told the story:

> When Farim saw her, he ran to meet her and greet her tenderly. After the moth-er had showered the tokens of her love on her child, she said to Farim: "Now let us return to our master!"
>
> "Mother, that I cannot do."
>
> "But come, what are you afraid of?"
>
> "No, Mother, I cannot. Although I never disobeyed you, this time I cannot do your will."
>
> "But your sisters are waiting for you impatiently. Come with me; if you like it here so much, you may return here later on."
>
> This, of course, was a trick on the mother's part, for the daughters were not with her.
>
> "If my sisters want to see me, let them come here, where the gate is always open, and nobody will do them any harm. But return to the master I cannot. Rather stay here thyself, Mother, for then we shall be together."
>
> Then the mother reminded her son of all she had done for him from the very beginning of his existence.
>
> "All that is true, dear Mother, but I cannot come with you."
>
> At last the enraged mother, wetting her right index finger with saliva, and taking with it some dust from the ground, anointed the boy's forehead with it, solemnly swearing: "Thou art henceforth dead for me, and my eyes shall never see thee again." Thereupon she ran away, without looking back once.[74]

In the narratives of enslavement explored in this book, most of the former slaves remembered and recounted the violent moments of confrontation with the slave raiders with a sameness and repetition that echoes the ac-counts of missionaries and explorers and also emerges in the narratives of slave owners. But never, in any narration of the slaves' experiences of forced separation, have I come across an episode that bears witness to the psycho-logical complexities of masters and slaves, of slaves and their families, and of liberation. Even the biographer condemns Aquid for cursing her son and for leaving him without turning back, although it turns out quickly in this narrative that shortly after this terrible day, Daniel Sorur "heard that his mother had run away from her master, but had been caught and had been sentenced to the hardest kind of work under the strictest surveillance."[75] Even Daniel could barely imagine the sorrow and pain his mother felt as she bade him this most terrible of good-byes. Years later, when he wrote about this break from her, he described her oath "like an arrow that pierced my heart, but that solemn, long-awaited moment happened because of divine providence. I had to cooperate with this action of grace in order to free myself from my fate as a slave and acquire my liberty as a child of God; otherwise I would have remained a slave of the devil."[76] If this meant that Aquid had become a slave of the devil, her image for him must have remained a confusing one of love, betrayal, and a loss more terrible than their original kidnapping. Maybe she cursed him for abandoning her. Maybe she was threatened by Ahmad wad Dafa'ala, who insisted she get Daniel back. Perhaps she could not look back because her circumstances (forced into this confrontation by her master) kept her from showing her tears of pride, maybe even joy, at her son's independence and persistence. Is there a chance that she actually blessed her son? They never saw each other again.

Slave and Priest

Daniel Sorur found comfort in Catholicism and showed great zeal and talents to his teachers. Monsignor Comboni loved him, but that affection could not hide Daniel from other missionaries' racial ambivalence, the same kind that Caterina Zenab, Bakhita Kwashe, and Sister Mary Josephine had faced. Comboni left the choice of which two African boys would accompany him to Italy in 1875 to the superior of the El Obeid institute, Giovanni Losi. Losi was the spiritual director for all of the young Sudanese students, and he recommended two different boys, both from Darfur. The first did not accept the invitation, but Arturo Morzal did, and Comboni hoped to replace the first with Daniel Sorur. Losi refused, citing Daniel's poor health. He shared with Daniel that Comboni wanted him to come but also his lack of faith in the boy's physical strength. As Daniel remembered, "His words brought me much sorrow, and I told him that I didn't want to go in a country with only white people and that I no longer wanted to become a priest." But Comboni prevailed, and Daniel went with Arturo Morzal, his companion in religious studies for years to come.[77]

This tension and racial anxiety recur often in Daniel Sorur's writings. In fact, part of his success as a writer and orator was his questioning of a European audience's belief in the equality of Africans. He challenged even those who pledged their support for abolition in Africa and mourned how perpetual the curse of Ham was for blacks: "We have always been mistreated without obtaining anyone's help." But citing the emancipation of African American slaves, Daniel Sorur lamented the lack of attention of European rulers and their subjects to the plight of other slaves. By resting their sense of blacks' vulnerability to enslavement on the Hamitic curse, Europeans displayed their own lack of Christian faith. "Perhaps my lamentation does not seem justified. However, I admit that many upon hearing the situation of slaves in Africa, have pity on them but do not try to help lift them from their bondage. Thus, will all of us ever be freed?" Even if awareness of the unhappy arouses pity, "fortunate people do not move themselves to give assistance or to take action! Upon the name of Jesus Christ, I entreat all of those belonging to the religion of Christ to come to your churches now and help us. Monarchs, who rule over great lands, I beseech you to have pity on the black slaves. Please try to free them from the Turks! And the rest of you who are blessed and happy, if you are moved by their misery, I ask you to be the liberators of these wretched people."[78]

After this passage in the narrative, Daniel Sorur used his own body and experience, relating how he, his mother, and his sisters were abducted, turning himself once more into the image of a slave who hopefully can attract the Christian pity of his readers. He even pointed out to his readers, when relating acts of cruelty against other slaves, that "I have seen such things with my own eyes when I was a slave."[79] If his readers could not act on the pity that he worked so hard to make them feel, then he wondered, "Do you believe and are you truly convinced that African people are also children of God?"[80]

Daniel's years in Europe gave him a clarity about racism that he continually had to address:

During the brief time of my life when I was solely among Europeans, I had the opportunity to make many observations about the ways blacks are talked about and judged. They are awed to hear that Africans are intelligent people capable of being educated in every intellectual discipline. The people try to dissuade others from sacrificing themselves for the spiritual uplifting of all Africans. They maintain that blacks are not part of the human race, or at least half-man, and occupy a space between monkey and man.[81]

He observed that scientists were of little help: "Many know that some scientists maintain that the black race is one of many that are destined to disappear with the passage of time. To prove this assertion, they have cited the disappearance of many ancient peoples, especially from the East, who have left very little, if any, traces of their existence."[82]

Father Daniel appreciated the fellowship and respect he received from large parts of the Christian community, within which he could also find great comfort in moments of racial pride and solidarity. Almost all of his writings show his eagerness to work with and talk to other former slaves, to teach the liberated, and to relate their stories. When he was ordained in Cairo, he looked back at the celebration with pride: "For you must know that a black man had never before been ordained priest in Cairo—I was the first. When so many Catholics in that great city got wind of the event, they were filled with pleasure and joy. This was why so many people from outside, both religious and common citizens, attended the ceremony. The Blacks also came forward—to see one of their own made priest—they were half mad with joy."[83]

Where Is Home for the New Christian Man?

Father Daniel spent many happy years in Egypt, enjoying his work, his students, and professional respect. But in regard to finding home, he took a profoundly intellectual approach. He was invited by the editor of the Italian journal *Nigrizia* to write an article about his tribe, the Dinka, which was published in 1887 and continues to be quoted by Italian scholars today. It is unclear whether he saw the editor's preface, which implored its European readers to be "indulgent towards any blemish he might find here considering the writer is an African and from Central Africa."[84] Maybe that compelled him to explore more carefully his origins, or maybe, as Fulvio de Giorgi suggests, the psychological pressures of identifying himself clearly required him to reexamine "the nature of his own character on the basis of

Christian and European culture, as well as his African heritage."[85] Father Daniel also had to carry his appearance, his body, his identity as a black man and an African through many different cultures in which his very presence would connote many different things. As de Giorgi writes, "His name itself was a testimony to it: Pharim, son of Den, coming from the Denka tribe, called Sorur by his Arab master, which meant 'joy,' and finally baptized with the Christian name Daniele, chosen and given to him by Mons. Comboni, who, in giving him his own name, established a strong, symbolic bond of fatherhood and perhaps even psychological 'ownership,' albeit in the context of Christian liberty and ecclesiastical fraternity."[86] So, as Father Daniel himself asked in the title of another essay, "What Is My Homeland?"[87] Not quite able to trust his memory to find his birthplace on a map, he read through the works of European explorers of Central Africa that were widely and contemporaneously published in the years of his own publishing activity. Daniel Sorur read works by Georg Schwein-furth, Antoine Horner, and Stanley and Richard Speke, among many others, but he also used the details of his personal memory. In so doing, writes de Giorgi admiringly, Sorur "accomplished a voyage of memory with European ethno-cartographic filters." But unlike the viewpoint of the European voyagers, Africa for Sorur could not be "elsewhere"—he had to locate himself, his family, and his birthplace inside the "anthropological interpretation" of the Europeans.[88]

Here is how he described his own work toward naturalization as a Dinka:

> The education that they [the Dinka] give to their children is limited to the man-agement of livestock and domestic work. With an education like that, I could not even come to learn the name and the geographical location of my tribe and native land. How distressing this was! I was born there and wanted to gather all my memories to at least come to better know the place of my birth. Reminiscing about the voyages that I undertook, I always wanted to know the places where I had been. Now I hope to determine with utmost accuracy the specific tribes present in the corner of the world from which I come.[89]

He remembered some names of tribes and tried to sort out, through memo-ries of trade, battles, and "pastoral excursions," where they were geographically in relation to his home. After considerable research, he resituated the other tribes, such as the Shilluk and the Nuer, with the riverine maps of the explorers:

> In the area formed by the Nile and the Bahr-el-Arab, I did not find any mention of the Giur tribe and the Bahr-el-Ghazal. I am certain that there are not any other streams like the ones there that we passed during our escape. Thus it could not be anything but the tribe of Giur in which I was born, in the Bahr-el-Ghazal, as I wrote in my autobiography.
>
> Thus, with the descriptions of the neighboring tribes and the places of their travels, I can say with some probability that I am a native of the Giur tribe and probably from the [west] of the Bahr-el-Ghazal.[90]

That was how Daniel Sorur Pharim Deng found his way home. He never saw it again, but at least he was as clear as he could be about where he came from.

The Country of
Saint Josephine Bakhita

Writing recently about his experiences as a black man and Italian citizen, Pap Khouma describes the paradoxes of negotiating with the police, municipal bureaucrats, neighbors, and suspicious white Italians who often equate black skin with immigrant or illegal status. His skin color contradicts his Italian identity card for those whose imaginations do not include him in their mental map of Italian citizenship:

> Whoever lives with these situations every day for over twenty-five years, eventually must come to accept them, brush them off and pretend as if nothing has happened in order to live without going insane, or becoming mistrustful, grim, or prejudiced himself. Nevertheless, he often risks misinterpreting situations, seeing racists emerge from all sides, of losing his head, and yelling at and insulting random people.
>
> Once, when I attended a musical festival in Agazzano, in the province of Piacenza, the Italian flag in the middle of the piazza went up in flames without a reasonable explanation after nearly everyone had left. I was careful not to put out the fire, even though I was very close to it. What would those present have thought and how would they have reacted if they saw me, an "extracomunitario [non-EU citizen]," in the piazza of a small town with the Italian flag aflame between his hands? Too many symbols mixed together. I let the flag burn and didn't provoke the anger of anyone.[1]

When Josephine Bakhita first arrived in Italy from Sudan in the mid-1880s, her dark face was far less recognizable to Italians, and her journeys across European borders not even well known enough to stereotype her as an extracomunitario. Bought as a slave and working in northern Italy as a nanny, Bakhita made a name for herself through her commitment to the Catholic Church. In 2000, nine years before Pap Khouma published his article, Bakhita was canonized as a saint, her image, life, and suffering celebrated by thousands in Saint Peter's Square and millions across the world. Her race and her belief are intimately tied together in the stories about her and, as the following quotations show, in the ways in which she is remembered:

> Faced with this humble African woman who underwent the ignominies of slavery, there is no need to experience uneasiness or reverential aloofness.[2]

> Half Sudanese, half Italian, Bakhita was an immigrant before the time.[3]

> Bakhita was a Negress, much loved by whites. Nowadays one might take this for granted, but perhaps this was not so much the case. During these years when the nasty word "racism" has once again [been] resurrected, an immigrant in the early twentieth century, who lived in an epoch when racism produced unspeakable horrors, stands up as a reference point for the suffering of all her fellow immigrants.[4]

Josephine Bakhita at prayer, 1933. From Zanini, *Bakhita*.

But these quotations come from a Catholic writer and another Italian journalist, both of whom love Bakhita as a historically unique member of their community.

As these quotations demonstrate, Saint Josephine Bakhita's trajectory through history is much longer than her life was. Her historical wingspan stretches from the decades of intense slave trading in nineteenth-century Sudan to more recent years of African migration to Europe and the Middle East. The narrative of Bakhita's life has made her the representative of slaves from over a century ago to Darfur or southern Sudanese refugees in the news today—her features an emblem for theirs. Although Bakhita is very much a part of Sudanese, Italian, and Catholic history, her traces— sanctuaries, housing settlements, social centers—can be found in cities from Khartoum to Seattle to Manila. This chapter explores Bakhita's many histories and legacies. It also explores how she was able to elevate herself from the social isolation of enslavement into the activist missionary order of the Canossian Daughters of Charity, and from the Canossian Daughters into a citizenship of sainthood far broader than the borders of any one country. Even with Saint Bakhita's incredible gifts of connection, love, and belonging, what keeps her immortal is her power to stand for those with no citizenship.

Black Mother, Tell Us Your Story!

I first saw a picture of Mother Josephine Bakhita in 1988 in a church in Zamalek, Cairo, where a southern Sudanese friend of mine worshipped. The church, Saint Joseph's, was holding a festival in Bakhita's honor, celebrating the not-yet-completed process of her beatification. In 1992, I saw Blessed Josephine Bakhita's picture again, reproduced many times on the walls of the Sacred Heart Cathedral in Abbasiya, Cairo, where my friend now not only worshipped but had also sought asylum, her political status in Egypt ruined by new immigration laws. Bakhita's status had also changed. Pope John Paul II had finalized her beatification, and we were at another, larger festival celebrating Bakhita's huge step closer to canonization. As in the last Bakhita festival I had attended, the nuns and the priests had laid out posters, prayer sheets, and booklets in many languages, commemorating this blessed life and the docility, so cherished by Monsignor Daniel Comboni, that made Mother Bakhita a soul to emulate. It seemed, from these short readings, that slavery had prepared Bakhita well for sainthood.

The sites of the two churches where I had seen her picture were originally established as Catholic teaching institutes by Monsignor Comboni in the 1870s, and although Mother Bakhita was not liberated by Comboni or his missions, her order, the Canossian Daughters of Charity, remains closely connected to Comboni's. By 1997, however, her framed picture or poster appeared on many churches in Cairo, some Anglican, others Episcopalian, marking these places as sites of sanctuary for Sudanese refugees in Egypt. Hundreds of people like my old friend turned to these churches for help as they struggled with the United Nations High Commission for Refugees for visas that would legalize their stay in Egypt.

In the Catholic Jubilee year of 2000, Mother Bakhita was canonized. Her sainthood was celebrated the world over. For her sister Canossian Daughters in Rome, Venice, Egypt, and Sudan, there was a particular tenderness in this sanctification of so beloved a sister, one whom many of them had known. For African American Catholics, Bakhita's canonization presented a new way of incorporating slavery into religious history and a sense of belonging in the church. And for Sudanese refugees in Egypt and southerners internally displaced in Khartoum, Bakhita's canonization offered the chance to feel a specific identification and pride, even though their economic and political circumstances in Egypt worsened. When, in 2004 at the Sacred Heart Cathedral I asked a group of refugee women about the significance of Bakhita and the experience of slavery, one responded passionately: "Bakhita is the first Sudanese to have history."[5]

What kind of history did she mean? Although there are important differences of experience, Saint Josephine Bakhita followed in the historical footsteps of Caterina Zenab, Bakhita Kwashe, Sister Mary Josephine Zeinab, and Father Daniel Sorur Pharim Deng. All of them traveled hundreds of miles in enslavement and thousands of miles for their faith. All of them left some record of their experience, especially Father Daniel. Three of them joined religious orders. With the exception of Sister Mary Josephine, all returned to Sudan after their religious training, though never to their birthplaces. Saint Bakhita never left Italy once she became a nun, but her history connects her intimately to Sudanese history. In truth, Bakhita's history is uniquely powerful in the way that it reaches deeply into Sudanese history, Egyptian history, Italian history, Catholic history, immigration history, and the ever-changing history of African refugees.

Bakhita's Life

The details of Bakhita's early life first became known when she dictated them to another nun, Sister Teresa Fabris, in 1910 at the request of their mother superior. Bakhita said that she was recounting her life as a slave, but she shared memories of her life as a free girl in Darfur, in an area known as Ogossa, or Olgossa, near the Jabal Agilere or Algere Mountains.[6] Bakhita, her sister nuns, and biographers came to the conclusion that she was born in 1869 or 1870. She constituted her family as her father, mother, three brothers, and three sisters, one of whom was her twin. Her parents must have told her about some of these siblings, four of whom had died before she was born. They were born into the Daju tribe, a group whose borders now cross into Chad, and in the late nineteenth century they were predominantly farmers, specializing in growing grains like sorghum, corn, and millet.[7] They were also increasingly endangered by the slave raids, probably of al-Zubayr Rahman Pasha's forces, who by the 1870s were increasingly in control of Darfur.

Bakhita's dictation reflects some of the social and economic changes that made the Eden of her childhood vulnerable:

> We lived happily with no knowledge of the coming sorrows. One day my mother decided to bring us to the fields where there were various plantations, beasts of burden, and laborers, in order to see if there was available work. My oldest sister did not feel like going and asked to stay at home with my younger sister. A little afterward, when we arrived in the fields, chaos ensued. People were shouting and fleeing. Everyone thought that the slave traders had arrived to take people away. We immediately returned home. We learned from my youngest sister, who was completely shaken and trembling, how the Arabs had taken away my older sister, and how she herself had just enough time to hide behind the wall of a crumbling, abandoned house; otherwise she would have been taken away as well. I remember distinctly how much my mother cried and how much we cried with her. That evening, when my father returned from work, he

became hysterical when he heard the news. With his fellow workers, he tried to find information on the whereabouts of my sister, but it was all in vain. We never knew anything more about my sister.[8]

This happened before Bakhita had turned nine, so it is clear that her family had absorbed the stress of children dying and the trauma of this slave raid that took the sister from their lives. This was not an economically self-sufficient family but one who had to seek work from other plantations, although Bakhita did not share any real awareness of whether or not circumstances had always been like that for them. It is also clear that although she says they had been very happy, the entire tribe lived with the fear of slave raids and suspected the threat as soon as a hue and cry was sounded from far away.

When Bakhita turned nine, she was walking with a friend in nearby fields when two men she identified as "Arabs" kidnapped her: "One of them grabbed me forcefully with one hand and with the other removed a large knife from his belt and pointed it at my side. The other directed a gun at my shoulders and told me: 'If you shout you die. Come, follow us!'" They walked through the brush, through the night; Bakhita said she was "calling my mother and father with anguish in my soul, but no one could hear me."[9] What this account does not say, but every other narrative about Bakhita does, is that this was the time she literally lost her family name. It is an ironic literary process that moves Bakhita from first-person to third-person narration: "During the journey they asked her name. She wanted to respond but could not. The fear, sadness, and exhaustion had taken away her memory, and from that moment she could not remember anymore. Thus, the two ironically gave her the name Bakhita, which means lucky."[10] She never revealed, maybe never remembered, her own childhood name.

Bakhita continued to dream about her family while locked in a *zariba* for about a month, until a slave merchant bought her. She now joined a caravan of three men, three women, and a girl not much older than she was. The adults wore neck chains, but the little girls walked unchained at the end of the line. When they reached the market, the merchant placed them all in a larger room in his home while arranging their purchase. Bakhita and the other girl actually escaped, but only for a few days, until they were delivered to another slave merchant. This time they made their way to Kordofan, where an "Arab captain" bought Bakhita and her friend as a present for his son when he married.[11] Bakhita remembered being treated well, until one day her master beat her viciously, leaving her injured and in bed for more than a month.

Three months later, a Turkish general bought her. Her duties in his house were to help his mother and his wife, dressing them, fanning them, and doing their hair. Bakhita remained in this house for three years and was beaten and whipped often. At one point, Bakhita and the other slaves were forcibly scarred; this was done, Bakhita remembered, "according to Turkish custom; the slaves had to honor their masters by having designs etched onto their bodies."[12] During the month that it took Bakhita to recover, the Egyptian armies in Kordofan confronted more news about the Mahdi's forces and their increasing victories in cities like El Obeid. The "Turkish" general, who was either Circassian or Egyptian, decided to leave Sudan with his family.[13] He brought his family and ten slaves to the capital and began looking for buyers. And here, in Khartoum, still in 1882 a very international city of European and Middle Eastern diplomats, Turco-Egyptian soldiers, northern Sudanese chiefs, merchants, and a huge population of slaves, the Italian consul, Callisto Legnani, bought Bakhita from the general. Bakhita worked in this household of "peace and tranquility" for a little more than two years. By 1884, the Mahdi's army was closing in on Khartoum, and the Egyptian government had sent General Charles Gordon to evacuate its troops. European diplomats were warned to leave; accordingly, Callisto Legnani was called back to Italy. Bakhita begged to go with him, and he took her and a young black man to Suakin. There they heard that the Mahdi's siege of Khartoum had succeeded: Gordon was dead and the city conquered. Bakhita remembered, "If I had remained there, I certainly would have been taken away. And then what would have happened to me?"[14]

They took a ship across the Red Sea, and then the Mediterranean Sea to Genoa. At the Genoese hotel where they stayed at first, the owner asked to buy the young man traveling with them. Soon after, the wife of another good friend of the diplomat asked her husband "why he had not bought another young slave for their daughter? In order to satisfy his friend, the diplomat gave me to them as a gift."[15] Bakhita was given to Augusto Michieli and his Russian wife, Turina; when their daughter Mimmina was born in 1886, Bakhita worked as her nanny. Bakhita felt well treated by this family and returned with them to Suakin, where they owned the Grand Hotel. They remained there for nine months, and Augusto Michieli decided the family should remain there. He sent his wife, daughter, and Bakhita back to Italy to consolidate their affairs, and the women remained in the Michieli house in Mirano for two years.

When it was time for Turina to return to Sudan, she left her daughter and Bakhita in the care of a friend, Illuminato Cecchini, a devout Catholic and advocate for peasants. He helped arrange Bakhita's instruction in the catechumen with the Canossian Daughters in Venice, and Bakhita and Mimmina lived with the nuns. Bakhita found herself feeling profoundly at home, deeply curious, and open to religious instruction. When Turina returned to take her and Mimmina back to Sudan, Bakhita, now about twenty or twenty-one years old, refused to go.[16] Turina struggled with Bakhita, and the mother superior of the Canossian Daughters appealed to the patriarch of Venice (the future Pope Pius X) to intercede. Turina countered by appealing to an aide of the king. Turina insisted that Bakhita was her rightful slave, which the church refused, saying slavery was illegal in Italy. The court case that followed became very famous in Italy, with this young African woman asserting her right to freedom. She won her case. Turina took Mimmina to Sudan, and Bakhita soon returned to the Institute of the Catechumens. Bakhita downplayed her act of defiance in her account and emphasized her joy about where freedom was taking her: "It was November 29, 1889, when I entered the catechumen. I passed the time with my instruction. I received the holy baptism on January 9, 1890, with a joy that only the angels could describe. I was given the name Giuseppina Margherita Fortunata [Lucky], that in Arabic is Bakhita. On the same day I received my confirmation and communion. It was an unforgettable day!"[17] Bakhita had decided to enter the convent as a religious. With much more ease than her predecessor, Sister Mary Josephine, she began her novitiate in 1893 and became a sister of the Canossian Daughters of Charity in 1896. Fourteen years later, she told all of this to her colleague, Sister Teresa. From that moment on, Bakhita's life was in the church's hands.

Bakhita's Life in Print

After that first dictation, Bakhita's convent was requisitioned as a military hospital during World War I. Bakhita had become the cook of the convent and helped the nurses with the soldiers when necessary, as it often was. The presence of a black nun surprised the soldiers, and her many experiences with them began to spread her fame. In 1922, she became the doorkeeper of the convent, the first face that visitors saw. By 1929, Bakhita again dictated her experience of slavery to another nun.[18] Soon, a local schoolteacher, Ida Zanolini, interviewed Bakhita at the behest of the superior general of the order, Mother Maria Cipolla. Zanolini's account, *Storia meravigliosa* (Tale of Wonder), was serialized. It first appeared in *Vita canossiana* in 1931 and was published as a book later that year. Bakhita's story was a tremendous success and was quickly translated into different languages. Visitors flocked to her, coming to her small convent in Schio (not far from Venice) to speak with "Mother Moretta." And as Roberto Zanini describes, "The Superiors of the various Canossian convents, solicited by the Sisters who had read with great interest Signorina Zanolini's book, clamored for her presence. They wanted to know her and make her known."[19] In the years 1933, 1935, and 1937, new editions of *Tale of Wonder* were published. The official photographer of the Holy See read her story and came personally to meet her and photograph Bakhita, to "leave behind a visible documentation of the life of such an extraordinary person."[20] Photographers visited Bakhita and printed her image throughout Italy.

Bakhita became so well known that the highest authorities of the Canossian order asked her to tour Canossian convents throughout Italy to help raise funds for Canossian and Comboni missions. During 1932–34, Bakhita toured the country, accompanied by Sister Leopolda Benetti, an experienced missionary who introduced Bakhita to audiences in church squares, parish halls, convents, and schools. "Everyone wanted to see the black Sister who had come from Africa and had been a slave," but Bakhita's public appearances proved difficult for her. Her sisters often found her, when alone, on her knees and crying, and one nurse remembered the sadness with which Bakhita answered her question of what was wrong: "It is not a matter of pain in my body, no! The fact is that everybody looks at me as if I were a rare beast. I like to work, I like to pray for them all, but I would prefer to avoid these crowds! And then they keep on calling me 'poor thing! Poor thing!' I am not a poor thing: I belong to the Paron [Master] and to His home. It is those who do not belong to the Lord who are poor things, not me!"[21] Sister Leopolda Benetti remembered, after Bakhita's death, "the mayhem that would occur when Bakhita left" each of these stages. "Everybody wanted to kiss her Medal, to hear a word from her; some even claimed for her signature on *Storia Meravigliosa*, forgetting that she could not even write!"[22]

Her exhaustion slowed the pace after about four years, and Bakhita resided in Milan from 1937 until 1939 as the doorkeeper for the International Canossian Missionary Novitiate. Again she was the first face seen by visitors, and by now a very famous face. Her health deteriorated, however, and Bakhita returned to the smaller convent in Schio where she had spent so many years. She suffered at the end of her life from severe respiratory ailments and died of pneumonia on February 8, 1947. That year another edition of *Tale of Wonder* was published in her honor. It has been reissued three more times since then, in 1950, 1961, and 2000, the year of her canonization.

Immediately after her death, church officials began a different type of documentation of Bakhita's life and sanctity. They began to gather testimonials from nuns and priests who had known her, from adults who as children had been cared for by her, and from the sick who claimed her intercession had cured them of their disease. These summations were printed under the title "Beatificationis et Canonizationis Servae dei Iosephina Bakhita Acta" for the Ordinary process held at Vicenza during 1955–57, and then more than a decade later at the beginning of Bakhita's Apostolic process in 1968–69. In 1975, the Canossian Daughters put forth another group of materials for the Sacred Congregation that met to judge the sanctity of candidates for canonization (Pro Causis Sanctorum). And, as described earlier, by the early 1980s and the outbreak of the Sudanese civil war, the Canossians had published thousands of booklets and pamphlets in Sudan and Egypt about Bakhita, all based on *Tale of Wonder*.[23]

Bakhita as an Immigrant

From Bakhita's arrival in Genoa in 1885 to her death in Schio in 1947, her presence in Italy raised issues that had not yet been resolved in Italian social, political, or religious culture. Slavery presents the first of these questions. The lives of the other *morette*, all redeemed by missionaries or Monsignor Comboni himself, put Italian Catholic missionaries well ahead of other Europeans in their zeal for abolition and their ability to create training institutions for liberated African slaves. Although Bakhita joined a religious order that was and remains deeply connected to the Comboni order and its missions, she herself was not redeemed but bought by an Italian diplomat who represented the government of King Victor Emanuel II. Roberto Zanini states that Calisto Legnani "had known Msgr. Comboni and had been influenced by him, and this had no doubt been one of the reasons why he decided to redeem our future Saint."[24] While it is true that Bakhita remembered him with affection and that he treated her well, she never stated that she was not his slave—in fact, she dictated to Sister Teresa in 1910 that he gave her to the Michielis. Turina Michieli insisted, when Bakhita refused to return once more to Sudan, that she was indeed her slave and was behaving ungratefully for the gentle treatment she had received in their household. The controversy over Bakhita's refusal—"Excuse me, Signora, but I'm not leaving here"—shocked all eyewitnesses and provoked this florid (and popular) reenactment, written by Ida Zanolini:

> The Signora laughed at this unexpected answer and looked at Bakhita, stunned by her completely new behavior. Even the Superior and Mother Fabretti looked at her with amazement.
>
> Bakhita stood in the middle of the room motionless, humble but decisive, and looked at the Christ figure. The Signora laughed again: "What sort of talk is this? Perhaps the fresh air of Venice has addled your brain? Little Madam! Who's given you ideas above your station? Aren't you forgetting that by law you belong to me and I have the right to demand your obedience? But I know what you're up to; you've become so cozy over the months with these Sisters that you don't want to leave them. Well, my dear, in life you often have to let your heart be silent. Isn't that true, Mother Superior?"
>
> A slight nod of the head was the reply of the good Mother who looked extremely embarrassed.
>
> "So, Bakhita, get ready. You should be used by now to a change of places and faces."[25]

Zanolini captures here what contemporary understandings of the legality of slavery were in the late 1880s. Although Pope Pius IX acted as a sponsor for Monsignor Comboni in the mid-1860s and slavery itself had been abolished on Italian soil, it was only in 1860, for example, that the church "stopped teaching that it was not a sin for a Catholic to possess another human being."[26] Italy was that same year in the process of uniting, so it is quite possible that there existed a diversity of legal opinion among the various provinces and kingdoms on the legality of slavery, even by the 1880s.

The Risorgimento had cost Pope Pius IX his temporal power and, eventually, almost all of the Vatican States. As we have seen with Sister Mary Josephine in her small convent in the Marches province, religious orders were shut down or cut off from state funding. Bakhita's case offers a glimpse into how difficult it was for the religious orders to stand up to the government, but also how the Canossian Daughters reached out to the patriarch of Venice, who would become pope in 1903, to advocate for Bakhita. As Lucetta Scaraffia has argued, this pope supported women and the poor. The Canossian Daughters represented a new, more activist community, founded by a former marchioness, Saint Magdalen of Canossa, who used her own wealth to create the order in 1812.[27] Even if Mother Fabretti, the superior who ran the Venice convent, was unsure how to act in the face of Turina Michieli's assertions of ownership over Bakhita, she was able to use her connections with the radically political and pro-church Illuminato Cecchini, Bakhita's mentor, to reach his good friend, Cardinal Patriarch Giuseppe Sarto. Like Cecchine, Cardinal Sarto opposed the unified Italian government "with firmness in the face of the advancement of Modernism."[28] In the course of Bakhita's trial, those forces of "modernism" supported the Michielis' claims over Bakhita, while the church, with Cardinal Sarto's particular help, considered her enslavement illegal. This was a huge gain not only for Bakhita but also for politics over temporal power, still being negotiated between the Italian state and the church.

As Italian social and religious politics changed over time, Bakhita's status as a famous African nun also presented new opportunities for the government and difficult challenges for her. By 1922, Mussolini was prime minister of Italy. He made the unification of Italy his great priority through his movement of fascism. As has been written, "Fascism tried to annex the glory of unification to itself." With his energies focused on intense nation-alistic solidarity and the creation of an Italian empire in northern and east-ern Africa, Mussolini reconciled the Roman Catholic Church with the new kingdom of Victor Emanuel III in 1929.[29] In 1932, Bakhita began her inten-sive touring across Italy, and the Italian invasion of Ethiopia dramatically increased her invitations. "When the African war broke out," Ida Zanolini wrote, "enthusiasm for Bakhita reached new heights. One day the crowd that surrounded her in the streets was so great that it even stopped the tram and for a brief time paralyzed the traffic."[30] By 1936, Mussolini's ef-forts to reach out to religious orders extended to a state celebration held in Rome in honor of new missionaries preparing to work in Addis Ababa. Bakhita was invited, met with Mussolini and the other missionaries, and was quoted as saying, "Let us hope that at least the Missions will profit, especially my people!"[31]

It is hard to imagine how Bakhita regarded fascism, and easier to envi-sion how powerful the message of colonialism could have been, especially when combined with what to her would have been the clear positives of missionary work. For many Italians, however, Bakhita herself was a textbook wrapped in a habit, exemplifying Africa and what they knew of Africa. But the extreme outpouring of Italians' fascination with, and often love for, Bakhita contrasted widely with the laws and behavior that tried to shape the colonial administration of Ethiopia. While Italians greeted Mussolini's declaration of empire in 1937 with enthusiasm, they also shared growing concerns about the mixed-race children produced by Ethiopian and Eritrean women and Italian soldiers. Legislation was passed "that sought to limit and finally prohibit sexual and marital rela-tions between colonizers and their colonial subjects." This legislation was not successful but, as Derek Duncan has written, certainly helped create an image of Eritrean women as prostitutes.[32] In important ways, though, the missionary houses countered these attempts at segregation and the derogation of African women by bringing Eritrean children closer to Ital-ian Catholic culture. As Jacqueline Andall has concluded, the missionary schools "were intended to raise Italo-Eritreans to be good Italian citizens and equally, in the contemporary context, while again, not an explicitly stated objective of religious institutions, migrants' children were effectively being raised as Italians."[33] Andall considers that this debate about race remains ongoing in Italy, and no doubt Pap Khouma would concur.

Bakhita's Body as Slave, as Nun, and as Icon

Bakhita herself figured prominently in this debate: a noncolonized former slave whose conversion occurred in Italy and not Sudan, a woman who had become the picture of Africa for many, a chaste and virginal counter to the image of African women as prostitutes, and a quiet but determined integrator, ever aware of her racial difference. How did she navigate herself through such terrain, and how did her adoring crowds imagine her? From the many documents about her, and the visual record she left behind, Bakhita's body, like all bodies, moved through different passages but not just biologically. Bakhita's body publicly bore the marks of slavery, held a surprise for first-time Italian onlookers, and eventually gained the protection of the church and the dignity offered by her Canossian habit, which helped her look like her sisters in many important ways.

We first see Bakhita's vulnerable body in her own description of herself when she was enslaved at nine. The gun pointed at her shoulders, the knife uncomfortably close to her side, Bakhita presented her much younger self as fragile and mute—her mouth shut down with her memory (thus the loss of her original name). As she grows, while a slave of the Turkish general, her body is repeatedly beaten and always hungry, but these injuries are small in comparison to the most visible bodily legacy of Bakhita's enslavement: the forced scarification. Bakhita never described her body as carefully as she told the story of watching a companion slave cut with a razor and then salt rubbed into her wounds:

> When the girl was taken away, I was to be put in her place, but I couldn't move. After a harsh look from my master's wife, with her whip in hand, I immediately lay down on the mat. My mistress told the Arab woman to spare my face, but instead carve six cuts on my breasts. With her tools, she began to give me six wide cuts on my breasts, whose scars I still have today. Then followed the seventy cuts on my stomach and finally the forty-eight on my right arm. I felt like I was about to die at every moment, especially when she rubbed the salt on me. Immersed in a lake of my own blood, I was then carried away on the mat, and afterward

I blacked out. When I regained my senses, I saw that some of the slaves surrounded me, who were touched and even suffering on account of my suffering.
For more than a month, all three of us were forced to lie on mats without being
able to move, except to reach the rag that we used to dry the water that continually oozed from our wounds.[34]

These scars forever marked her, but they also linked her emotionally to the
other slaves who were her companions during this time of her life. It is only
during the first days of her capture that Bakhita remembered herself alone
(made more so by the hostility of the slave raiders). In this passage, as in
others, Bakhita presented scenes in which she and other Sudanese slaves
were in constant communication, listening to and comforting each other
with stories and shared experience.

Once in Italy, Bakhita had to negotiate a different kind of fellowship,
within a religious community that saw first her black skin, and within her
own mind, now very conscious of that color. When finally, after her trial,
she was brought to the Institute of the Catechumens, her difference from
the other Christian women struck her, and she later told another nun, in
the Venetian dialect she always used, "It is here that I became a child of
God, I, a poor black girl, a poor black girl!"[35] Other nuns sometimes did
not offer much help, for example, when one asked her as she changed the
sheets of a convent bed, "How do you manage not to smudge the white
linens with your black hands?" Bakhita had come into a society where, as
Zanini wrote, "a black human being had never been seen, except on postcards, on picture books of colonial propaganda or on commercials of some
exotic product or of some Circus, not to mention some famous shoe polish
and soap 'strong enough even to whiten the skin of Africans.'" In empathy
with Bakhita, he emphasized how hard this must have been and how hurt
she must have felt, "who had hesitated so long before asking for admis-
sion to the convent just because of the color of her skin."[36] It seems the
legacies of Father Daniel and Sisters Bakhita Kwashe and Mary Josephine
could not even reach across one decade to help Bakhita. In those years of
the early 1890s, Father Daniel and Sister Bakhita were either in Egypt or
Sudan, but Sister Mary Josephine was in Italy in her cloistered convent.
No wonder Bakhita was overjoyed when she met another Sudanese nun,

Sister Agostina, in the 1930s while Bakhita was busily touring on her way to Padua. Sister Agostina was a few years older than Bakhita's older sister, the sibling first kidnapped in Darfur, and had been rescued from slavery by an Italian missionary. "They were so taken up with the remembrance of their lost families that they came to suspect to be real blood sisters," Zanini wrote.[37] Perhaps no translators were needed, no Venetian dialect and no Italian, and these two sisters could speak to each other from old places in their hearts.

Bakhita also found comfort in her work with children in her home convent in Schio. On her tours, however, her encounters with children were more difficult because she frightened them. Although she always won them over, it seems her sister companions and the local mother superiors learned to expect the first reaction: "To see Mother Moretta," one remembered, "was to run for your life."[38] Even children who knew her well and loved her surprised her by asking to see her scars, a difficult self-exposure for an adult nun in general, and for Bakhita in particular. Sister Noemi Raccanello remembered one such scene:

> Once I saw her in the playground surrounded by a group of children, who, happy to have her with them, never ended querying her. Rather indiscreetly one of them asked her to let them see the tattoo she had on her body. To my surprise I saw her modestly undoing the pin, which held her shawl at the neck, and reveal some of the scars. "Poor things," she explained later to those who knew her well and were aware of her sense of modesty, "why not please them? Who knows, after seeing this, they may be more grateful to the Lord for being born in Italy?"[39]

Her sister nuns remembered that she usually responded to the constant attention to her skin color with jokes and wit. In the early 1930s, *Tale of Wonder* sold for two Italian lire. One evening an unexpected visitor came to Schio, surprising everyone while the sisters, including Bakhita, were at recreation. The Reverend Mother informed Bakhita that a visitor was waiting, and "Bakhita's spontaneous reaction set everybody laughing: Mother, people read me for 2 lire, how much should they pay for seeing me?"[40]

When she was an old woman in Schio, however, Bakhita's body was seen as having great and sanctified power. Allied planes bombarded northern Italy heavily, but Schio escaped such damage. All attributed this to Bakhita, who by then was being called a saint.[41] When she died, however, her sister nuns and the larger church treasured her corpse. Her remains were brought into the chapel of the convent for her wake, and the local residents flooded in to see her, to touch her and her clothing. The testimony of Sister Clotilde Sella bears witness to how she was mourned:

> Sunday morning (February 9, 1947) the body of Mother Bakhita was brought into the chapel next to our church. The body remained flexible, and many of the local mothers took the arm of Mother Bakhita and put it over their children's heads as a sign of protection. Late on Monday evening, when the body was placed in a zinc coffin, the body was still lukewarm in the back and still flexible. Her facial expression was so serene that not even the children were afraid to look at her. On Sunday morning, as soon as the news of Mother Bakhita's death was announced in the church by the high priest, there were numerous requests from the congregants to see the corpse and intercede on her behalf. I saw every type of person present, not only from the working class, but doctors and other dignified people as well. Dr. Mazzon was surprised because on Monday afternoon the body was still flexible. He talked with his colleagues, who perhaps thought this was characteristic of Africans. Many touched Bakhita's body with objects. They cut her covering into small pieces in order to bring away something to remember her by. Wives and brides-to-be rubbed their rings against Bakhita's bejeweled hand in order to have protection over their families. We had to delay closing the coffin because the workers of Lanificio Rossi who didn't get out of work until 8:00 had asked to be able to see her body one last time.[42]

Even though the doctors thought the warmth of her body might be an African trait, in death Bakhita was no longer an "other." She belonged to Schio, to Catholics, to Italians, and to God.

Universal Sister

Bakhita returned to Sudan posthumously in February 1993, a year after her beatification. Pope John Paul II brought her back in his sermon to a huge crowd in Green Square, before an enormous portrait of Bakhita and a gigantic iron statue of Christ. Not only did the pontiff commemorate Bakhita's profound spirituality and faith but he introduced her as well into the religious politics of the Sudanese civil war. "Bakhita learned from the tragic events in her life to have complete trust in the One who is present everywhere. Using religion as a pretext for injustice and violence is a terrible abuse and must be condemned by all who have genuine belief in God," the pope said. Offering even more context for this first Mass given in a country governed by Islamic law, the pope added, "I came to Khartoum in a spirit of friendship and esteem; I leave you with the hope that a better rapport between North and South, and between the followers of different religious traditions may soon become a reality. God Bless Sudan!"[43]

The pope's politicized words of hope made Bakhita actively relevant to the suffering of southern Sudanese refugees in the early 1990s, but the war continued, and more and more southerners fled the country. They brought terrible stories to the churches in Egypt where they sought sanctuary. Reports increasingly emerged in the international media, in the Christian press, and in publications of human rights agencies of a revival of slave raids launched against southern communities.[44] As early as 1987, northern Sudanese scholars and activists, such as Suleiman Ali Baldo and Ushari Ahmad Mahmud, also publicized the reintroduction of slavery in Sudanese society and were forced into exile soon after.[45] Bakhita's life as a slave could no longer be relegated to nineteenth-century Sudanese history but mirrored contemporary experience as well. Her canonization in 2000 broadcast this message with even more power.

The narratives of Bakhita's life provide a vocabulary about slavery and its history for many Sudanese, although it remains a deeply sensitive issue. For southern Sudanese, many of whom are Catholic, the church has provided a means of discussing it without revealing too much that is personal, even if they know someone who has been enslaved. The women that Abuna Ibrahim and I interviewed at the Saint Bakhita Center in Cairo made this clear. They spoke of the late nineteenth century as the era of slavery (*zaman al-raqiq*), yet this era seemed to reach across decades. As Regina James spoke of it, "We experience the same thing. We are living the life of Bakhita. Everything comes from God. Bakhita is a miracle from God. In order not to be angry, pray to God. We experience the same thing: torture, lost in the street, beaten. In the streets here, people just beat you."[46] And all in the room agreed that they hear the word *'abid* (slave) hurled at them all the time. Bakhita helped them shape this history for themselves and helped them to find some dignity in their circumstances.

Armel Brice Adanhounme writes that in the face of civil wars and massive forced migration in Africa, Bakhita redeems the memory of slavery in the name of all slaves.[47] For him, the hagiography of this saint becomes "a principle of the enculturation of faith, where the Eucharist of the master washing the slave's feet subverts the civilities of the theology of sensualists of this world."[48] He notes one of the most powerful statements Bakhita ever made was in response to a question of how she would behave if she met those who enslaved her: "If I met up with those slave traders who kidnapped me and even those who tortured me, I would get down on my knees to kiss their hands, because if it weren't for them, I wouldn't be a Christian or a religious today."[49] Adanhounme explains how this statement turns the history of slavery around. In his reading of her, Bakhita actually makes demands of the church:

> For Bakhita, slavery was born of ignorance, so she proposed herself as the one to teach the liberty of Christ to those she called "poor unfortunates." Bakhita is not only a victim, but like a "passionate participant" in slavery; her methodology is contained in her last words, calling for the heavy chains of slavery to be lifted from her. What a testament for the Christian churches and the Africans who are its members! How to preach the evangelism of liberty and liberation in a context where children continue to be enslaved? Even more generally, how can Christianity, conscious of its heritage and collusion with the enslavement of blacks, proclaim the redemption of Africa for which it had previously predicted eternal damnation?[50]

This mystical, activist Bakhita transforms the historical event of slavery into a theological approach. Even for anthropologists, she "teaches us how one can regain being the subject [*comment l'on peut redevenir sujet*], not object."[51] But the most beautiful point Adanhounme makes is that Bakhita offers an innovation in the methodologies we use to look back at historical slavery. Bakhita helps us reread, reinterpret the enslavement of blacks "as an opportunity for salvation, and not with the old model seeing it as an emptiness that had to be overcome. Blacks do not have an ontological void to fill, but rather a theological space to fulfill."[52]

Saint Bakhita has also changed the language of slavery's legacy for black Catholics in the United States. M. Shawn Copeland has explored how slavery's past has racially divided American Catholics:

> In response to the blatantly false dichotomy inserted between "black" and "Catholic," black Catholic theologians have had to come to grips with our angular cultural, existential, and ecclesial situation, that is, to come to take up apologetics. The word apologetics comes from the Greek "apologia," which denotes "in defense of." Thus, black Catholic theologians have been compelled not only to account for our belief as theistic, Christian and Catholic, but also to account for our belief as it has been formed, nurtured and mediated in the context of brutal chattel slavery, deprecation of black culture and black bodies, protracted anti-black racism and persistent discrimination even within our church.[53]

The gift of Bakhita and other African "men and women of exemplary prayer and love and asceticism," such as Benedict the Moor, Martin de Pores, Tertullian, and Saint Augustine, is how they "enhanced Catholic tradition."[54] And those scholars like Dom Cyprian Davis, who have shaken the "lives and stories of enslaved and free people of color," offer a way to look at faith; they "incarnate faith as the free act that it is."[55] Copeland asserts that the exploration of these narratives that tell of the damage caused by slavery are not to be retold for "voyeuristic fascination, but to make unseen suffering and oppression visible, to make reconciliation possible." Instead, "the study of history opens us to a vision of the church as mystery, as a graced counter-sign, 'an incarnational bridge, a sacramental union that makes us [all] pilgrims, climbing [together] through time and space.'"[56]

Bakhita On-Screen

In 2009, the Italian TV channel Rai aired the two-hour film *Bakhita*, which dramatized her childhood, her experience as a slave, and the trial that made her free. Although the film took great liberties with the narrative, particularly about her Italian owners, it delved deeply into the racial prejudice that Bakhita confronted among the villagers near Genoa and even among some of the older Canossian nuns in Venice. The film starred the Senegalese actress Fatou Kine Boye, whose beautiful clear-eyed face and huge smile offered some of the personal magnetism that Saint Bakhita herself must have possessed. *Bakhita* tried very hard to look at Italian society from her perspective, as shown in the scene when she first sees Venice. The actress captured both the fear and amazement that Bakhita must have felt, and the film drew large audiences throughout Italy. It was covered in the newspaper *Corriere della sera*, and the Canossian Daughters in Rome warmly recommended it.[57] The film is now internationally distributed through YouTube, as well as on DVD.

In the spring of 2011, Catholic missionaries showed the film to children in southern Sudan. First they handed out large cards with Bakhita's picture to the children. One of the missionaries wrote about the event on his blog, showing how her image was brought even more personally home: "We handed them out to the crowd of 2000 or more people who had gathered just before beginning a dramatized video account of St. Bakhita's life. Amazingly, at the end of the evening I did not see even one that had been thrown away or dropped on the ground. We asked each person who received the card to consider it as a personal invitation to holiness, a holiness that St. Bakhita proves is possible for all Sudanese."[58]

Bakhita's photograph on the shirts of Sudanese children. From http://cfrsudan.blogspot.com.

As I sat on a bench at a metro station in Rome, holding the Zanini book about Bakhita while I waited for the train, the woman sitting next to me saw the saint's portrait on the front and began speaking to me in rapid Italian about how much she loved Bakhita, the beauty of the film, and the power of the story. Perhaps the power of her story and her image can resonate with black Italians like Pap Khouma and for African immigrants to Italy, who represent an unpopular vision of the continent. And perhaps Bakhita can change how we read and tell the history of slavery. It cries out for retelling.

Epilogue

In the draft law, it was solemnly stated that the freedom of blacks in the Empire had been secured in the eyes of the law. . . . Special passports were to be given to those domestic slaves who accompanied their masters on trips and to those freed blacks who left the Empire for abroad. Any domestic black who had no special passport was to be regarded as a slave and to be duly manumitted. Court procedures were to be initiated against those who attempted to take them abroad.

Y. Hakan Erdem,
Slavery in the Ottoman Empire and Its Demise, 1800–1909

This passage describes a small part of a group of laws drafted by the Ottoman government in 1882 to regularize the abolition of the slave trade in Africans and to punish those who continued to import black slaves into the empire. As the drafts of these laws make clear, the documentation of travel for black Ottoman subjects had become controversial, and Ottoman officials paid careful attention to the issue of passports for them. Negotiations continued through 1883 between Ottoman officials and the sultan, Abdulhamid II, and then between the sultan and the British embassy in Istanbul. They foundered over this question of travel and documentation: the British expressing concerns that all domestic slaves be issued "special certificates" when accompanying their masters on trips abroad and that proper papers be furnished "to all Ottoman vessels manned wholly or in part by African slaves."[1]

Sultan Abdulhamid II resisted the ratification of these laws, and negotiations dragged on through the decade, but the draft laws concerning the slave trade in Africans did pass in 1889 and were cemented with the Brussels Anti-slavery Conference later that year.[2] As the language of the negotiations makes clear, the very act of travel had become proscriptive, at least for black Ottoman subjects, who would from then on need passports or certificates permitting them voyage to and from the empire. And once Abdulhamid was deposed in 1909, the government of the Young Turks turned its attention to the release of Circassian slaves in the sultan's palaces. This was done to provide an example to the rest of the Ottoman population and to establish better relationships with the Circassians in the Caucasus, "at least some of whom had come to loathe the employment of their kin as slaves in the increasingly Western-oriented atmosphere of the early twentieth century."[3]

The Young Turks released these Circassian slaves, most of them women, in Istanbul and contacted Circassian settlements throughout Anatolia for their relatives to pick them up at Topkapi Palace.[4] This act of manumission also released these women into the tumultuous and rapidly changing political geography of the late Ottoman Empire, where the vagueness of imperial borders was sharpening into the more focused lines of nation-states. In the 1880s, Ottoman officials could register their opposition to the prohibition of the African slave trade by reminding the sultan that such laws had ignited controversy and turmoil along the important slave-trading networks of the Red Sea and the Indian Ocean, notably in the Hijaz. They could question the passing of such a law for Circassians by simply stating that "there remained no country called Circassia."[5] But in the years immediately preceding World War I, those certainties were evaporating for Ottomans. The old networks of the slave trade, in both Africans and in Circassians, now contradicted the assertion of a new, modern Ottoman state as imagined by the Young Turks. They released these hundreds of royal slaves in hopes, perhaps, of sending them "home." But the historical literature falls silent on how these former slaves were able to travel and what kind of documentation was necessary for them to do so. After World War I and the empire's end, the lines of the Ottoman map were redrawn into mandates of power for the British and the French. Did these changes turn the former slaves into refugees, along with so many millions of others who were displaced?

Old Maps, New Passports

Most of the writers in this book who owned slaves were nationalist leaders whose narratives reflect their increasingly keen sense of political participation in a particular country—Egypt, Sudan, or in the case of the late Ottoman Empire, the new nation of Turkey. They faced political uproar as dramatic as any experienced by their slaves, but these men and women possessed a clear sense of national belonging. Although Babikr Bedri and Halide Edib Adivar confronted exile in their lifetimes (he fled to Upper Egypt after the Mahdiyya; she temporarily exiled herself from Turkey in the early years of Ataturk's rule), they knew where to find their homes. I assume that Halide had the correct passport to enter New York City in the 1920s.

As this book has tried to show, the ideas of citizenship, migration, and homeland were infinitely more complicated for the former slaves. Their first journeys were violent and forced. Subsequent voyages, undergone when they were free, had to be made in secret or under the aegis of missionaries who could negotiate for their passport documentation with Ottoman, Egyptian, or European authorities. None of them—Şhemsigül, Salim, Iqbal, Sa'id Ağa, Daniel Sorur Pharim Deng, or Bakhita—ever returned to their places of origin.

That does not mean, though, that people from their homelands have not reclaimed them. While their narratives incorporate very few, if any, maps, their stories do offer paths back to their origins, particularly for later generations of people forced to travel similar roads. In her seminal essay "Prehistories of Globalization," Seteney Shami traces "the relationship between motion and identity" by juxtaposing the narratives of Şhemsigül, the Circassian slave in mid-nineteenth-century Egypt, and Shengul, a young Circassian woman who left Turkey in 1991 for her "homeland" in the Caucasus. Like Şhemsigül's story of loss, Shengul returns to the place of her family's origins feeling like a lonely foreigner. Shami sensitively discusses the great parallels between these movements—one from homeland into diaspora; the other out of diaspora back to the homeland—but what is most poignantly presented is Shengul's awareness of Şhemsigül's story. When asked by Seteney Shami, Shengul responded, "You mean the story of the girl who is sold to Egypt, raped by the slave trader, and beaten by his wife?" This awareness stunned Shami, but Shengul explained that a synopsis of the original article written by Ehud Toledano had been published in Turkey (in Turkish) in a volume called *Circassians in Print*.[6] Shami concluded, "Şhemsigül has now become part of Shengul's repertoire. Hers is not a forgotten story any more."[7] Yet, this reclamation comes clouded with some shame: "'I felt very sorry for this girl when I read the story,' Shengul said. 'I thought of translating the article into Circassian and publishing it here. Then I thought I should not give the Russians any more ammunition. They sold us in the past. I should not give them any more power in the present.'"[8] Shengul's origins uneasily bear the stain of slavery. Its history connects her to her home, but it is too shameful.

For slaves in the late decades of the Ottoman Empire, like refugees fleeing Sudan in more recent years, their identities and often their skin color stigmatized them. They needed papers to move from one country to another, whether they had chosen to make those voyages freely or had been forced into migration. Intermediaries like Monsignor Daniele Comboni spoke for them to the authorities until they were fluent enough in foreign languages to speak for themselves and to be able to persuade others of the authenticity of their own identities. They moved under cover through war zones like the Mahdiyya in Sudan along the Nile into Egypt, and from there to Italy or to England.

As discussed in the beginning of this book, refugees from Sudan staged massive demonstrations against the United Nations High Commission for Refugees in Cairo during the fall of 2005, protesting the legal limbo of their status in Egypt and their inability to get the requisite documentation to work legally in Cairo, to educate their children, or to be resettled in countries like the United States, Canada, or Australia. When the Egyptian police attacked the camps that the protesters had erected in Mustafa Mahmud Square, many fled even farther north across the Sinai into Israel. They fled, under cover, through the tensions of the Arab-Israeli conflict. Once there, as one refugee nicknamed Bob recounted, the power of a strong narrative was urgent. Facing Israeli border guards, Bob remembered, "We told them stories we knew from the news and maps to support the lie, but everything else was true."[9] When Bob and his companions told stories of their experience and used maps to support their lies, they presumed that in that summer of 2004 Israelis had heard about the violence of the Janjaweed in

Darfur. They also knew that had the guards found out they had been living for years in Egypt, the Sudanese would immediately be returned there. So he erased this part of his map, omitting years lived in Cairo after he made his way from Darfur.

In an admirable effort to show respect to these journeys, in *Out of Exile* Craig Walzer introduced each displaced person's experience with a map. All of the maps center on Sudan and Egypt. What distinguishes each map are small stars that point out the origins of each narrator's journey, with the names of their villages or cities. While this may help the reader to know the origins of this diaspora, only the narratives give the full extent of where these people have been, why they have been there, and what they have done.

As the refugees described in *Out of Exile* all make clear, correctly calibrating the details of where you were, when you were there, and what happened to you while you were there can make all the difference for officials responsible for the granting of asylum or even the documents that can legalize refugee status. As another refugee, Tarig Omar, described his experience in Cairo, trying to convince interrogators from the United Nations High Commission on Refugees is excruciating without the proper training: "I was lucky, but just imagine—thousands of refugees come and they have to give testimonies, but they don't know what to write or how to write it. It's not their job to be a lawyer, to know the law, or how to prepare a testimony in a good, legal way. Many times I wonder, what if I had not met the lawyer Mr. Suleiman, and if he hadn't introduced me to Barbara? I think I would not have gotten refugee status."[10] Even with that refugee status, Tarig was left for years in Egypt, being considered for resettlement in countries such as the United States, Canada, or Australia or waiting for Sudan to be safe enough for his return.

Perhaps the stories of slavery presented in this book can add dignity to the historical situation in which these refugees find themselves. At the time of this writing, the maps of their journey may be dramatically and permanently altered with the establishment of the world's newest state, South Sudan. May they return home freely, wherever they decide that home exists.

Reference Matter

Notes

Prologue

1. Forcier, "Divided at the Margins."

2. Abeer Allam and Michael Slackman, "Egyptian Police Kill at Least 23 Unarmed Sudanese Migrants," *New York Times*, December 30, 2005.

3. Michael Slackman, "After Cairo Police Attack, Sudanese Have Little but Rage," *New York Times*, January 3, 2006.

4. Gamal Nkrumah, "The Noose Tightens," *Al-Ahram Weekly*, January 5–11, 2006. Almost five years to the day, Egyptians protesting these same conditions launched a revolution against the government of President Husni Mubarak. The police also used water cannons against protesters as they prayed. This time, the police did not win the fight.

5. Mona Eltahawy, "The Arab World's Dirty Secret," *New York Times*, December 10, 2008.

6. Sills, "Surveying the Map of Slavery," p. 321.

7. Douglass, "Introduction," p. 8.

Chapter 1

1. The genre of *khitat* refers to what Nasser Rabbat calls "topographical/historical studies of cities." These "traditionally reported on a city's monuments, neighborhoods, and streets—in short, its architecture and urban history." For an insightful explanation of the history of this genre in Egypt, see Rabbat, "The Medieval Link," p. 30.

2. AlSayyad, "'Ali Mubarak's Cairo," p. 59.

3. Ibid.

4. Ibid., p. 60.

5. Mehrez, *Egyptian Writers*, p. 66.

6. Ibid., p. 68.

7. Hunter, *Egypt under the Khedives*, pp. 124–31.

8. J. Abu-Lughod, *Cairo*, p. 105.

9. Ibid., p. 56.

10. Mubarak, *Al-Khitat*, 3:53 (1886–89). For this chapter, I am relying on the older version of *Al-Khitat*. It is interesting, as I turned between the different editions, how the title of the 1886–89 edition is listed, by 'Ali Mubarak, as *Al-Khitat al-jadidah al-tawfiqiya*. But the 1994 edition, and most bibliographies and libraries, list it as *Al-Khitat al-tawfiqiya al-jadidah*, perhaps giving more honor to Khedive Tawfiq, under whose auspices the work was finished, than I have.

11. This passage is from ibid., 1:2–3, but I used the graceful translation provided by Michael J. Reimer in "Contradiction and Consciousness," p. 61.

12. AlSayyad, *Cairo*, p. 217. For a careful rendering of 'Ali Mubarak's position during the 'Urabi rebellion, see Schölch, *Egypt for the Egyptians*, pp. 264–68.

13. Ibid., p. 218.

14. Mehrez, *Egyptian Writers*, p. 67.

15. Rabbat, "The Medieval Link," p. 32.

16. Nora, "Between Memory and History," pp. 8–9.

17. The two most complete studies of slavery in Egypt depend quite heavily on 'Ali Mubarak as one of their primary sources of information: Baer, "Slavery in Nineteenth-Century Egypt" (1967); and Hilal, *Al-Raqiq* (1999). It is worth noting that more than three decades separate these two studies; even though Hilal has had access to archival material Baer never had, both saw in 'Ali Mubarak the best place to start.

18. The word *mamluk* means "owned" or "in the possession of."

19. In this discussion of slaves and slavery in *Al-Khitat*, I have chosen to adopt the same vocabulary that 'Ali Mubarak used.

20. Troutt Powell, *A Different Shade of Colonialism*, chap. 3.

21. Rabbat, "Who Was al-Maqrizi?," pp. 3–4.

22. Rabbat, "The Medieval Link," p. 32.

23. Like many Egyptian intellectuals of his time, 'Ali Mubarak does not identify the diverse ethnicities of Turkic, Turkish-speaking soldiers of the Fatimid, Mamluk, or Ottoman armies. They are always referred to as "Turks." This may have been learned from Europeans, who, as Metin Kunt has stated, referred to the Ottoman domains as "Turkey" when "none in the Islamic world nor any in Asia in general would have recognized the term." Kunt added, "In the Turkish language itself, the word 'Turkiye' had to be invented as a translation of European usage only around the turn of the twentieth century." See Kunt, *Ottomans and Safavids*, p. 191.

24. Lev, *State and Society in Fatimid Egypt*, p. 43.

25. Mubarak, *Al-Khitat*, p. 51 (1994).

26. Mubarak, *Al-Khitat*, 1:52 (1886–89).

27. Ibid., p. 42.

28. Ibid., p. 52.

29. Bacharach, "African Military Slaves."

30. These descriptions also come from J. Abu-Lughod, *Cairo*, p. 57.

31. Ibid., p. 54; see also p. 48.

32. Mubarak, *Al-Khitat*, 1:69 (1994).

33. J. Abu-Lughod, *Cairo*, p. 48.

34. Fayza Hassan, "How Green Was This Valley?," *Al-Ahram Weekly On-line*, October 22–28, 1998.

35. J. Abu-Lughod, *Cairo*, p. 93.

36. Ibid., p. 102.

37. Ibid., p. 105.

38. Toledano, "Late Ottoman Concepts," p. 494.

39. One reason that 'Ali Mubarak may have chosen to characterize all white slaves as *mamluks* was the incredible ethnic and racial diversity of the different Mamluk sultanates. From 1250 to 1390, the Arab historians characterized the Mamluks as *dawlat al-atrak*, or the Turkish sultanates. From 1390 to 1517, Circassian Mamluks, originally from the Caucasus, ruled Egypt and Syria. For more information, see Northrup, "The Bahri Mamluk Sultanate," pp. 250–51; and Garcin, "The Regime of the Circassian Mamluks," 1:640–1517.

40. Ayalon, "The Mamluks," p. 90.

41. Shaw, *History of the Ottoman Empire*, 1:113.

42. Ibid., p. 114.

43. Winter, "Re-emergence of the Mamluks," p. 96.

44. Ayalon, "The Mamluks," p. 91.

45. Winter, "Re-emergence of the Mamluks," p. 96.

46. Ibid., p. 97.

47. Ibid., p. 98.

48. Crecelius and Djaparidze, "Georgian Mamluks of Egypt," p. 327.

49. Koremezli, "Place of the Ottoman Empire," pp. 5–7.

50. Toledano, *Slavery and Abolition*, p. 32.

51. Ibid.

52. Ibid.

53. Shaham, "Masters, Their Freed Slaves," p. 165.

54. Ibid., p. 166.

55. Hilal, *Al-Raqiq*, p. 193.

56. Ibid., p. 209.

57. Baedeker, *Egypt, Handbook for Travellers*, p. 51.

58. Gerber, *Social Origins*, p. 150.

59. Walz, *Trade between Egypt and Bilad as-Sudan*, p. 3.

60. Ibid., p. 29.

61. Baer, "Slavery in Nineteenth Century Egypt," p. 419.

62. Walz, *Trade between Egypt and Bilad as-Sudan*, p. 25.

63. Baer, "Slavery in Nineteenth Century Egypt," pp. 427–29.

64. Ibid., p. 427.

65. O'Fahey, "Slavery and Society in Dar Fur," p. 85.

66. Sikainga, *Slaves into Workers*, pp. 8–13.

67. Johnson, "Structure of a Legacy," p. 79.

68. Hilal, *Al-Raqiq*, pp. 11–117.

69. Troutt Powell, *A Different Shade of Colonialism*, p. 118.

70. Baer, "Slavery in Nineteenth Century Egypt," pp. 420–21.

71. Hilal, *Al-Raqiq*, p. 239.

72. Naqod, *'Alaqat al-riqq fi al-mujtama' al-sudani*, p. 79.

73. For fuller discussions of this period in Egyptian history, see Fahmy, *All the Pasha's Men*; and Pollard, *Nurturing the Nation*.

74. Mubarak, *Al-Khitat*, 2:4 (1886–89). It was unusual for native-born Egyptians to be sent on these delegations. Dr. Nabrawi's talent had to have been outstanding.

75. Ibid., 17:4.

76. *Jariyah* is an Arabic term for a female slave commonly used in the days of 'Ali Mubarak. He also sometimes feminized the term *mamluk*.

77. Mubarak, *Al-Khitat*, 17:4 (1886–89).

78. Ibid., 8:82.

79. Ibid., 11:70–71.

80. Ibid., p. 71.

81. Ibid., 12:112 (Siwa); 15:5 (Kirdassa).

82. See Baer, "Slavery in Nineteenth Century Egypt," p. 418. Baer traced all of the references to slavery in 'Ali Mubarak's *Khitat*.

83. Mubarak, *Al-Khitat*, 14:53 (1886–89). Lucie Duff Gordon also recounted details, as she heard them, of what she called a "massacre at Gao," a village not far from the house in which she stayed in Luxor. In her account, however, the *shaykh* was never killed. Gordon, *Letters from Egypt*.

84. Mubarak, *Al-Khitat*, 14:53 (1886–89).

85. Hilal, *Al-Raqiq*, p. 218.

86. L. Gordon, *Letters from Egypt*.

87. Tignor, Review of Lady Duff Gordon's *Letters from Egypt*, p. 227.

88. 'Ali Mubarak's gratitude to the black official 'Anbar Effendi can also be found, though not written with as much detail, in his novel *'Alamuddin*. For a discussion of this experience, see my book *A Different Shade of Colonialism*, chap. 1.

89. Mubarak, *Al-Khitat*, 9:37–38 (1886–89).

90. Ibid., p. 38.

91. Ibid., pp. 38–39. For a full summary of 'Ali Mubarak's professional trajectory, see Hunter, *Egypt under the Khedives*, pp. 124–27.

92. Mubarak, *Al-Khitat*, 9:39 (1886–89).

93. Ibid. This famous section of *Al-Khitat* was also quoted in Mubarak, *Hayati*, pp. 8–9.

94. Hilal, *Al-Raqiq*, p. 261.

95. Ibid., p. 39.

96. Hunter, *Egypt under the Khedives*, p. 124.

97. Ibid., p. 126.

98. Mubarak, *Al-Khitat*, 9:47 (1886–89).

99. I. Abu-Lugod, "Transformation of the Egyptian Elite," p. 336.

100. Ibid.

101. Ibid., p. 337.

102. Ibid., p. 339.

103. McGregor, "Circassian Qubbas of Abbas Avenue, Khartoum," pp. 30–31.

104. Hunter, *Egypt under the Khedives*, pp. 131–35. Scholch also discussed, in wonderful detail, 'Ali Mubarak's intense negotiations with the leaders of the 'Urabi rebellion, in *Egypt for the Egyptians*, pp. 263–64, 267–68.

105. For more complete discussions of the 'Urabi Rebellion, refer to, e.g., Scholch, *Egypt for the Egyptians*; and Berque, *Egypt*.

106. Bierman, "Disciplining the Eye," p. 18.

107. Ibid., p. 21.

108. Ibid., p. 18.

109. Ibid., p. 13.

Chapter 2

1. I have written extensively about the simultaneity of the 'Urabi and Mahdi's rebellions and their impact on the relationship between Egyptian and Sudanese societies in *A Different Shade of Colonialism.*

2. Bedri, *Memoirs*, 1:vii. I have used both the Arabic versions of *Tarikh hayati* and the three translated volumes of *The Memoirs of Babikr Bedri*. To make translation easier, I excerpted the long passages found in this chapter from the English version.

3. Ibid., p. viii.

4. G. Sanderson, "The Modern Sudan," p. 445.

5. Ali, "Shaykh Babikr Badri's Autobiography," p. 75.

6. Hodgkin, "Educational Development in the Sudan," pp. 335–36.

7. Asad, "Memoirs of Babikr Bedri," p. 184.

8. Ibid.

9. Bedri, *Memoirs*, 1:219.

10. Ibid., p. 107.

11. Ibid., p. 109.

12. Ibid., pp. 225–26.

13. Grandin, "La vie très exemplaire," p. 530.

14. Ibid., p. 531.

15. Ibid., pp. 531–32.

16. This can be better demonstrated in my *Different Shade of Colonialism*, chap. 3.

17. Rhodes House Archives, Box G-26, "Letter to His Highness, Isma'il Pasha, Viceroy of Egypt."

18. Troutt Powell, *A Different Shade of Colonialism*, p. 118.

19. Foreign Office 141/95, anonymous letter to Raouf Pasha, governor general of Sudan, October 10, 1880.

20. C. Gordon, *Journals of Major-Gen. C. G. Gordon.*

21. All of the references to al-Zubayr are positive, and if his slave trade participation is mentioned (as it often is), Gordon uses it as a sign of al-Zubayr's potential for governance and leadership.

22. C. Gordon, September 17, 1884, 1:102.

23. F. Shaw, "The Story of Zebehr Pasha," p. 334.

24. Ibid., p. 334.

25. Ibid., p. 336.

26. Ibid., p. 569.

27. Ibid., p. 576.

28. Ibid.

29. Ibid., p. 577.

30. Ibid., p. 579.

31. Ibid., p. 581.
32. Ibid.
33. Ibid., p. 340.
34. Hilal, *Al-Raqiq*, pp. 356–59; 'Issa, *Hikayat min Daftar al-Watan*, pp. 240–41.
35. F. Shaw, "The Story of Zebehr Pasha," p. 340.
36. Ibid., p. 581.
37. Callaway and Helly, "Flora Shaw/Lady Lugard," pp. 83–84.
38. Bedri, *Memoirs*, 1:103n3. See also Hill, *Biographical Dictionary*, p. 391.
39. Bedri, *Memoirs*, 1:38.
40. Ibid., p. 112.
41. Ibid., p. 8.
42. Ibid., pp. 21, 37, 38, 41.
43. Ibid., pp. 53, 59, 89, 122.
44. Ibid., p. 141.
45. Ibid., pp. 156, 181,192, 204, 215.
46. Sikainga, *Slaves into Workers*, p. 29.
47. Bedri, *Memoirs*, 1:21.
48. Ibid., p. 25.
49. Ibid., p. 141.
50. Ibid., p. 152.
51. Ibid., p. 156.
52. Ibid., p. 180.
53. Ibid., p. 181.
54. Ibid., p. 184.
55. Ibid., p. 192.
56. Ibid., p. 204.
57. Ibid., p. 210.
58. Ibid., p. 215.
59. Ibid., p. 36.
60. Ibid., p. 38.
61. *Sabah al-khayr* means "good morning" in Arabic.
62. Bedri, *Memoirs*, 1:40.
63. Ibid.
64. Ibid., p. 41.
65. Ibid., p. 44.
66. Ibid., p. 48.
67. Ibid., pp. 49–50.
68. Ibid., p. 46.
69. Patterson, *Slavery as Social Death*, pp. 40–41.
70. Bedri, *Memoirs*, 2:125.
71. Ibid., p. 218.
72. Ibid., pp. 240–41.

73. Bedri, *Memoirs*, 1:241.
74. Sikainga, *Slaves into Workers*, p. 61.
75. Bredin, "Life Story of Yuzbashi 'Abdullah Adlan," p. 51.
76. Ibid., p. 76.
77. Ibid., pp. 130–31.
78. Ibid., pp. 131–32.
79. G. Sanderson, "The Modern Sudan," p. 451. On the next page, Sanderson distinguishes Babikr Bedri's autobiography as an example of one family's alliances.
80. L. Sanderson, "Memoirs of Babikr Bedri," p. 156.
81. Idris, *Conflict and Politics*, p. 25.
82. Ibid., pp. 31–32.
83. Ibid., p. 32.
84. Woodward, *Sudan*, p. 27.
85. Sikainga, *Slaves into Workers*, p. 66.
86. Manning, *Slavery and African Life*, pp. 161–62.
87. Sikainga, *Slaves into Workers*, p. 37.
88. Ibid.
89. Bedri, *Memoirs*, 2:80–81.
90. Ibid., p. 87.
91. Ibid., p. 88.
92. Ibid., p. 90.
93. Ibid., pp. 94, 104.
94. Ibid., p. 100.
95. Ibid., p. 111.
96. Ibid., pp. 118–19.
97. Ibid., pp. 126, 241.
98. Ibid., p. 241.
99. Ibid., pp. 242–43.
100. Ibid., p. 314.
101. Ibid., p. 316.
102. Ibid., p. 338.
103. Ibid., p. 359.
104. Ibid.
105. Ibid.
106. Ibid., p. 156.
107. Ibid., pp. 163–64.
108. Ibid., p. 311.
109. Ibid., pp. 312–13.
110. Ibid., p. 313.
111. Ibid., pp. 127, 132, 136.
112. Ibid., pp. 179–81.
113. Ibid., p. 161.

Chapter 3

1. Sudan Archive (hereafter SAD), 12/51.
2. SAD, 427/7/16 (v), Journal of R. V. Savile, February 10, 1910.
3. Troutt Powell, "Bodies Caught on Film."
4. McBride, *Impossible Witnesses*, p. 5.
5. Wilson, *I Was a Slave*, pp. 55–56. How was a collective memory of slavery shaped? Anthropologists of Sudanese culture have reinforced Salim's lament in studies about the growth of different kinds of spirit-possession cults among urban communities of slaves, former slaves, and sometimes slave owners living in Khartoum in the late nineteenth century, in which stories and figures important in the history of Sudanese slavery were reenacted, taking temporary "possession" of people in the cult. For more information on this, see Makris, *Changing Masters*; and Boddy, *Wombs and Alien Spirits*. These are important studies, critical for a deeper understanding of the legacy of slavery in the Nile Valley. Though spirits representing different figures of the slave trade or enslavement experience "possessed" many, those practicing *zar* and *tumbura* (ceremonies of spirit possession) did not "own" their memories in the ways that published narrators (slave autobiographers?) of their own enslavement did. The narratives of *zar bore* and *tumbura* practices are never circulated under the names of those who lived such experiences.
6. This is the name of the village as spelled out by Salim in his narrative.
7. Wilson, *I Was a Slave*, p. 217.
8. Johnson, "Salim Wilson," p. 27.
9. Walz, "Bakhita Kwashe."
10. It is important to note that she herself was never a slave.
11. Johnson, "Divinity Abroad," p. 174.
12. Sharkey, "Christians among Muslims," p. 58.
13. Ibid., p. 65.
14. Ibid., pp. 71–72.
15. Mynors, "Adventures of a Darfur Slave," p. 273.
16. Ibid.
17. Ibid.
18. Ibid.
19. Ibid., p. 274.
20. Ibid.
21. Ibid., pp. 274–75.
22. Ibid., p. 275.
23. Wheeler, "Freed Slaves," p. 17.
24. Ibid.
25. Gomez, *Exchanging Our Country Marks*, p. 154.
26. Ibid.
27. Ibid., p. 167.
28. Wood, *Blind Memory*, p. 241.

29. This was arguably the case, despite the fact that complex and fascinating accounts of slavery had been published in English for centuries. Olaudah Equiano first published *The Interesting Narrative of the Life of Olaudah Equiano, or Gustavus Vassa, the African* in 1789, some twenty years after Phillis Wheatley, the former slave and poet, published her work. It is interesting to think that only recently, the authenticity of Equiano's origins in Africa were challenged by the scholar Vincent Carretta, in *Equiano, the African*. For a brief and interesting discussion of this, see "Olaudah Equiano: A Critical Biography," http://www.brycchancarey.com/equiano/biog.htm.

30. Wood, *Blind Memory*, p. 243.

31. Ibid.

32. Johnson, "Divinity Abroad," p. 177.

33. McBride, *Impossible Witnesses*, p. 3.

34. Ibid.

35. Ibid.

36. Ibid., pp. 5–6.

37. Wilson, *Jehova-Nissi*, p. 4.

38. Ibid., p. 5.

39. Kathish, *The Ethiopia Valley*, p. 4.

40. Ibid.

41. Davis and Gates, *The Slave's Narrative*, p. xxiii.

42. Ibid., p. xxviii.

43. Ibid.

44. Johnson, "Black Evangelist," p. 32.

45. Interestingly, this published version of Salim's life does not include a preface by an editor or the author.

46. Rydell, "'Darkest Africa,'" p. 138.

47. Ibid., p. 142.

48. Wells et al., *The Reason Why*, p. 10.

49. Robert Rydell notes in his introduction to *The Reason Why* that a special Jubilee day was set aside for black audiences. The African American paper the *Indianapolis Freeman* objected to this, with the headline "No Nigger Day!" The editors of this paper also objected to the pamphlet that Douglass and Ida B. Wells were planning, in an editorial titled "No 'Nigger Day,' No 'Nigger Pamphlet'!" Douglass and Wells worried that this, too, would humiliate African Americans "in the eyes of the world" (Wells et al., *The Reason Why*, p. xxvii).

50. Wilson, *I Was a Slave*, pp. 152–53.

51. Ibid.

52. Ibid., p. 154.

53. Ibid., p. 153.

54. Ibid., p. 129.

55. Ibid.

56. Ibid., p. 144.

57. Davis and Gates, *The Slave's Narrative*, p. xxvii.

58. Ibid.
59. Wilson, *I Was a Slave*, pp. 167–68.
60. Ibid.
61. Ibid., pp. 201–2.
62. Ibid., p. 203.
63. Ibid., p. 204.
64. Ibid., pp. 206–7.
65. Ibid., p. 216.
66. Ibid., p. 222.
67. Ibid., p. 227.
68. Ibid., p. 230.
69. Ibid., p. 233.
70. Ibid., pp. 234–35.
71. Johnson, "Divinity Abroad," pp. 176–77.
72. Ibid., p. 237.
73. Ibid., p. 238.
74. Johnson, "Black Evangelist," p. 29.
75. Ibid.
76. Ibid., p. 33.
77. Kathish, *The Ethiopia Valley*, p. 40.
78. Ibid., p. 44.
79. Ibid., p. 45.
80. Ibid., p. 46.
81. Wilson, *I Was a Slave*, p. 16.
82. Johnson, "Divinity Abroad," p. 179.
83. Fryer, *Staying Power*, pp. 228–29, 300.
84. Rossum, "'A Vision of Black Englishness,'" p. 14.
85. Wilson, *I Was a Slave*, p. 7.
86. Johnson, "Black Evangelist," p. 38.
87. Lienhardt, *Divinity and Experience*, p. 105.
88. Johnson, "Black Evangelist," p. 36.

Chapter 4

1. Badran, *Feminists, Islam, and Nation*, pp. 33–34.
2. Edib, *Memoirs*, p. 4.
3. Sonmez, "The Novelist Halide Edib Adivar," pp. 1–2.
4. Baron, *Egypt as a Woman*, pp. 185–86.
5. Ibid., p. 18.
6. Ibid.
7. Troutt Powell, *A Different Shade of Colonialism*, chap. 2.
8. Sophie Basch, preface to Hanoum, *Le harem imperiale*, p. xvii.
9. During these same decades, Egyptian and Ottoman authors also addressed the issue of slavery in their plays and novels. For example, in the late 1860s, Ahmet Midhat

Pasha, a prolific writer of novels and plays in Turkish, wrote a play called *Esaret* (The slave girl), deeply critical of how the slave trade separated children from their families. Other Ottoman playwrights also staged plays about slavery and marriage, as did the Cairo-based novelist Jurji Zaydan, in particular his novel *Al-Mamluk al-sharid* (The noble slave).

10. Huda Sha'rawi died before completing the dictation of her memoirs to her secretary, 'Abd al-Hamid Fahmy Mursi, and it was he who translated her French dictation into Arabic, edited the notes, and prepared them for publication. See Kahf, "Packaging 'Huda,'" p. 152; and Al-Guindi, "Veiling Resistance," p. 60.

11. Toledano, *Slavery and Abolition*, p. 54.

12. Baron, *Egypt as a Woman*, p. 165.

13. Toledano, *Slavery and Abolition*, p. 59.

14. In his important and influential chapter, "The Other Face of Harem Bondage," in *Slavery and Abolition*, Ehud Toledano discusses how he found Şemsigül's narrative in the police registers, known as the Zabtiyya, in the National Archives of Egypt. Liat Kozma, in *Policing Egyptian Women*, has also explored these registers to find voices of slaves and other marginalized women.

15. Toledano, *Slavery and Abolition*, p. 62.

16. Ibid., p. 67.

17. Ibid., p. 72.

18. Ibid., p. 80.

19. Derluguian, *The Unlikely Abolitionists*, p. 16.

20. Ibid., p. 58.

21. Ibid., p. 61.

22. Sha'rawi, *Mudhakirat*, pp. 37–38.

23. Her maternal great-grandfather had been accused by Shaykh Shamil of collaborating with the Russians, and a generation later, Huda's father was accused by Egyptian nationalists of colluding with the British to weaken the nationalist revolt of Colonel Ahmad 'Urabi Pasha. Huda spent many pages in the beginning of her memoirs defending the memory of her father and did so again in reconstructing the bravery of this maternal relative.

24. Sha'rawi, *Mudhakirat*, p. 39.

25. It is important to remember that Huda's father died suddenly when she was five years old. She worked hard to reconstruct tender moments from his life.

26. Sha'rawi, *Mudhakirat*, p. 40.

27. "The Circassian Exodus," *Times of London*, February 7, 1860.

28. Ibid.

29. "The Circassian Exodus," *Times of London*, December 7, 1864.

30. Hanoum, *Le harem imperiale*, p. 52.

31. Ibid., p. 56.

32. Ibid., pp. 74–75.

33. Ibid.

34. Ibid., p. 101.

35. Ibid., p. 103. These translations from the French are mine, but I have also cross-checked this with the translations made in 1925 from the English edition: Hanimefendi, *Imperial Harem of the Sultans*, p. 87.

36. Hanimefendi, *Imperial Harem of the Sultans*, pp. 79–80.

37. Ibid., p. 80.

38. Ibid., p. 92.

39. Ibid., p. 95.

40. Ahmed, "Between Two Worlds," p. 162.

41. Ibid.

42. Sha'rawi, *Mudhakirat*, p. 41.

43. Ibid., p. 51.

44. Ibid., p. 52.

45. Kahf, "Packaging 'Huda,'" p. 160. The translation is Kahf's.

46. Ibid.

47. Sha'rawi, *Mudhakirat*, p. 71.

48. Ibid., p. 74.

49. Ibid., p. 89.

50. Ibid.

51. European-style department stores began to be established in Cairo and Alexandria in the late nineteenth century. Uri Kupferschmidt names the stores of the Austrian Orosdi-Back family being established in Egypt in the 1860s; both she and Beth Baron note that these and other chains were well established by the 1880s. Assuming from Huda's memoirs that she was still quite a young woman when visiting the department store, we can estimate that Huda experienced this encounter in the late 1890s or perhaps at the turn of the century. See Baron, "Unveiling in Early Twentieth-Century Egypt," p. 374; and Kupferschmidt, "Who Needed Department Stores in Egypt?," pp. 178–82.

52. Sha'rawi, *Mudhakirat*, p. 60.

53. Kahf, "Huda Sha'rawi's *Mudhakirat*," p. 7.

54. Sha'rawi, *Mudhakirat*, p. 60.

55. Edib, *Memoirs*, p. 7.

56. Ibid., p. 49. Zeynep Beril Saydun also mentions Halide's observations about race in her society, in *Construction of Nationalism and Gender*, pp. 36–39.

57. Edib, *Memoirs*, p. 82.

58. Ibid., p. 83.

59. These memoirs were written first in English in 1924–25, when Halide was in exile in New York City and teaching at Columbia University, not far from Harlem. Her vocabulary of racial identity here is in English, not Turkish. It is fascinating to think that she may have had experiences during the Harlem Renaissance that contributed to her racial lexicography as well.

60. Edib, *Memoirs*, p. 90.

61. Ibid., pp. 166–67.

62. Ibid., p. 167.

63. Ibid., p. 168.

64. Ibid.

65. Ibid., p. 169.

66. Ibid., p. 231.

67. There remains a possibility, which I have not been able to document, that Huda and Halide had opportunities to meet. Huda attended the International Women's Conference in Istanbul in 1935, held, interestingly enough, in Yildiz Palace, one of the places Leyla Saz Hanimefendi used to describe the experiences of slaves. Halide was no longer in exile at that time and was a prominent politician in Istanbul. Huda surprised everyone, notably Ataturk, Turkey's first president, with her fluent Turkish. See Ibrahim, *Huda Sha'rawi*, 1:214–15.

68. Erdem, "Preface," in Olpak, *Biographie d'une famille d'esclaves*, pp. 14–15. This manuscript is translated from Turkish into French. The French translation into English is mine.

69. Olpak, *Biographie d'une famille d'esclaves*, p. 27.

70. Ibid., pp. 29–30.

71. Ibid., p. 32.

72. Ibid.

73. Ibid., p. 33.

74. Ibid., p. 39.

75. Ibid., p. 24.

Chapter 5

1. Nikkel, "Salim Charles Wilson," p. 15.

2. Walz, "Bakhita Kwashe."

3. Comboni to Father Mazza, Alexandria, January 2, 1861, no. 53, www.comboni .org/index.php?sez=scritti&id=53.

4. Troutt Powell, *A Different Shade of Colonialism*, chap. 5.

5. Comboni to Mazza, Aden, January 23, 1861, no. 57, www.comboni.org/index .php?sez =scritti&id=57.

6. Comboni to Mazza, Aden, January 13, 1861, no. 56, www.comboni.org/index .php?sez =scritti&id=56.

7. Wheeler, "Freed Slaves," p. 21.

8. Johnson, "Divinity Abroad," p. 178.

9. Wheeler, "Freed Slaves," p. 21.

10. Comboni to Mazza, Aden, January 13, 1861, no. 56.

11. Comboni to the president of the Society of Cologne, Cairo, December 27, 1867, "The First African Colony in Central Africa at the Feet of Pius IX," www.comboni.org/index.php ?Lingua=EN&ca=10008&CodScritto=229&s-1.

12. Ibid.

13. Ibid.

14. Ibid.

15. As listed by Comboni himself in his letter to the president of the Cologne Society for the Aid of Poor Blacks, October 4, 1863, www.comboni.org/index.php?sez =scritti&id=105.

16. Walz continues, in "Bakhita Kwashe," by adding that in "all of the literature of the period dealing with the educated graduates of the Italian schools, whether in Verona or elsewhere in Europe, these terms were used. Even after they returned to the Sudan, *moretta/moretto* continued to be applied to these adepts, regardless of whether or not they were in the mission.

17. Comboni to president of the Society of Cologne, October 4, 1863, no. 105, paragraph 759.

18. Duncan, "Italian Identity and the Risks of Contamination," p. 101.

19. Ratti, "Comboni Sisters."

20. Wheeler, "Freed Slaves," p. 22.

21. Walz, "Bakhita Kwashe."

22. Ibid.

23. Ibid.

24. Ibid.

25. Ibid.

26. Ibid.

27. Ibid.

28. Comboni to Mother Emilie Julien, Khartoum, June 4, 1873, no. 503, www.comboni .org/index.php?sez=scritti&id=503.

29. Walz, "Bakhita Kwashe."

30. Ibid.

31. Ratti, "Comboni Sisters," p. 84. Ratti does not specify the source of this conversation.

32. Walz, "Bakhita Kwashe."

33. Ibid. This institute became Saint Joseph's Church and still works with Sudanese, Somali, and Eritrean refugees.

34. Ibid.

35. Ratti, "Comboni Sisters," p. 85.

36. Pierli and Ratti, "Sr Mary Josephine Zeinab," p. 34.

37. Ibid., p. 35.

38. Ibid., p. 36.

39. Ibid.

40. Ibid., p. 37.

41. Ibid.

42. In September 1860, Italian forces seized the fortress of the neighboring city of Castelfidardo from the French armies defending it for the Papal States. For a discussion of the battle, see www.comune.castelfidardo.an.it/Visitatori/Storia/pillole/battaglia.htm.

43. Beales and Biagini, *Risorgimento*, p. 1.

44. "The Syllabus of Errors Condemned by Pius IX," http://www.papalencyclicals .net/Pius09/p9syll.htm.

45. Halperin, "Church and State," p. 74.

46. Ibid., p. 75.

47. Ibid., p. 76.

48. Ratti, "Comboni Sisters," p. 38.

49. Ibid., p. 39.

50. Ibid.

51. Ibid., p. 40.

52. Ibid.

53. Scaraffia, "Christianity Has Liberated Her," p. 250.

54. Ibid., p. 254.

55. Ibid., p. 257.

56. Ibid., p. 259.

57. Ibid., p. 264.

58. Pharim Deng was his given name, his master named him Sorur (Arabic for "plea-sure" or "joy"), and Daniel was his baptismal name. All of the journeys of the former slaves in this book can be mapped by their names.

59. From "Slave and Priest" (biography in English), translator unknown, ACR, Sezi-one A, Casella 30, Busta 1-1, "Daniele Surur," pp. 16, 24.

60. Ibid.

61. De Giorgi, "Tra Africa e Europa," pp. 70–71. Translated by Daniel Lammendola.

62. These basic details of Daniel Sorur Pharim Deng's life are drawn from "Slave and Priest," the manuscript from the ACR; Nikkel, "Daniel Sorur Farim Deng," p. 43; and de Giorgi, "Tra Africa e Europe," pp. 67–70.

63. De Giorgi, "Tra Africa e Europe," pp. 71–72.

64. Comboni to Surur and Morzal, Rome, July 23, 1877, www.comboni.org/index.php ?sez=scritti&id=709.

65. Nikkel, "Daniel Sorur Farim Deng," pp. 43–44.

66. De Giorgi, "Tra Africa e Europe," p. 74.

67. Ibid. He does not offer details of this encounter in his article but cites one of So-rur's own writings, "Nero della tribu dei Denka." De Giorgi also found details from an obituary about Daniel Sorur: "Il Rev. P. Daniele Sorur. Nero della tribu dei Dinka. Mis-sionario dell'Africa centrale. Cenni biografici," p. 45.

68. De Giorgi, "Tra Africa e Europe," p. 75.

69. Ibid., p. 71.

70. See Saidiya Hartman's touching book *Lose Your Mother*.

71. Daniele Sorur Pharim Deng, "La pene dei neri schiavi in Africa." The edition I found in the Archivio Comboniani was edited by Father Renato Boccassino and pub-lished in *Euntes Docete* 1 (1964): 59. English translation by Daniel Lammendola, pp. 5, 7.

72. Deng, "La pene dei neri schiavi," p. 62 (English, pp. 6–7).

73. Deng, "La pene dei neri schiavi," p. 72.

74. "Slave and Priest," ACR, pp. 25–26.

75. Ibid., p. 26.

76. De Giorgi, "Tra Africa e Europe," p. 70n11. De Giorgi, quoting from D. Sorur, "Memorie scritte dal R. P. D. Sorur Pharim," *Nigrizia* (1888): 113.

77. De Giorgi, "Tra Africa e Europe," p. 71n16 (also quoting from Sorur, "Memorie scritte," pp. 114–15).

78. Deng, "La pene dei neri schiavi," p. 56 (English, pp. 4–5).

79. Ibid., p. 74 (English, p. 14).

80. Ibid., p. 62 (English, p. 7).

81. De Giorgi, "Tra Africa e Europe," p. 98, quoting from D. Sorur, "Che cosa sono I Negri? [Who are the Blacks?]," ACR, pp. 1–4, 34–35.

82. Ibid.

83. Nikkel, "Daniel Sorur Farim Deng," p. 44.

84. Ibid., p. 44n2.

85. De Giorgi, "Tra Africa e Europe," pp. 78–79.

86. Ibid., p. 78.

87. "Qual'e il mio paese natio?," ACR, A/30/2/0, as quoted in De Giorgi, "Tra Africa e Europe," pp. 79–80. Daniel Sorur also published memoirs in *Nigrizia* in 1888. Volume numbers for *Nigrizia* are not available, and I ask that readers rely on De Giorgi's copious notes.

88. De Giorgi, "Tra Africa e Europe," p. 86.

89. Ibid., p. 87.

90. Ibid., p. 92.

Chapter 6

1. Pap Khouma, "My Life Obstacles as a Black Italian," *La repubblica*, December 12, 2009, http://www.repubblica.it/cronaca/2009/12/12/news/io_nero_italiano_e_la_mia _vita_ad_ostacoli-1820188/.

2. D'Attilia, "A Tribute from an Admirer," p. iii.

3. Zanini, *Bakhita*, p. 5.

4. Ibid., p. 8.

5. This interview was conducted in Arabic at the Saint Josephine Bakhita Center for Women at the Sacred Heart Cathedral in June 2004, with the help of the Canossian Daughters of Charity in Cairo and Father Cosmo, the priest at Sacred Heart. The interview with these gracious women could not have been conducted without the gentle help and concern of Abuna Ibrahim Riyad, a Coptic priest of the Church of the Sacred Virgin, Dokki, Cairo.

6. "Notebook of the Black Canossian Mother," p. 1. Memoirs of Sister Giuseppina Bakhita dictated by her to a nun in Schio (1910), held in the Canossian Daughters of Charity Archive. English translation by Daniel Lammendola. See also Zanini, *Bakhita*, p. 16. Zanini agrees that Bakhita mentioned these mountains very specifically, many years after she had last seen them.

7. Beswick, *Sudan's Blood Memory*, p. 153. See also "The Daju Peoples of Sudan and Chad," http://strategyleader.org/profiles/daju.html.

8. "Notebook of the Black Canossian Mother," p. 1.

9. Ibid.

10. Sacra Congregatio (1975), p. 2, Canossian Daughters of Charity Archive. Translated by Daniel Lammendola. This document belongs to a huge file created to propose Bakhita's beatification and canonization to the Vatican.

11. "Notebook of the Black Canossian Mother," p. 2.

12. Ibid., p. 5.

13. I am following Bakhita's orally dictated map of cities here. She seems to have had an especially clear sense of geography and where she was during these years.

14. "Notebook of the Black Canossian Mother," p. 6.

15. Ibid.

16. Ibid., pp. 6–7.

17. Ibid., p. 7.

18. Zanini, *Bakhita*, p. 184.

19. Ibid., pp. 184, 79.

20. Ibid., p. 79.

21. Ibid., p. 81.

22. Ibid., pp. 81–82.

23. "Beatificationis et Canonizationis Servae dei Iosephina Bakhita," Sororis Professae Instituti Filiarum a Caritate, Sacra Congregatio Pro Causis Sanctorum, Positio Super Virtutibus (1975). These are official documents of the Catholic Church prepared for Bakhita's beatification and canonization held in the Canossian Daughters of Charity Archive. They also include the testimonies of many of Bakhita's contemporaries. I cannot express enough gratitude to Mother Velia and Mother Erica for their generous help in gathering more than five hundred pages in testimonials on Bakhita's behalf when I visited the headquarters of the Canossian Daughters of Charity in Rome in May 2009. Mother Velia remembered meeting Saint Bakhita and the warmth of her smile.

24. Zanini, *Bakhita*, p. 43.

25. Zanolini, *Tale of Wonder*, p. 123.

26. Adanhounme, "Du bon usage," p. 144.

27. See the Web site of the Canossian Daughters of Charity, http://www.canossiansisters.org/who.html. The Canossian Daughters' first mission overseas began in 1860.

28. Zanini, *Bakhita*, pp. 68–69. Zanini writes that it was this future pope (and saint) who examined Bakhita at the Institute of the Catechumens.

29. Beales and Biagini, *The Risorgimento*, p. 3.

30. Zanolini, *Tale of Wonder*, p. 201.

31. Zanini, *Bakhita*, p. 80nn4, 5. Zanini thinks she meant the Sudanese and Africans as a whole in her statement about "my people."

32. Duncan, "Italian Identity," p. 101.

33. Andall, "Immigration and the Legacy of Colonialism," p. 205.

34. "Notebook of the Black Canossian Mother," p. 5.

35. Zanini quotes her as saying, "Mi, povera negra, mi povera negra!" Bakhita never learned Italian but communicated increasingly well in Venetian dialect. On her many tours across the country, other nuns translated for her. Zanini, *Bakhita*, p. 66.

36. Ibid., p. 155.

37. Ibid., p. 86.

38. Zanolini, *Tale of Wonder*, p. 201.

39. Zanini, *Bakhita*, p. 142.

40. Ibid., p. 139. Apparently Bakhita also amused her sister nuns by dancing traditional dances during recreation and getting them to join her. In the 2009 Italian television film about her, she wins over the villagers of Mirano by teaching them to dance.

41. Ibid., p. 184.

42. Sacra Congregatio, 1975. This quotation comes from the collected summaries of her life (from the text XXXIII 6 Ord. *ex off.*, Sister Clotilde Sella, *Summ.*, pp. 227–28), paragraph 517.

43. Zanini, *Bakhita*, pp. 100–101.

44. Jok, *War and Slavery in Sudan*, pp. 28–41.

45. Mahmud and Baldo, *Human Rights Abuses*, pp. 1–33.

46. Interview held at the Sacred Heart Cathedral, Sakakini, Cairo, June 2004.

47. Adanhounme, "Du bon usage," p. 135.

48. Ibid., p. 136.

49. Guerrini, "Bakhita," p. 20.

50. Adanhounme, "Du bon usage," p. 137.

51. Ibid., p. 142.

52. Ibid., p. 153.

53. Copeland, "Building Up a Household of Faith," p. 56.

54. Ibid., p. 58.

55. Ibid.

56. Ibid., p. 62.

57. *Corriere della sera*, March 22, 2009. The DVD is now available with English subtitles.

58. Father Herald Joseph Brock, "CFR Sudan Mission," http://cfrsudan.blogspot.com/2009/06/mission-team-6-torit-3_05.html.

Epilogue

1. Erdem, *Slavery in the Ottoman Empire*, p. 140.

2. Ibid., p. 144.

3. Ibid., pp. 147–48.

4. Ibid., p. 148.

5. Ibid., p. 139.

6. Shami, "Prehistories of Globalization," p. 201.

7. Ibid., p. 202.

8. Ibid.

9. "We Wanted Israel's Protection. That Was All," in Walzer, *Out of Exile*, p. 221.

10. "A Good Actor in a Bad Movie," in ibid., p. 76. Barbara, in this quote, is Dr. Barbara Harrell-Bond, formerly of the Center for Forced Migration Studies at the American University in Cairo.

Bibliography

Archives

Archivio Comboniani Roma (ACR)

Canossian Daughters of Charity Archive, Rome. This archive includes "Vicentina Beatificationis et Canonizationis Servae dei Iosephina Bakhita," Sororis Professae Instituti Filiarum a Caritate, Positio Super Virtutibus; all of the documents and testimonies for beatification and canonization of Josephine Bakhita; and *Quaderno di madre moretta canossiana* [Notebook of the black Canossian mother].

Foreign Office, Public Record Office, Kew Gardens, London

Rhodes House Archives, Oxford University, British and Foreign Anti-Slavery Society Papers

Sudan Archive, University of Durham (SAD), UK

Online Archives

Missionari Comboniani, "Scritti" [Letters], www.comboni.org/index.php?sez=scritti&id

Papal Encyclicals, http://www.papalencyclicals.net

Published Sources

Abu-Lughod, Ibrahim. "Transformation of the Egyptian Elite: Prelude to the 'Urabi Revolt." *Middle East Journal* 21, no. 3 (1967).

Abu-Lughod, Janet L. *Cairo: 1001 Years of the City Victorious.* Princeton, NJ: Princeton University Press, 1971.

Adanhounme, Armel Brice. "Du bon usage de la mémoire de l'esclavage des noirs comme un possible capital de redemption: L'exemple de Bakhita" [How the good use of the memory of the slavery of blacks can be a possible source of redemption: The example of Bakhita]. *Theologiques* 13, no. 2 (2005).

Ahmed, Leila. "Between Two Worlds: The Formation of a Turn-of-the-Century Feminist." In *Life/Lines: Theorizing Women's Autobiography,* edited by Bella Brodzki and Celeste Schenk. Ithaca, NY: Cornell University Press, 1988.

Al-Guindi, Fadwa. "Veiling Resistance." *Fashion Theory: The Journal of Dress, Body, and Culture* 3, no. 1 (1993).

Ali, Nasr el Hag. "Shaykh Babikr Badri's Autobiography: *Ta'rikh hayati.*" *Sudan Notes and Records* 48 (1967).

AlSayyad, Nezzar . "'Ali Mubarak's Cairo: Between the Testimony of '*Alamuddin* and the Imaginary of the *Khitat*." In *Making Cairo Medieval*, edited by Nezar AlSayyad, Irene A. Bierman, and Nasser Rabbat. Oxford, UK: Lexington Books, 2005.

———. *Cairo: Histories of a City*. Cambridge, MA: Harvard University Press, 2011.

Andall, Jacqueline. "Immigration and the Legacy of Colonialism." In *Italian Colonialism: Legacy and Memory*, edited by Jacqueline Andall and Derek Duncan. Oxford: Peter Lang Press, 2005.

Asad, Talal. "The Memoirs of Babikr Bedri." *Africa: Journal of the International African Institute* 40, no. 2 (1970).

Ayalon, David. "The Mamluks: The Mainstay of Islam's Military Might." In *Slavery in the Islamic Middle East*, edited by Shaun Marmon. Princeton, NJ: Markus Wiener Press, 1999.

Bacharach, Jere L. "African Military Slaves in the Muslim Middle East." Black Past.org: Remembered and Reclaimed. 2007–11. http://www.blackpast.org/?q=perspectives/african-military-slaves-muslim-middle-east.

Badran, Margot. *Feminists, Islam, and Nation: Gender and the Making of Modern Egypt*. Princeton, NJ: Princeton University Press, 1995.

Baedeker, K. *Egypt, Handbook for Travellers*. Leipzig: Baedeker, 1885.

Baer, Gabriel. "Slavery in Nineteenth Century Egypt." *Journal of African History* 8, no. 3 (1967).

Baron, Beth. *Egypt as a Woman: Nationalism, Gender, and Politics*. Berkeley: University of California Press, 2005.

———. "Unveiling in Early Twentieth-Century Egypt: Practical and Symbolic Considerations." *Middle East Studies* 25, no. 3 (1989).

Beales, Derek, and Eugenio F. Biagini. *The Risorgimento and the Unification of Italy*. London: Longman, 2002.

Bedri, Babikr. *The Memoirs of Babikr Bedri*. Translated by Yousef Bedri and George Scott. Vols. 1–2. London: Oxford University Press, 1969.

Berque, Jacques. *Egypt: Imperialism and Revolution*. Translated by Jean Stewart. New York: Praeger, 1972.

Beswick, Stephanie. *Sudan's Blood Memory: The Legacy of War, Ethnicity and Slavery in South Sudan*. Rochester, NY: University of Rochester Press, 2004.

Bierman, Irene A. "Disciplining the Eye: Perceiving Medieval Cairo." In *Making Cairo Medieval*, edited by Nezar AlSayyad, Irene A. Bierman, and Nasser Rabbat. Oxford, UK: Lexington Books, 2005.

Boddy, Janice. *Wombs and Alien Spirits*. Madison: University of Wisconsin Press, 1989.

Bredin, G. R. F. "The Life Story of Yuzbashi 'Abdullah Adlan." *Sudan Notes and Records* 42 (1961).

Callaway, Helen, and Dorothy O. Helly. "Flora Shaw/Lady Lugard." In *Western Women and Imperialism*, edited by Nupur Chaudhuri and Margaret Strobel. Bloomington: Indiana University Press, 1992.

Carretta, Vincent. *Equiano, the African: Biography of a Self-Made Man*. Athens: University of Georgia Press, 2005.

Comboni Institute. *Daniel Comboni: Missionary, Father and Prophet.* Verona: The Comboni Institutes, Coop. Novastampa di Verona, n.d.

Copeland, M. Shawn. "Building Up a Household of Faith: Dom Cyprian Davis, O.S.B. and the Work of History." *U.S. Catholic Historian* 28, no. 1 (2010).

Crecelius, Dan, and Gotcha Djaparidze. "Relations of the Georgian Mamluks of Egypt with Their Homeland in the Last Decades of the Eighteenth Century." *Journal of the Economic and Social History of the Orient* 45, no. 3 (2002).

D'Attilia, Miela Fagiolo. "A Tribute from an Admirer." In *Bakhita: A Saint for the Third Millennium*, edited by Roberto Italo Zanini. Rome: Orca Printing and Advertising, 2000.

Davis, Charles T., and Henry Louis Gates Jr. "Introduction." In *The Slave's Narrative*, edited by Charles T. Davis and Henry Louis Gates Jr. New York: Oxford University Press, 1985.

De Giorgi, Fulvio. "Tra Africa e Europa: Daniele Sorur Pharim Den" [Between Africa and Europe: Daniele Sorur Pharim Den]. *Archivio Comboniano Anno* 42, no. 1 (2004).

Deng, Daniele Sorur Pharim. "La pene dei negri schiavi in Africa" [The suffering of black slaves in Africa]. Edited by R. Boccassino. Rome: Euntes Docete, 1964.

Derluguian, Liubov. *The Unlikely Abolitionists: The Russian Struggle against the Slave Trade in the Caucasus, 1800–1864.* PhD diss., Department of History, State University of New York, Binghamton, 1997. OCLC's Experimental Thesis Catalog (United States).

Douglass, Frederick. "Introduction." In *The Reason Why the Colored American Is Not in the World's Columbian Exposition*, edited by Robert W. Rydell. Urbana: University of Illinois Press, 1999.

Duncan, Derek. "Italian Identity and the Risks of Contamination: The Legacies of Mussolini's Demographic Impulse in the Works of Comisso, Flaiano and Dell'Oro." In *Italian Colonialism: Legacy and Memory*, edited by Jacqueline Andall and Derek Duncan. Oxford: Peter Lang Press, 2005.

Edib, Halide Adivar. *Memoirs of Halide Edib.* Piscataway, NJ: Gorgias Press, 2004.

Erdem, Y. Hakan. "Preface." In *Biographie d'une famille d'esclaves: Kenya—Crete—Istanbul* [Biography of a family of slaves: Kenya—Crete—Istanbul], by Mustafa Olpak. Paris: Librairie Ozgul Kitabevi, 2006.

———. *Slavery in the Ottoman Empire and Its Demise, 1800–1909.* New York: St. Martin's Press, 1996.

Fahmy, Khaled. *All the Pasha's Men.* Cambridge: Cambridge University Press, 1998.

Forcier, Natalie. "Divided at the Margins: A Study of Young Southern Sudanese Refugee Men in Cairo, Egypt." Center for Migration and Refugee Studies, American University in Cairo, November 2009.

Fryer, Peter. *Staying Power: Black People in Britain since 1504.* London: Humanities Press, 1984.

Garcin, Jean-Claude. "The Regime of the Circassian Mamluks." In *The Cambridge History of Egypt*, vol. 1, *Islamic Egypt, 640–1517*, edited by Carl Petry. Cambridge: Cambridge University Press, 2008.

Gerber, Haim. *The Social Origins of the Modern Middle East.* Boulder, CO: Lynne Rienner Publishers, 1987.

Gomez, Michael A. *Exchanging Our Country Marks: The Transformation of African Identities in the Colonial and Antebellum South.* Chapel Hill: University of North Carolina Press, 1998.

Gordon, Charles G. *Journals of Major-Gen. C. G. Gordon, C.B. at Khartoum.* Introduction and notes by A. Egmont Hake. Leipzig: Bernard Tauchnitz, 1885. [Printed from the original manuscripts.]

Gordon, Lucie Duff. *Letters from Egypt, 1862–1869.* New York: Praeger, 1969.

Grandin, Nicole. "La vie très exemplaire du shaykh Babikr Bedri (1861–1954)" [The very exemplary life of Shaykh Babikr Bedri (1861–1954)]. *Cahiers d'études africaines* 22, no. 87 (1982).

Greene, Sandra. *West African Narratives of Slavery: Texts from Late Nineteenth- and Early Twentieth-Century Ghana.* Bloomington: Indiana University Press, 2011.

Guerrini, M. Mariarosa. *Bakhita: Daughter of Africa and "Universal Sister."* Rome: Curia Generalize, Figlie della carita Canossiane, 2000.

Halperin, S. William. "Church and State in Italy during the Last Years of Pius IX." *Church History* 5, no. 1 (1936).

Hanimefendi, Leila Saz. *The Imperial Harem of the Sultans: Memoirs of Leyla (Saz) Hanimefendi.* Istanbul: Peva Publications, 1995.

Hanoum, Leila. *Le harem imperial au XIXe siècle* [The imperial harem in the 19th century]. Paris: Éditions Complexe, 2000.

Hartman, Saidiya. *Lose Your Mother: A Journey along the Atlantic Slave Route.* New York: Farrar, Straus and Giroux, 2007.

Hathaway, Jane. *The Politics of Households in Ottoman Egypt: The Rise of the Qazdaglis.* Cambridge: Cambridge University Press, 1997.

Hilal, 'Emad Ahmad. *Al-Raqiq fi misr fi'l-qarn al-tasi' 'ashr* [Slavery in nineteenth-century Egypt]. Cairo: Al-Arabil, 1999.

Hill, Richard L. *Biographical Dictionary of the Anglo-Egyptian Sudan.* Oxford: Oxford University Press, 1951.

Hodgkin, Elizabeth. Review of *Educational Development in the Sudan 1898–1956*, by Mohamed Omer Beshir, and *The Memoirs of Babikr Bedri*, by Babikr Bedri, translated by Yousef Bedri and George Scott. *Journal of Modern African Studies* 8, no. 2 (1970).

Hunter, Robert F. *Egypt under the Khedives, 1805–1879: From Household Government to Modern Bureaucracy.* Cairo: American University in Cairo Press, 1984.

Ibrahim, Georgette Atiya. *Huda Sha'rawi: Al-zaman w'al-riyada* [Huda Sha'rawi: The era and the explorations]. Vol. 1. Cairo: Dar Atiya, 1998.

Idris, Amir. *Conflict and Politics of Identity in Sudan.* New York: Palgrave Macmillan, 2005.

'Issa, Salah. *Hikayat min daftar al-watan* [Stories from the national record]. Cairo: Dar al-Ahali, 1992.

Johnson, Douglas H. "Divinity Abroad: Dinka Missionaries in Foreign Lands." In *Vernacular Christianity: Essays in the Social Anthropology of Religion Presented to Godfrey Lienhardt*, edited by Wendy James and Douglas H. Johnson. New York: Lilian Barger Press, 1988.

———. "Salim Wilson: The Black Evangelist of the North." *Journal of Religion in Africa* 21 (1991).

————. "The Structure of a Legacy: Military Slavery in Northeast Africa." *Ethnohistory* 36, no. 1 (1989).

Jok, Jok Madut. *War and Slavery in Sudan.* Philadelphia: University of Pennsylvania Press, 2001.

Kahf, Mohja. "Huda Sha'rawi's *Mudhakkirati*: The Memoirs of the First Lady of Arab Modernity." *Arab Studies Quarterly* 20, no. 1 (1998).

————. "Packaging 'Huda': Sha'rawi's Memoirs in the United States." In *Going Global: The Transnational Reception of Third World Women Writers*, edited by Amal Amireh and Lisa Suhair Majaj. New York: Garland Publishing, 2000.

Kathish, Hatashil Masha. *The Ethiopia Valley: The Story of the People Called the Dinkas.* Birmingham, UK: C. Caswell, n.d. (ca. 1908).

Koremezli, Ibrahim. "The Place of the Ottoman Empire in the Russo-Circassian War (1830–1864)." Master's thesis, Bilkent University, Ankara, 2004.

Kozma, Liat. *Policing Egyptian Women: Sex, Law and Medicine in Khedival Egypt.* Syracuse, NY: Syracuse University Press, 2011.

Kunt, Metin. "Ottomans and Safavids: States, Statecraft and Society, 1500–1800." In *A Companion to the History of the Middle East*, edited by Youssef M. Choueri. Blackwell Companions to World History. Malden, MA: Blackwell Publishing, 2005.

Kupferschmidt, Uri. "Who Needed Department Stores in Egypt? From Orosdi-Back to Omar Effendi." *Middle East Studies* 43, no. 2 (2007).

Lev, Yaacov. *State and Society in Fatimid Egypt.* Leiden, Netherlands: Brill, 1991.

Lienhardt, Godfrey. *Divinity and Experience: The Religion of the Dinka.* Oxford: Oxford University Press, 2003.

Mahmud, Ushari Ahmad, and Suleiman Ali Baldo. *Human Rights Abuses in the Sudan: The Diein Massacre: Slavery in the Sudan.* Khartoum, 1987.

Makris, G. P. *Changing Masters: Spirit Possession and Identity Construction among Slave Descendants and Other Subordinates in the Sudan.* Evanston, IL: Northwestern University Press, 2000.

Manning, Patrick. *Slavery and African Life: Occidental, Oriental, and African Slave Trades.* Cambridge: Cambridge University Press, 1990.

McBride, Dwight A. *Impossible Witnesses: Truth, Abolitionism and Slave Testimony.* New York: New York University Press, 2001.

McGregor, Andrew. "The Circassian Qubbas of Abbas Avenue, Khartoum: Governors and Soldiers in 19th Century Sudan." *Nordic Journal of African Studies* 10, no. 1 (2001).

Mehrez, Samia. *Egyptian Writers between History and Fiction: Essays on Naguib Mahfouz, Sonallah Ibrahim and Gamal al-Ghitani.* Cairo: American University in Cairo Press, 2005.

Mubarak, 'Ali Pasha. *Al-Khitat al-tawfiqiya al-jadidah li misr al-qahirah wa mudunuha wa biladuha al-qadimah w-al-shahirah* [roughly and unpoetically translated as The new plans of Khedive Tawfiq for Cairo, Egypt, and her old and famous cities and villages]. 20 vols. Cairo: Bulaq Press, 1886–89.

————. *Al-Khitat al-jadidah al-tawfiqiyah li misr al-qahira.* 16 vols. Cairo: Al-Hi'yah al-'amma lil-kitab, 1994.

_____. *Hayati* [My life]. Edited by 'Abd al-Rahim Yusuf Gamal. Cairo: Maktabat al-adab, 1989.

Mynors, T. H. B. "The Adventures of a Darfur Slave." *Sudan Notes and Records* 30 (1949).

Naqod, Muhammad Ibrahim. *'Alaqat al-riqq fi al-mujtama' al-sudani* [The relationships of slavery in Sudanese society]. Cairo: Dar al-Thiqaqafa, 1995.

Nikkel, Marc. "Daniel Sorur Farim Deng: Comboni's Adoptive Son." In *Announcing the Light: Sudanese Witnesses to the Gospel*, edited by Andrew C. Wheeler. Nairobi: Pauline Publications Africa, 1998.

_____. "Salim Charles Wilson: Black Evangelist of the North." In *Announcing the Light: Sudanese Witnesses to the Gospel*, edited by Andrew C. Wheeler. Nairobi: Pauline Publications Africa, 1998.

Nora, Pierre. "Between Memory and History: *Les lieux de mémoire*." *Representations* 26 (Spring 1989).

Northrup, Linda S. "The Bahri Mamluk Sultanate, 1250–1390." In *The Cambridge History of Egypt*, vol. 1, *Islamic Egypt, 640–1517*, edited by Carl Petry. Cambridge: Cambridge University Press, 2008.

O'Fahey, R. S. "Slavery and Society in Dar Fur." In *Slaves and Slavery in Muslim Africa*, vol. 2, *The Servile Estate*, edited by John Ralph Willis. London: Frank Cass, 1985.

Olpak, Mustafa. *Biographie d'une famille d'esclaves: Kenya—Crete—Istanbul* [Biography of a family of slaves: Kenya—Crete—Istanbul]. Paris: Librairie Ozgul Kitabevi, 2006.

Patterson, Orlando. *Slavery and Social Death: A Comparative Study*. Cambridge, MA: Harvard University Press, 1985.

Pierli, Francil, and Maria Teresa Ratti. "Sr Mary Josephine Zeinab: 'The Chosen One from the Nuba Mountains.'" In *Announcing the Light: Sudanese Witnesses to the Gospel*, edited by Andrew C. Wheeler. Nairobi: Paulines Publications Africa, 1998.

Pollard, Lisa. *Nurturing the Nation*. Berkeley: University of California Press, 2005.

Rabbat, Nasser. "The Medieval Link: Maqrizi's *Khitat* and Modern Narratives of Cairo." In *Making Cairo Medieval*, edited by Nezar AlSayyad, Irene A. Bierman, and Nasser Rabbat. Oxford, UK: Lexington Books, 2005.

_____. "Who Was al-Maqrizi? A Biographical Sketch." *Mamluk Studies Review* 7, no. 2 (2003).

Ratti, Maria Teresa. "Comboni Sisters: Missionary Women in the Evangelization of the Sudan." In *Gateway to the Heart of Africa: Missionary Pioneers in Sudan*, edited by F. Pierli, M. T. Ratti, and A. C. Wheeler. Nairobi: Paulines Publications Africa, 1998.

Reimer, Michael J. "Contradiction and Consciousness in 'Ali Mubarak's Description of Al-Azhar." *International Journal of Middle East Studies* 29, no. 1 (1997).

Rossum, Deborah J. "'A Vision of Black Englishness': Black Intellectuals in London, 1910–1940." *Stanford Electronic Humanities Review* 5, no. 2 (1997).

Rydell, Robert W. "'Darkest Africa': African Shows at America's World's Fairs, 1893–1940." In *Africans on Stage: Studies in Ethnological Show Business*, edited by Bernth Lindfors. Bloomington: Indiana University Press, 1999.

Salih, Tayeb. *Season of Migration to the North*. New York: New York Review of Books, 2009. [First published in Arabic in 1967, and in English in 1969.]

Sanderson, G. N. "The Modern Sudan, 1820–1956: The Present Position of Historical Studies." *Journal of African History* 4, no. 3 (1963).

Sanderson, Lilian. "The Memoirs of Babikr Bedri." *Journal of African History* 11, no. 1 (1970).

Saydun, Zeynep Beril. *Construction of Nationalism and Gender in Halide Edib's Autobiographical Writings.* Trier, Germany: Wissenschaftlicher Verlag, 2008.

Scaraffia, Lucetta. "Christianity Has Liberated Her and Placed Her alongside Man in the Family." In *Women and Faith: Catholic Religious Life in Italy from Late Antiquity to the Present*, edited by Lucetta Scaraffia and Gabriella Zarri. Cambridge, MA: Harvard University Press, 1999.

Scholch, Alexander. *Egypt for the Egyptians: The Socio-political Crisis in Egypt, 1878–1882.* Reading, UK: Middle East Centre, St. Antony's College, Oxford [by] Ithaca Press, 1981.

Shaham, Ron. "Masters, Their Freed Slaves, and the *Waqf* in Egypt (Eighteenth–Twentieth Centuries)." *Journal of the Economic and Social History of the Orient* 43, no. 2 (2000).

Shami, Seteney. "Prehistories of Globalization: Circassian Identity in Motion." *Public Culture* 12, no. 1 (2000).

Sha'rawi, Huda. *Harem Years: Memoirs of an Egyptian Feminist (1879–1924).* Edited, translated, and introduced by Margot Badran. London: Virago Press, 1986.

———. *Mudhakirat* [Memoirs of Huda Shar'awi]. Cairo: Dar al-Hilal, 1981.

Sharkey, Heather J. "Christians among Muslims: The Church Missionary Society in the Northern Sudan." *Journal of African History* 43 (2002).

Shaw, Flora. "The Story of Zebehr Pasha, as Told by Himself." *Contemporary Review* 52 (1887).

Shaw, Stanford J. *History of the Ottoman Empire and Modern Turkey.* Vol. 1. Berkeley: University of California Press, 1976.

Sikainga, Ahmad Alawad. *Slaves into Workers: Emancipation and Labor in Colonial Sudan.* Austin: University of Texas Press, 1996.

Sills, Adam. "Surveying the Map of Slavery in Aphra Behn's *Oroonoko*." *Journal of Narrative Theory* 36, no. 3 (2006).

Sonmez, Emel. "The Novelist Halide Edib Adivar and Turkish Feminism." *Die Welt des Islams*, n.s., 14 (1973).

Tignor, Robert L. Review of *Letters from Egypt*, by Lady Duff Gordon. *African Historical Studies* 4, no. 1 (1971).

Toledano, Ehud. *As If Silent and Absent: Bonds of Enslavement in the Islamic Middle East.* New Haven, CT: Yale University Press, 2007.

———. "Late Ottoman Concepts of Slavery (1830s–1880s)." *Poetics Today* 14, no. 3 (1993).

———. *Slavery and Abolition in the Ottoman Middle East.* Seattle: University of Washington Press, 1998.

Troutt Powell, Eve M. "Bodies Caught on Film: Photographs of Slaves in Sudan." In *The Ashgate Research Companion to Modern Imperial Histories*, edited by Philippa Levine and John Marriott. London: Ashgate Press, 2012.

———. *A Different Shade of Colonialism: Egypt, Great Britain, and the Mastery of Sudan.* Berkeley: University of California Press, 2003.

Walz, Terence. "Bakhita Kwashe (Sr. Fortunata Quasce). 2007." http://www.dacb.org/stories/sudan/bakhita_kwashe.html.

———. *Trade between Egypt and Bilad as-Sudan (1700–1820)*. Cairo: Institut Francais d' Archéologie Orientale du Caire, 1978.

Walzer, Craig, ed. *Out of Exile: Narratives from the Abducted and Displaced People of Sudan*. San Francisco: Voice of Witness, 2009.

Wells, Ida B., Frederick Douglass, Irvine Garland Penn, and Ferdinand L. Barnett. *The Reason Why the Colored American Is Not in the World's Columbian Exposition*. Edited by Robert W. Rydell. Chicago: University of Illinois Press, 1999.

Wheatley, Phillis. "On Being Brought from Africa to America." Accessed May 4, 2012. http://allpoetry.com/poem/8514755-On_Being_Brought_from_Africa_to_America-by-Phillis_Wheatley.

Wheeler, Andrew C. "Freed Slaves and the Origins of the Sudanese Church." In *Announcing the Light: Sudanese Witnesses to the Gospel*, edited by Andrew C. Wheeler. Nairobi: Paulines Publications Africa, 1998.

Wilson, Salim C. *I Was a Slave*. London: Stanley Paul, n.d. (ca. 1939).

———. *Jehova-Nissi: The Life Story of Hatashil-masha-katish, of the Dinka Tribe of the Sudan*. Birmingham, UK: C. Caswell, 1901.

Winter, Michael. "The Re-emergence of the Mamluks following the Ottoman Conquest." In *The Mamluks in Egyptian Politics and Society*, edited by Thomas Phillip and Ulrich Haarmann. Cambridge: Cambridge University Press, 1998.

Wood, Marcus. *Blind Memory: Visual Representations of Slavery in England and America, 1780–1865*. New York: Routledge, 2000.

Woodward, Peter. *Sudan, 1898–1989: The Unstable State*. Boulder, CO: Lynne Rienner Publishers, 1990.

Zanini, Roberto Italo. *Bakhita: A Saint for the Third Millennium*. Rome: Orca Printing and Advertising, 2000.

Zanolini, Ida. *Tale of Wonder: Saint Giuseppina Bakhita*. Rome: Canossian Daughters of Charity, General House, 2000.

Index

Page numbers in italic type indicate illustrations.

Lev, Yaacov, 16
Levant Herald (newspaper), 127
Lienhardt, Godfrey, 113
Livorno, Geremia da, 157
Losi, Giovanni, 179
Ludwig I, King of Bavaria, 153
Lugard, Frederick, Lord, 45

Magdalen of Canossa, Saint, 196
Mahdi and Mahdiyya: Bakhita and,
    161–62; Bedri and, 39–41, 50–51, 55,
    59; British opposition to, 45, 64, 77, 86;
    Comboni and, 175; death of Mahdi,
    57; defeat of, 65; siege of Khartoum,
    191; and slavery, 57, 66; victories of,
    56, 82–83, 152
Mahmud, Ushari Ahmad, 202
Majnun Layla, 43
Mamluks (white slaves): in Egypt, 19–25;
    Egypt ruled by, 20–22, 24–25; ethnic
    diversity of, 217n39; history of, 20;
    identity of, 14; and race, 17
Manning, Patrick, 67
Maqrizi, Taqi al-Din al-, 9, 13, 15, 30
Marno, Ernst, 151–52
Marriage, 63–65, 144
Al-Masry al-youm (newspaper), 2
Mazza, Nicola, 149–51, 157
Mazza Institute, Verona, 149–50, 157
McBride, Dwight, 90
McGregor, Andrew, 36–37
Mehmet, Deli, 122–23
Mehrez, Samia, 9, 12
Memory: history vs., 13; of slavery, 81,
    222n5
Michieli, Augusto, 192, 195
Michieli, Turina, 192, 195
"Middle passages," 127–29
Midhat, Ahmet, *Esaret*, 224n9
Migration, of slaves, 209–10
Military: slavery and, 20–21, 27; and
    Turkish language, 36–37
Missionaries. *See* Catholic missionaries
Missionary Institutes, Cairo, 151
Morette, 155, 156, 163, 195, 228n16
Morzal, Arturo, 174–75, 179
Motherhood, slavery and, 121–23

Mubarak, 'Ali, 7–38, 44; Bedri compared
    to, 40; *Al-Khitat al-jadidah al-tawfiqiyah
    li misr al-qahirah*, 4, 7–38, 215n10; life
    of, 9–10, 32–36; ministerial career of, 10
Mubarak, Husni, 215n4
Murgan, 78, 78–80
Mursi, 'Abd al-Hamid Fahmy, 225n10
Mussolini, Benito, 196–97
Mustansir, Ma'd al-, 15–17
Mutanabbi, Abou-Tayyib al-, 42
Mynors, T. H. B., 86

Nabrawi, Ibrahim Bey al-, 23, 28–29,
    217n74
Names, personal, 4, 21, 82, 93, 157, 182,
    190, 229n58
Narration of slave stories: Ahmed and,
    84–88; circulation and awareness
    of, 209–10; by female slaves, 136–37,
    141; language of, 81, 86–87, 90–94,
    99; Murgan and, 79–80; purpose and
    function of, 204; Wilson and, 80, 91–99
Nationalism, 118, 209
New York Times (newspaper), 1
Nigrizia (journal), 181
Nkrumah, Gamal, 2
Nora, Pierre, 13
Nujumi al-, Wad, 59

Ohrwalder (priest), 175
Olivieri, Niccolò, 82, 149–50, 164–66
Olpak, Mustafa, 144–47
Omar, Tarig, 211
Omdurman, battle of (1898), 43, 61, 63–64,
    68
Order of Saint Joseph, 160
Ottoman Empire, *xv*; abolition of slavery
    in, 207–8; Caucasian emigration to,
    127–28; Egypt and, 118, 121; postwar,
    145; slavery in, 19–24; social transfor-
    mations in, 118–19

Padmore, George, 112
Palestine, 107–8
Pan-Africanism, 112
Passports, 207–8
Patterson, Orlando, 60

CPSIA information can be obtained
at www.ICGtesting.com
Printed in the USA
JSHW022358190722
28236JS00012B/41